Praise for *Labor Day*

"*Labor Day* belongs on the nightstand next to *What to Expect When You're Expecting*. It's a must-have book for mothers, mothers-to-be, and anyone who cares about what birth looks like today."
—MOLLY RINGWALD, actress, singer, and
author of *When It Happens to You*

"One of the most important preparations for labor is reading actual stories from actual women in labor. *Labor Day* provides a tremendously varied, honest, and beautiful set of stories to learn from and grow with, no matter where you are in your parenting journey."   —MAYIM BIALIK, Ph.D., actress, neuroscientist

"Pregnancy made my body ravenous for food and my brain ravenous for stories like these, stories of how other women had crossed the great divide. In delivery rooms, in the backseats of cars, and at home, these women tell their birth stories so clearly that they must have had stenographers present on the scene. I loved reading this book with my baby asleep in the next room, and will give it to every pregnant woman I know from here on out, forever."
—EMMA STRAUB, author of *Laura Lamont's Life in Pictures*

"I read *Labor Day* the way I ate my first meal after giving birth: I knew I loved labor stories, but I didn't know I was absolutely starving for them. Ravenous. And they satisfied me; they filled me with wonder and tears and quite a few laugh-out-loud guffaws. And mostly they filled me with gratitude that real women shared their real experiences so that all of us can reexperience the wild joy and terror and beauty of giving birth."
—ELIZABETH LESSER, cofounder of Omega Institute and
author of *Broken Open: How Difficult Times Can Help Us Grow*
and *The Seeker's Guide: Making Your Life a Spiritual Adventure*

"*Labor Day* is such a gift. I've probably read or heard hundreds of birth stories, but once I picked up *Labor Day*, I could not put it down. Birth stories, especially those told by mothers who are also writers, are riveting. From Heidi Julavits reflecting on the value of a doula by reminding us that 'pain, when explained, can be much less painful' to Eleanor Henderson's depiction of being 'dazed with happiness,' this collection beautifully covers a huge range of birth experiences. Each fascinating detail, from the banal to the exalted, gives a glimpse of just what can happen when a baby is born." —CATHERINE TAYLOR, author of *Giving Birth: A Journey into the World of Mothers and Midwives*

Labor Day

Labor Day

TRUE BIRTH STORIES

BY

TODAY'S BEST WOMEN WRITERS

Edited by

Eleanor Henderson

AND

Anna Solomon

FARRAR, STRAUS AND GIROUX

NEW YORK

⊙

Farrar, Straus and Giroux
18 West 18th Street, New York 10011

Amy Brill's "One Year, Two Births" previously appeared, in slightly different form,
in *Redbook* as "Happiness Is . . . an Awesome Car."
Marie Myung-Ok Lee's "What to Expect When You're Not Expecting"
previously appeared on *The Atlantic*'s website.
Jane Roper's "Twice Delivered" previously appeared, in slightly different form,
in her memoir *Double Time.*

Library of Congress Cataloging-in-Publication Data
Labor day: true birth stories by today's best women writers / edited by
Eleanor Henderson, Anna Solomon. — 1st Edition.
    pages   cm
    ISBN 978-0-374-23932-9 (hardback) — ISBN 978-0-374-71145-0
(ebook)
    1. Labor (Obstetrics)—Anecdotes.   2. Childbirth—Anecdotes.
3. Motherhood—Psychological aspects.   4. Authors—Family
relationships—Anecdotes.   I. Henderson, Eleanor, editor of compilation.
II. Solomon, Anna, editor of compilation.
RG651.L23 2014
618.4—dc23
                                                        2013041341

Designed by Abby Kagan

Farrar, Straus and Giroux books may be purchased for educational, business, or
promotional use. For information on bulk purchases, please contact the Macmillan
Corporate and Premium Sales Department at 1-800-221-7945, extension 5442,
or write to specialmarkets@macmillan.com.

www.fsgbooks.com
www.twitter.com/fsgbooks • www.facebook.com/fsgbooks

1   3   5   7   9   10   8   6   4   2

FOR OUR MOTHERS,
ANN BABCOCK HENDERSON
AND
ELLEN RACHEL SOLOMON,
WITH GRATITUDE

Contents

Labor Day

Introduction: Expect the Unexpected

Angelina and Gisele prepared their tubs. Christina Aguilera scheduled an elective C-section. Kate Middleton broke ground by asking her prince to stay in the delivery room instead of heading to the links. As choices of when, where, and how to give birth have become more numerous and more stark, American mothers are preparing for labor with one common thing in their diaper bags: birth plans. Such plans have become as ubiquitous as stretch-mark creams and layettes, and as the first decision many make as parents, they're charged with meaning. What began as an expression of personal preference has quickly come to represent a declaration of our philosophies, our politics, and our identities—as mothers and as women.

The story of birth in the twenty-first century is undeniably different from the one it was thirty years ago, when *What to Expect When You're Expecting* first empowered mothers-to-be with essential guidance through the forty weeks of pregnancy. Since then, thousands of new books—and documentaries and articles and blogs—have sought to prepare women for the final push of pregnancy, their labor day. A vast and diverse industry has grown up around birth in the United States, from "boutique" labor and delivery suites that offer mani/pedis and vaginal-rejuvenation therapies to "alternative" birthing centers that provide the chance to labor without drugs or medical intervention. A generation ago, many of our mothers went into the hospital with a comb and nightgown; we go in armed with our birthing ball and pump, our iPod loaded with rain forest sounds. They took a Lamaze class—maybe; we take classes in breast-feeding and infant care and prenatal yoga, where we do our Kegel exercises in obedient unison. As often as not, they expected to birth on their backs, with their husbands cheering them on from the hallway (or the nearest bar).

We, on the other hand, are encouraged—by doctors and co-workers, family and friends—to tackle our labors as we might a new job, to make detailed birth plans, to hire doulas who will advocate for these plans, to train our partners as our coaches and cord cutters. Oh, and do we want that cord to be cut right away, or after it has stopped pulsing? Do we want eye ointment administered? Do we want to delay the first bath? With these choices comes information, a tidal wave of statistics and warnings: often contradictory, sometimes frightening, always addictive. On the one hand, many doctors won't allow patients to attempt a vaginal birth after having had a C-section (VBAC) and warn that going beyond forty-one weeks or having a larger baby endangers our babies and us. On the other hand, natural-birth advocates warn that epidurals will lead to Pitocin, which will lead to other interventions; that C-sections cause infection; and that episiotomies are akin to genital mutilation. Today, many Western women are told they can have babies well into their forties, yet anyone over thirty-five still falls into "advanced maternal age" and is encouraged to undergo extra tests, which bring added anxiety.

Armed with all this information, with countless choices, with squat bars and whirlpool tubs and "walking" epidurals, we are meant to feel empowered. We enter a heady zone of birth preparation; here, it seems, we can bring the uncontrollable under our control. But often, our plans prove somewhere in between irrelevant and useless. (Angelina never got to use that birthing tub. When her baby presented breech, she had a C-section.) For the lucky few, birth goes beautifully—short, free of complication, perhaps even sublime. More commonly, our labors tackle us, rather than the other way around; our deliveries are not always as we imagined or wanted. We may be left feeling disappointed, embarrassed, having failed to meet our own and others' expectations. Too often, we mothers are guilty of perpetuating this sense of inadequacy ourselves by making a fuss about our "successes," earned or not.

Under such pressure, prepared to the hilt, are we really any better off than our mothers? And if not, where do we turn?

To stories.

In the summer of 2005, we—Eleanor Henderson and Anna Solomon—sat on the patio of the Storm Café in Middlebury, Vermont, overlooking Otter Creek. We'd met just days before at the Bread Loaf Writers' Conference, where we were working as waiters. That night, with three other new girlfriends, we were taking a break. We talked about newly minted husbands and newly minted M.F.A.'s. And, of course, about books and babies. We wanted both, badly, soon. But which would come first?

As it turned out, our babies beat our books down the birth canal. And for a while, as we gestated, the only books at our bedsides were books about babies: what to expect when you're pregnant, and in labor, and beyond; what to do to soothe round ligament pain; how close your contractions should be before calling your doctor; whether you needed a bassinet or a cosleeper or both. Bookstores, we found, were filled with pregnancy journals and parenting bibles, month-by-month manuals and gear guides that were little more than product catalogs. But the shelves were virtually empty of artful, entertaining, unvarnished accounts of labor and delivery. That was what we wanted, we realized. We wanted the extraordinary, the ordinary, the terrifying, the profane, and, sure, the sublime, too. We wanted the truth.

So Eleanor sent out a missive to her friends. How did it happen for you? Did your water break? Did you get an epidural? What did it feel like? Would you do it again? The e-mails came in spades, and in detail—mucus plugs, episiotomies, an entire sheet of Christmas cookies thrown up into a sick pan. These were the stories she needed to hear, and, of course, the friends who were writers told the best ones—the most insightful, the most reflective, the kind that invited you right into the delivery room to take a peek over the nurse's shoulder. When Anna sent along a four-page essay about her daughter's recent birth—comic, poignant, pee-soaked, and starring Manhattan's most eccentric ob-gyn—the idea occurred to us at the same time: These stories need to be collected and shared.

The time seemed ripe. Was it us, or was there a new baby bump featured in the checkout line each week? The reality-TV industry produced birth story after birth story (one too many for Eleanor's queasy husband). But behind the world's fascination with airbrushed bellies and dramatized labors, we sensed a more urgent narrative forming, a conversation about the choices available to mothers in the twenty-first century. We watched as "Why Women Still Can't Have It All" became the most circulated article in the history of *The Atlantic*, as *Time* magazine made "Are You Mom Enough?" a catchphrase, and as Mitt Romney unleashed binders full of outraged women into the Twitterverse. Ours is an era in which mothers can be CEOs, DIY homemakers, or combat soldiers with equal zeal (and self-consciousness); we can be tiger mothers or "attachment" parents; we can argue for self-sacrifice in one breath and for selfishness in the next; we can call ourselves feminists and we can call feminism dead. Of course, for many women across the United States and certainly across the globe, these choices are still limited, but those of us privileged enough can do and be almost anything—including paralyzed by the sheer number of possibilities.

With *Labor Day*, we wanted to give expression to the epic questions—of parenthood, fertility, marriage, work, equality—

that shape the birth experience for this new generation of mothers and mothers-to-be. To our delight, the writers we approached—poets, fiction writers, memoirists, playwrights; friends and strangers alike—delivered birth stories that do exactly that, and so much more. As the essays rolled in, we laughed. We wept. We groaned in recognition, and gasped with surprise. Each story brought with it new struggles and new triumphs. We found ourselves as immersed in our fellow writers' birth stories as we had been in our own.

It's an elemental, almost animalistic urge—the expectant mother's hunger for birth narratives. Surely our mothers and their mothers nurtured the same craving, a craving as old as storytelling, or childbirth itself. The writers featured in this anthology might even suggest that pregnancy brings the privilege of a higher emotional frequency, tuning us in to the stories of other women. "I felt porous," Rachel Jamison Webster writes of her pregnancy, "strummed by the nerves of the earth. I could feel a friend who was hurting or rejoicing across the country, and I would call and drop into the moment mid-conversation. I felt connected to everyone I loved, especially to other women, and I felt—and still feel—awed to be a portal through which another would enter her life."

Many of the conversations we drop in on in this book are in uncanny harmony with one another. Dani Shapiro, like Rachel Jamison Webster, feels surrounded by her ancestors as she gives birth. Ann Hood and Marie Myung-Ok Lee, both given Pitocin without permission, watch in exasperation as the items on their birth plans are derailed or just dismissed. Gina Zucker and Phoebe Damrosch bask in the triumphant pleasures of their postlabor meal. Mary Beth Keane and Edan Lepucki find themselves struggling postpartum with lingering doubts and regrets about their long, intense labors. Nuar Alsadir and Danzy Senna are both haunted by the feeling that their induced babies, now children, know they were born too early. Susan Burton and Claire Dederer hold the details of their birth stories close, too precious to share. Arielle

Greenberg and Heidi Pitlor write about the heartbreaking loss of their babies late in pregnancy, as well as the joy of the births that followed. (While we don't want to reduce them to their darkest moments, we feel it's important to note that certain details in these essays, as well as in those by Amy Herzog and Rachel Jamison Webster, might upset some new and expectant mothers. But these essays also bear witness to the extraordinary resilience of mothers and those who support them, without which the story of birth would not be complete.)

Other stories reflect collisions, of experience and perspective. While pregnancy eases Dani Shapiro's anxiety, for Lauren Groff it brings on depression. While pushing comes as naturally as breathing to some of us (Phoebe Damrosch, Amy Brill, Anna), for others (Rachel Jamison Webster, Sarah A. Strickley, Eleanor) it requires learning to use muscles—including mental ones—we didn't know we had. Joanna Rakoff and Jane Roper must disprove the (male) doctors who tell them they won't have the strength or stamina to push out their babies, while Ann Hood and Heidi Julavits make transformative connections with the people who help bring their babies into the world. For Nuar Alsadir, seeing her baby's face for the first time presents a disconnect with the face she's imagined; for Lan Samantha Chang, it's instant recognition. And while Edan Lepucki and Joanna Rakoff both labor in the shadow of their mothers' legendary births (one a home birth, one propulsive), Dani Shapiro and Sarah Jefferis resolve that their own births mark a departure from motherhood as they've known it.

And so this book is born: a cacophonous, collective baby. The true stories in these pages are as varied as the women who crafted them. Here are women of diverse cultures, races, and sexual orientations, women in the big city and women in the country. Here are women intent on giving birth naturally and others begging for epidurals; women who pushed for hours and women whose labors were over practically before they'd started; women giving birth to twins and to ten-pound babies. Here are women giving birth at home, in hospitals, in tubs, on the bathroom floor, and, yes, in the car. Here are women facing agonizing complications and loss— infertility, miscarriage, stillbirth. Here are women reveling in labor, fearing labor, defeated by labor, fulfilled by it—and always amazed by it. These stories bear no moral, espouse no single method, or dismiss any other. They simply do what great stories do best: tell one particular experience so vividly that any reader can find herself in it.

In *Labor Day: True Birth Stories by Today's Best Women Writers*, we put aside our birth plans. We don't prepare, but reflect. We remember, regret, rejoice, and reveal. We tell the whole truth and nothing but the truth—what wasn't washed away by the amnesia of oxytocin, anyway. As distinct as these thirty truths are, they are bound by the common thread of the most universal experience there is, the oldest art in the world. We hope these essays reach you with the same simple but profound sense of anticipation and celebration in which they were conceived—by a group of women sitting around a table. We might have been any women at any time in history, sitting around a table, or a quilt, or a fire—dreaming about babies, telling our own stories, and discovering ourselves in one another's.

ELEANOR HENDERSON AND ANNA SOLOMON
APRIL 2014

What I'm Trying to Say

ANNA SOLOMON

Contractions started around five on Friday afternoon.[1] They were mild at first, mild enough that I doubted they were real. I could walk. I did walk, around our neighborhood, thinking, Am I having contractions? When Mike got home, we rented a movie and bought a box of brownie mix, and after dinner (what did we eat? I remember only the brownies, my wanting them) I mixed and baked the brownies. Later I would wonder, What was I thinking, making brownies? But for a while then, they still tasted good to me, and I wasn't in so much pain that I couldn't enjoy the movie, too—though I don't remember what it was now, and I don't think we finished watching it. The contractions got stronger, then stayed the same through the night, somewhere between five to ten minutes apart, varying in length. I couldn't sleep, and by morning I decided I needed an epidural. I'd been unsure about the epidural question—I thought I would

[1] This was the first essay in the collection, its seed, if you will, a spontaneous response to an e-mail from a very pregnant Eleanor ("I need the details," she instructed), and as such we wanted it to appear here largely unaltered. But since I wrote it, my perspective—on doctors, on pain, on women's bodies and joy and grief and just about everything else—has changed. Thus, these asides.

see what it was like, that if I could do it without, I'd rather, but that I wouldn't go crazy about it. Now I thought, I can't do it without. I need to sleep. That was my main priority—to rest. Which people had told me the epidural let you do. So we called Dr. Yang,[2] who said she doubted I was in labor but that sure, I could meet her at her office at nine.

A word about Dr. Yang, whom other patients sometimes refer to as "the Yangster," who my sister-in-law warned me was "a little intense," and whom I generally just call "my crazy Chinese doctor." She is temperamentally similar in some ways to the Chinese grocer in our corner bodega, except that instead of yelling at me, "This is DAIKON!" (when I called one night in my seventh month, terrified by the white puffy flesh suddenly bulging from the part of my stomach where I imagined my baby's head to be) she yelled, "That is your COLON, ANNA! It's coming through the tissue! It's just ABDOMINAL SEPARATION! YOU HAVE TO RELAX!"

We made the trip from Brooklyn to TriBeCa, our still-shiny labor ball stowed in the backseat. It was a Saturday, the bridge mercifully empty. At Dr. Yang's office, we were let in by a group of Chinese construction workers, busy affixing a new door. Dr. Yang, the leader explained, would be back to meet us; she'd had to go to the hardware store for a tool.

Dr. Yang is a solo practitioner, I should explain, which in her case means not only that she delivers every baby of every patient but also oversees every hinge being fitted to her doors.

We went into a room at the back and waited. I got very angry, waiting. I'd been angry at Dr. Yang before, many times, but now I felt angry in the way a laboring woman feels angry. She had abandoned me, I decided. And now? Now? What did this portend about my labor and delivery? Would she leave as the baby was coming out to go buy a box of nails?

[2] Not her real name.

Dr. Yang arrived some ten minutes later. Okay, Anna, let's see, let's see. Oh, I can see just looking at you, you're not in labor!

Of course the second she walked in the room, my contractions had diminished.

After her examination, she declared, See! You are only fifty percent effaced, and barely dilated even a centimeter!

I started to cry. But I'm exhausted! I said. I did not say, I want an epidural, because I knew now how stupid and impossible that idea was. I can't keep going!

My guess is you'll go into labor in the next day or two.

But this *is* labor, I told her.

Well, she said. Look. Anna. You have a very strong mind. I know this about you. You can make many things happen with your mind . . .

You're saying this is all in my head?

What I'm trying to say . . . (This was Dr. Yang's favorite phrase.) Listen. You have a very strong mind. In China, this is a very prized attribute. I? I can lower my blood pressure by ten points just thinking about it. In China, people can move cups just looking at them! What I'm trying to say . . .

As she spoke, I was vaguely aware—and disappointed, and ashamed—that I wasn't in as much pain as I'd been earlier.

What I'm trying to say is you're feeling your pain at a ten, and I want you to feel it at a four.

But I need to sleep! I said, still crying.

Yes. Exactly. You need to rest. Sometimes that brings labor on itself.

But I can't sleep! I said. It's too painful! (And I *am* in labor, I wanted to add, but didn't.)[3]

---

[3] Looking back now, my wrestlings with Dr. Yang—often in my head—mostly seem like a waste of energy. Also, a symptom of my privilege, that first pregnancy. It had been so easy: We'd conceived on our first try; there had been no complications. My expectation—my assumption—was that all the

Here. Listen. I want you to go home, take an Ambien—I write you out a prescription—take the hottest bath you can stand, drink a glass of wine. Relax.

I thought pregnant women aren't supposed to take hot baths, I said.

Baloney, Dr. Yang said, as she had about many other myths I'd brought up during our visits. The baby is all there. She not bothered by the heat!

I explained to Dr. Yang that the one time I'd taken Ambien, two nights before my wedding, I'd awakened hours later on the bathroom floor. I hadn't even made it to the bed.

Then take half! she cried, and ushered us out.

I felt desperate on the way home. The next day or two?

But at home, I followed Dr. Yang's directions—except for the wine, which I thought would make me throw up. After the bath, I got into bed (it was about 11:00 a.m. now) and for the next couple hours I managed to sleep between—though not during—contractions. It was a vague, hazy sleep, the four- and five-minute snatches building on one another. When I woke up and went to the bathroom, I had blood in my underwear. Dr. Yang had said, When you're in labor, you'll have blood, you'll have all sorts of things coming out of you.

Hooray![4]

---

important things (a beating heart, blood flow, progesterone, amniotic fluid, et cetera) would be just fine. Now when I think of all that must happen in order for an embryo to be put together, to grow and thrive and be born into the world a healthy, sentient human being, my breath catches in awe and fear. I like to think that Dr. Yang, for all her eccentricities, gets that, too—the miracle—and that *that's* why she has little patience for the small stuff.

[4] Hooray! It makes me flinch now, my unthinking optimism. Between this first labor and the birth of my second child, I had three miscarriages, all washed in

It was about two now. From there, the contractions got steadily stronger. I rested my forearms on the ball, my knees on the floor, Mike pushing my hip bones together, as we learned in class. Nothing made it less painful, but at least we were doing something, and I couldn't *not* be on my knees. Between contractions, I closed my eyes and rested. That was what I did best, I think, during my labor, really rested between contractions, not fearing the next one, but really sinking into the relief of those moments.

This better be labor! I think I said a few times. And around five, I said, We have to go to the hospital. I don't care if Dr. Yang laughs and sends us back. We're going.

Mike called Dr. Yang. Dr. Yang loves Mike, and she said, Well, Mike, if *you* really think it's different from this morning, I'll meet you at the hospital. I have another patient already there.

The car ride was the worst part, by far. It took us about fifty minutes, across the bridge (which one did Mike take?), through lower Manhattan, up the West Side Highway, which is not a highway at all, but a misnamed series of traffic lights that seemed to be red, every one, the whole way. I was, as Mike told me later, mooing

---

blood. My friends had miscarriages, too—a number of them had three, like me. Others gave birth to dead babies, or to very sick babies. I lost my innocence. So when I went into labor the second time, if I had seen blood, I think I would have burst into tears. Instead, my water broke, clear and warm and, conveniently, on our all-weather deck. Mike and I looked at each other and started to laugh. I don't know if I believe in God, but it was the sort of moment where I'm tempted to. We were living in Providence, Rhode Island, by then, far from Dr. Yang, but as I readied the hospital bag, I could hear her voice, reprimanding and encouraging me: Of course that's your amniotic fluid, Anna! Don't forget a towel!

like a cow. I was grabbing at the doors, writhing to the floor. It was awful.[5]

In the lobby, the triage nurse didn't ask what we were doing there, but sent us up to labor and delivery. Dr. Yang was still with the other patient, so a resident examined me. I remember looking at her face, staring, willing her, thinking, If she tells me I'm only two centimeters dilated, I will die. I will die. I really will, right here. I will die.

But I wasn't. I was eight centimeters dilated. "Entering transition," as she put it.

Hooray! I thought. I'm in labor! Then I thought—and shouted— I want an epidural NOW!

In the delivery room, the nurse told me Dr. Yang would be there soon, and that she had to get an IV in me to deliver fluids so they could do the epidural.

But where's the epidural? I asked.

[5] Pain. When I was pregnant with our second child, Mike and I went for two "contemplative" childbirth-preparation sessions with the warmest, loveliest doula/birth instructor/massage therapist/yoga teacher I've ever met. I learned to visualize my uterus like a jellyfish, pulsating, dancing, doing the work it needed to do. I learned to think of each contraction as an opening, my cervix a sea anemone offering up its colorful tendrils, a releasing sort of embrace. I went from being dilated three centimeters to ten in less than thirty minutes, not enough time for the epidural I vaguely asked for, and yet somehow, though the pain filled me utterly, because I had a new way of thinking about it this time— the labor wasn't being *done* to my body, my body was *doing* it—I managed to feel centered: not the battered cow, but the undulating grass, the sky above, a wave out at sea, *the only wave*. Which is, I suppose, what Dr. Yang meant when she told me to feel my pain at a four instead of a ten. She meant I could think my way to a different relationship with the pain. So she was right after all—as she often was. But I was younger then, less focused, unable to listen. And she sounded so angry!

Anesthesiology's been backed up all day, I heard her say. (She couldn't have said this to me, right? Wouldn't that have been too cruel?)

What? What?

It's okay. Here, said the nurse, trying to get the IV in.

But I was so dehydrated, the first veins she tried disappeared, and then she burst the vein in my left hand, which would be bruised for weeks, and then she couldn't get it into my right hand. Finally, she got it into my right arm. At some point in all this, I said, I have to pee, I have to go to the bathroom, and she said, You just go now. Just go. And I did. I peed all over myself. It was the first time I'd peed all over myself since I was a kid, I guess. I was just like a damn baby.

I remember hearing her say at some point during this, We have pushing! And I realized I was pushing. She said, I think she's fully dilated, and I said, Where is Dr. Yang? And soon Dr. Yang was there, in a brightly flowered velour dress, with pink lipstick to match,[6] and she said something to me—she actually said this—about how the residents often overestimate how dilated women are. And I thought, Fuck you.[7] Where is my epidural? Am I shitting myself? Oh shit, I might be shitting myself. And the nurse said, She's fully dilated, I really think so and Dr. Yang

---

[6] I realize this sounds like a laboring woman's hallucination, but Mike will corroborate it.

[7] Two and a half years later, a couple weeks after my second miscarriage, I stood up from a furniture store's white couch and started hemorrhaging. I went straight to Dr. Yang, telling her I'd just filled a toilet with blood, and she said, You know, Anna, even a drop of blood can *look* like it fills a toilet. Again, I thought, Fuck you. Every nerve in my body filled with rage; if I'd had a plate, I would have thrown it. Instead, I pulled down my dark jeans, shaking, and she said, Oh. Then, after she finished pulling a clot out of me, she told me she'd be right back, ran downstairs to her suboffice apartment, and gave me one of her skirts to wear on the subway ride home.

checked me out and didn't confirm or not confirm this, but she said to me, Anna, if it feels better to push, you can push.

I'd already been pushing, but I kept at it. And it did feel better. It felt great. I mean, it hurt like hell, but it was something to do, not just enduring the waves of pain but pushing. I was grunting insanely, making disgusting noises. Mike was holding one leg, Dr. Yang the other, and on her face, I remember, was total, utter joy.

I said, Wait. Am I pushing out the baby? I really thought, until that point, that I was pushing because it felt better.

YES! she cried. Here. You can feel it.

And I felt Sylvie's head (Oh, I'm going to cry now), a mushy, hairy, slimy thing.[8] And I kept pushing. And when she came out (it was 7:33 now; I'd pushed for about twenty-five minutes; we'd been at the hospital about an hour and a half), it was like a building erupting from me. And once it was out, it was out. Over. Sylvie screamed, they brought her right to me, she had *so* much hair! There was a little stitching to be done, but I barely noticed. And

---

[8] With my son, there was no time to feel his somewhat less hairy head emerge. Sam's head flew out on my first push, the rest of him on my second. It was 2:03 p.m., less than two hours after my water had broken. (At 12:28, I'd sent an e-mail to Eleanor, telling her I might not have time to work on this anthology that day.) It was as if he knew how long we'd waited for him. We named him Samuel, after the biblical Hannah's Samuel. So maybe I do believe a little bit in God. Sam was born, like any second kid, into a different family: older, and with a child already embedded in its rhythms, and, in our case, stronger for having learned resilience. We had traveled through sorrow to a place where we'd started to wonder if we really wanted another child, and then, following Sam's conception and our first glimpse of his heartbeat (me, holding my hands over my eyes and peeping through my fingers, blood thrumming in my ears), an utterly joyful anticipation. When Sylvie was born, I had little idea how blessed we were, but as I labored with Sam, I was grateful in every cell of my body. I was grateful to be given another chance to push, grateful even for the pain, so grateful that as soon as I brought him to my breast, I thought, I want to do this again! (That urge has since passed.)

Sylvie looked at me, found my breast, and started to suck. The next day, the pediatrician put her finger in Sylvie's mouth and said, That's the best suck I've felt in a while. And it was true, from the beginning: Sylvie taught me how to nurse her.[9]

---

[9] I haven't seen Dr. Yang in almost three years. I returned her skirt long ago, and I was relieved to go through my pregnancy with Sam without being yelled at by my doctor. But when we sent out Sam's birth announcement, an e-mail came back from Dr. Yang: "It is so good to hear from you and the great news! How was the labor? Hope it was a piece of carrot cake! What a long journey from Sylvie to Samuel. Thank you for sharing the great news. Be well."

I was annoyed, at first, by her "long journey" comment. I'd never told her about the third miscarriage, and I wondered if she was criticizing me for taking nearly five years to have another child. Then I remembered her face as she helped Sylvie into the world, her joy, her flowered dress so out of place in that sterile room, her strong, thin arms handing my daughter to me, and I realized I was being silly. Dr. Yang had become as complex a presence in my life as the people I love. I did love her, I realized. So I sent her a simple e-mail back: "Thank you."

It Takes a Building

PHOEBE DAMROSCH

When I began planning my second birth, I tracked down the out-of-print children's book I had heard about—the only one I could find that depicted a home birth—to read with my toddler son. At one point, the boy in the book says about his mother, "Every few minutes she yells so loudly the whole town will know we're having our baby today!" The family in the book chops firewood in their yard—in other words, they don't live in a Brooklyn apartment building with an echoing air shaft and neighbors on all sides. If any town was going to know there was a baby on the way, it was going to be mine. This line haunted me.

Friends urged nonchalance; after all, the acoustic landscape of New York City contains Mr. Softee trucks, sirens, urban chickens, rehearsing jazz musicians, endless horn honking, and marital spats. But these friends didn't live above George. For months, we had been tiptoeing around, covering every floorboard with rugs, and leaving the apartment at 7:00 a.m. on weekends so our son wouldn't wake up "Man George" (thus named to distinguish him from Curious George). Man George complained when our teething baby cried at night. He banged on his ceiling in the afternoon when a tower of blocks toppled over. Once, when we overturned a bench, he bellowed so loudly, we jumped. He sent e-mails to our landlord and the building superintendent, calling us reckless, inconsiderate, careless, and uncivilized.

Looking back on it later, it was clear that Man George wasn't the real source of my anxiety going into my second birth. That was a much more complex affair. I worried about how the new baby would rearrange the dynamics of our family, knowing that it would be in ways I could never prepare for, just as his brother had done before him. I worried that my first son would be heartbroken, missing my ready arms and empty lap. I worried that my house would be a wreck, that I'd never have time to get a haircut, that I'd let my kids live on buttered noodles because I would be too tired to fight about it. And I worried about the pain. Oh Lord, the pain.

When my first son was born two years before, on a hot summer evening in Harlem, I'd had none of these concerns and no Man George to fret over. Below us lived an Italian man who made love to a series of enthusiastic women at all hours, above us an athletic set of six-year-old triplets. My moaning and pacing was sure to be drowned out.

I went into my first labor looking forward to it, wondering every morning whether this would be the day, going to sleep each night sure that I'd be up within hours. When the day finally arrived, two weeks after my due date, my husband, André, and I walked to the farmers' market and bought peaches and tomatoes, stopping to lean on park benches along the way. Contractions came and went, and I began to think this whole birth thing would be no sweat, despite the fact that I normally took an Advil at the slightest twinge of a headache. But I had also rowed crew and biked across the country. I could handle this. Women had been giving birth naturally for ages. My body was made for birthing. My baby knew how to come out. These were the truths I repeated to myself in the months leading up to that first birth. Still, this was theoretical. You can read all the books, spend every weekend breathing with your partner, collect birth stories from everyone you know, but there is no way to determine what your labor will be like.

After a few real contractions back at our apartment, I began to grasp the severity of my situation. I was on my hands and knees (the position I would remain in for all five hours of the labor), and after one really intense contraction, I lowered my head to the floor and wept, prostrating myself to the force that was quickly overtaking me. But then the next contraction came and there was no time to be in awe; there was simply a job to be done.

The pain had surprised me, but so did my labor personality. At one point, about three hours into active labor, when my midwife and my best friend had arrived, I decided that I had had enough. This is absurd and uncalled for, I remember thinking. If there were a customer service line to call, I would have asked to speak to a manager and not settled for anything less than an apology and promise of retribution. I decided to push the baby out right then. My midwife, hearing me start to grunt and groan like a weight lifter, informed me that I wasn't ready yet, that I was not completely dilated. I didn't care; I wanted the baby out. Sensing that I was determined, she offered to do a midwife trick and give my cervix a little help during the next contraction. Our baby arrived soon after this, in a tub in the kitchen. If I didn't have pictures, the memories might have been even more scattered: the towels warming in the oven, the placenta bobbing around in the salad-spinner bowl, eating bagels and farmers' market tomatoes on our couch with a two-hour-old baby on a pillow between us.

My first son was born on a Saturday night, and Monday morning I returned some books to the library, feeling ecstatic and capable of anything. After that labor, I was a superhero: a delusion I would wish on every new mother. But not everyone was as satisfied as I was. I had a friend who told me I had been selfish to have my baby at home, to put my son in danger for my own comfort. When you choose a home birth, defending yourself against comments like these becomes part of the experience. Sometimes it helps to have statistics in your back pocket, like the fact that a planned, low-risk home birth is as safe as a hospital birth, according to a large 2009 study published in the *Canadian Medical Association Journal.* But fact-checking aside, my friend's comment struck me as sad. As if the birth had only been about producing a healthy baby. That was incredibly important to me, of course, but so was producing a healthy, confident mother. So was allowing my son to come when he was ready. So was bringing him into our lives in the most intimate, loving, safe place we could. So was knowing that he was held from the moment he was born in the gentlest and most familiar hands. So was answering every cry, changing every diaper, finding our own answer to every question. Many women want these things for their births, but it is not always possible in a hospital with a clock ticking and so many rules to follow. One hospital in my area is nearing a 50 percent cesarean rate. For me, a cesarean was something very real to avoid, partly because I didn't want to recover from major surgery while caring for an infant and partly because I was concerned about the safety of myself and my child. The CDC reports that cesareans triple the risk of neonatal death, not to mention higher rates of life-threatening infections for the baby and mother, increased chances of uterine rupture in later pregnancies, increased allergies in babies, and the list goes on. But I didn't say these things to my friend, nor could I say them to most of the mothers I knew. To raise questions about why they were being induced or pushed into C-sections somehow came across as critical of them as mothers, which was the last thing I meant. What I meant is that all mothers deserve a beautiful birth. All babies deserve it. All families deserve it.

There is so much that goes unsaid. For example, I always thought that pregnancy, birth, and caring for a new baby were all part of a continuum or trajectory, but they were three totally separate experiences. Both of my pregnancies feel so personal that even now I don't think of myself as having been pregnant with either of my sons. I was just me, pregnant. Birth was an intense, painful, infuriating, challenging metamorphosis—but again, it was my own. And then there were my delicious boys with their dark eyes, wrinkled brows, and tiny, eager hands. Home birth brought the seams of those experiences close, but they remained three distinct pieces of a whole for me.

When it came time to prepare for my second birth, I had thought a lot about my first experience and decided that what I needed to do to make it less rushed and more enjoyable for everyone was to cultivate a more go-with-the-flow attitude. I did hypnobirthing training, learning to cue myself into a meditative, trancelike state in which I would allow birth to wash over me. I bought candles, lavender oil, and New Age music with lots of tinkling chimes (not my usual style). When the time came, I had only to lie on the bed, close my eyes, and allow my baby to come. Man George would never even know.

And yet, as I lay meditating in preparation, I couldn't shake my uneasy feeling. I still had to get from one side of the unknown to the other. I also had a dark secret that I can now reveal because it turned out to be laughable: I was absolutely certain that I would never love my second child as much as my first, though I promised myself that he would never know. How little did I know about love! Of course I would not feel about this tiny larva of a newborn as I did about the person I had spent the last two years falling in love with—but I would. My capacity to love and my capacity to withstand pain both surprised me.

Withstanding pain should not be confused with welcoming it. On the day of labor, guess who showed up? That bitch from the last birth. Except this time, she was a little whiny, too. "Why does it have to be this way?" I moaned to my midwife and my mom, who had driven down from Vermont on my due date, five days before. Every time I found a position that felt more comfortable— buoyed in the tub, lying back in the rocking chair—my midwife shook her head apologetically. The baby was lounging over on one side of my belly in what my husband referred to as a "gangsta lean." Our task was to get him to move toward the center, with his spine in line with my belly button. It's okay to take a break, she told me again and again, but when you are feeling brave, you need to get up and walk. I was not feeling brave. I was feeling pissed off.

By then, my midwife knew me well. During the prenatal home visits, I lay on my bed as she listened to the heartbeat and then held the stethoscope to my ears so that I could hear. My son played with the measuring tape while we talked, sometimes for close to an hour, about various things that were often related to pregnancy—all the medical stuff, but also good recipes for iron, how to handle my older son during the birth, my husband's role in labor, what attachments we needed to connect a hose to our bathroom sink.

Just before 9:00 p.m. on another hot August night, it was time. We had had good luck getting the baby to shift over by having me lie on my opposite side, and it was while I was in that position that my midwife informed me that if I wanted to have a water birth, I needed to get into the tub pretty quickly. I was not about to move, so I began pushing right where I was, on the bed my father had built. When I say that I began pushing, I simply mean that the contractions changed from being waves that I withstood to being surges that urged my body to bear down. Each contraction was a paradox: simultaneous passivity and activity. I was powerless to the force and rhythm of them, and yet each asked something different of me, from subtle shifts in breathing and posture in early labor to primal moaning and swaying in active labor to the final stage, in which every cell in my body felt that it was being called on to push. I can't imagine what I would have said to my husband if he had yelled "Push!" like they do in the movies. It would be like yelling "Sneeze!" to someone clearly about to. The baby was inching down the birth canal and, despite my better judgment, I was making that happen. When I look back on the final few minutes of the birth, I remember the ridiculousness of having a head in my vagina, that famous burning ring of fire, the slippery wriggle that followed, and then the relief. And a baby. Where did he come from?

While I showered, rubbing my doughy belly and feeling blissfully autonomous, my mother went downstairs to check on my older son, who was asleep at his friend's apartment on the first floor of our building. She found him awake and excited to meet his new brother. As soon as he entered our bedroom, he climbed into my lap—the giant that he now was in comparison. This is the child who never stops speaking from the moment he wakes up to the moment his head hits the pillow, but in that moment he was dumbstruck. He pointed and grinned and pointed again. He watched silently from my lap while our midwife weighed the baby in a red polka-dotted sling hooked up to a scale—nine pounds even. And then when she had finished and his new brother was swaddled and resting, he uttered his first comment. "Let's take the baby to the museum." Later I would wonder whether he meant for us to leave him there, but I think his motives were pure. We take all of our favorite houseguests to the Brooklyn Museum, across the street.

Just as André poured glasses of champagne for everyone, our midwife's beeper went off, letting her know that another mother was going into labor. She packed up her tub and wheeled it out. She'd call the next day and come back in three days. One boy fell asleep on our bed, another rocked in my mother's arms a few feet away. It was nearly 11:00 p.m. and I was starving. André lit some candles at our dining room table and put a few pillows on a chair for me. We raised our glasses to a job well done, to our new baby, to our growing family. And then we raised them to Man George. While I'd been laboring, he'd been cooking rice and beans, conch, and fried plantains. He'd put the food into matching casserole dishes on a painted tray and delivered it to André sometime in the early evening, though I'd been too deep in my labor fog to notice.

George would give us a few weeks before he started banging on the ceiling again. Tomorrow we would wake up in our own beds and there would be coffee. And a baby to begin to love.

Three

HEIDI PITLOR

A few years ago, when I carted my two babies around the grocery store or Target, people regularly approached us and asked me whether I'd had help conceiving them. Each time, I responded—with a mix of irritation on behalf of the many people who need infertility treatments and dumb, misplaced pride— "No. Twins run in my family. My grandmother was a twin." *Not that it's any of your business.*

I never laid out the whole story to these curious strangers, of course. I did not say that although I was lucky enough not to have needed infertility treatments, I did experience a terrible miscarriage not long before I conceived the twins. I had been six months pregnant with a boy. One September night, excruciating pains shot through my lower abdomen as if bricks were pressing into me from every angle. The pain continued on and off, though mostly on for a week, a week of many ultrasounds (all normal) and visits to doctors. ("It's normal. Just ligaments stretching," one said. "Buck up. Pregnancy hurts," another doctor told me, a man to whom I nearly replied, "Did yours hurt?") A week of nearly no sleep, a week of fear and horrible cramping and pain and a growing sense that this pain was anything *but* normal.

And then one morning, nothing. No pain. No burps or kicks

from within, no movement at all. Except a slight, almost peaceful floating sensation, as if a heavy water balloon were sloshing back and forth inside of me. *Strange*, I thought, but at least the pain had gone.

The next day, at a regularly scheduled checkup, I lay on the examining table while my midwife dragged a fetal Doppler around and across the small hill of my abdomen to measure the baby's heartbeat. She tapped the end of the microphone and tried again. At last, she looked at me kindly and shook her head. "I'll go get the ultrasound ready," she said. She touched my arm and left the room. I lay there alone for about five minutes, staring up at stickers of ducks waddling across the ceiling, these pudgy, smiling ducks meant to comfort women as they got Pap smears or pelvic exams. I glanced over at a poster mapping out the stages of fetal growth. I finally looked down at my belly and immediately closed my eyes. My heart thudded. The midwife reappeared and walked me down a hallway to a closet-size room with an ultrasound machine. Here, that unsympathetic male doctor tried and failed to find a baby's heartbeat. "It's gone," he said, and the midwife took my hand.

Back in the exam room, I called my husband, who, bless him, came within minutes. We held each other, utterly at a loss for words, and soon after met with another doctor, who asked me to decide whether I wanted to deliver the baby or have a D & C (dilatation and curettage) to remove the baby. "Think about it," she said, handing me a rose-colored pamphlet. She told me that most people chose to deliver so that they can hold their baby one last time. "It helps you understand that you really were a mother." But I had a friend who had lost a baby even further along in her pregnancy. She had labored and delivered in the maternity ward of a hospital, where a dozen balloons were mistakenly delivered to her room and then whisked away. Babies wailed up and down the hallway. New grandparents peered in her room asking if she knew where their daughter was. *No thank you*, I decided right then. *No labor and delivery for me.* Are you sure? Certain? *Yes, please*, I said again and again. *I'm sorry, but I'm clear about my choice.* I never wavered—I felt quite sure that I had been and still was, in some unnamable way, a mother. The doctor explained the procedure for the D & C: I would be induced within a few days and the surgery would take place a few days after that. So for more than five days I would carry this baby boy within me. For five days I would continue to appear pregnant. I was more than a little nervous.

The strange thing was that these five days, while heartbreaking, were also a sort of gift. I had the chance to hold him inside me just a little while longer, just me and him, a five-day-long goodbye.

I was prescribed antibiotics, which caused me to vomit in the parking lot of my doctor's office. The next day, the doctor inserted twenty dilators, what felt like toothpicks, into my cervix. The following day brought twenty more, and we waited for me to begin to dilate. The next day, we drove to the hospital and I was wheeled to a waiting area far from the maternity ward. A nurse asked if I would like a priest to be present before or after the procedure. I declined and said, "I'm Jewish, sort of," meaning that it had been a long time since I had gone to temple. I was given a general anesthetic and the surgery was performed. When I woke, a group was standing before me: my husband, my doctor, a nurse, and a smiling woman wearing a large maroon-and-orange hat and a red patchwork pantsuit that for some reason made me think of Mummenschanz.

My doctor appeared excited. "She's a rabbi," my doctor said, gesturing to the woman. "We found her in the hallway."

"Would you like to sing a song?" the rabbi asked, and, too groggy to do much more, I shook my head, said thank you anyway, and passed out again.

When I woke again, the rabbi had left. My doctor told me that the surgery had gone well and that, as requested, the baby had been wrapped inside a blanket that we had brought for him, a soft yellow blanket that my aunt had recently given us.

Legally, we were required to name him and make burial arrangements. He was given a death certificate (though no birth certificate) and cremated. We decided to spread his ashes in the ocean and planted a small white fringe tree in our backyard in his memory. It blooms only in June and for only a few weeks, but it makes its presence known with its strong smell of honeysuckle and delicate but dense, almost hairlike, white foliage.

Grief. Long October days of eating blueberry muffins and reading trashy magazines and crying. My stomach shrank to its previous size. I had been told how to handle lactation if it occurred, but fortunately, it never did. I missed my boy. I saw him everywhere still, in the faces of small boys on the street, in the few items of clothing we had received as early gifts, in the ultrasound photos of him that we had been given while he was alive. Friends and family visited, and probably because of their generous sympathy and love, I let myself fall apart.

But I was thirty-six and this had been my first pregnancy. I knew I wanted more than one child—and time did not stop. We had to start to try again soon. I was not emotionally ready, nor was my husband. Still, according to the laws of biology and the advice of my doctor, *we really had to try*. During the autopsy, tiny blood clots had been found in our baby—this may or may not have been the cause of death, but I was assigned a doctor for high-risk pregnancies. He suggested if and when I did conceive again, I take shots of Lovenox, a blood thinner, each day as a precaution. "It couldn't hurt," the doctor said.

My husband and I went back to work. Christmas and Hanukkah came. We traveled to the Berkshires and, in February, up to Stowe, Vermont. We tried again to conceive—nervously, obediently—and one winter morning, the pregnancy stick showed a positive. We were happy. A little. Looking down at that white stick with the pink stripe, I said to my husband, "I'll be *really* happy when I'm holding a baby."

After six or seven weeks, we went back to my ob-gyn's office for our first checkup. I'd had some spotting and assumed the worst. So back into the ultrasound room with the same midwife I went. But this time there was no unsympathetic doctor, and my husband was with me. The ultrasound technician flicked on the monitor and squirted gel across my stomach. All eyes (except mine) turned to the screen. The midwife gasped—and my immediate thought: "The baby is gone." Someone said, "Two," and my husband's eyes ballooned. "Twins." Nurses and midwives rushed into the room. Someone said, "It's a miracle"; someone else added, "Bless Jesus"; and I laughed, I think, and swallowed hard, because now I could lose two babies.

"It's unbelievable," I said. "And poetic."

Pregnancy number two is inseparable from pregnancy number one in my mind. I lost one and soon after got two. I do not know precisely why either happened. But I am aware that I am profoundly and eerily lucky.

I gave myself painful shots of Lovenox in my upper thigh twice a day. And my belly began to grow at an alarming rate. Every few weeks, I sat across the waiting room from women the size of refrigerators at my high-risk doctor's office. I tried to estimate how many babies they carried, how far along they were. At about four months, I myself looked seven months pregnant. The twins would be a boy and a girl. I saw them on those ultrasound screens, in their separate sacs, a yin and yang squirming beside each other, nuzzling my ribs and pelvis. Sometimes one would sleep while the other danced—my son was on my left side; my daughter lay along the length of my right. One would hiccup, the other punch at me. Five months passed and the prenatal tests were encouraging. But the six-month mark loomed, the point at which my first baby had passed away. And after that, well, my friend had lost her baby at eight months.

When you are pregnant with twins, you are told to gain weight quickly. The biggest risk is premature labor. *Keep those babies inside you as long as possible. Get them as close to a healthy birth weight as possible before they arrive.* So I ate—ice cream, mostly. Each day, I and they grew. Six months arrived and there was no pain, no sign of danger. Seven and my daughter began to drop, so bed rest was ordered. Each day, I lay across our couch, reading and watching home-improvement TV shows and eating ice cream. And expanding rapidly.

Seven and a half months, eight, and I could come off bed rest, but at this point, I could hardly walk. People told me that I looked as if I were wearing a costume—a car, maybe. I spent each day at my sister's house, as she lived minutes from the hospital where I planned to deliver. I set up camp on her couch and tried not to complain too much about my increasing discomfort. I could hardly breathe. I had a difficult time even then allowing myself hope that this pregnancy would yield happy results. I would not have a baby shower or, for that matter, buy much of anything for the babies until the last-possible moment.

Eight and a half months. The babies were measuring large—more than five pounds each. I begged my doctor to schedule an induction. I felt frantic to know when—and frankly that—these babies would arrive. At nine months she would, she said.

Thirty-seven weeks and two days. I could not move. I could not sleep. In the middle of one of many sleepless nights, I shook my husband awake (he'd been ordered downstairs to sleep elsewhere, as I required the whole of our queen-size bed, but for some reason, he had made his way back). "It's time," I said.

"Contractions?" he asked.

"Maybe," I said. I'd had Braxton-Hicks contractions and miscellaneous other pings and pangs for roughly five months now. *Sure, why not*, I was in labor. I don't know exactly what prompted this lie other than the increasingly obvious truth: *I couldn't remain in this condition for one more second.* And perhaps that I needed at least to *feel* that I could control the ending of this pregnancy.

Bless him again, my husband quickly got us ready and drove me to the hospital, where a nurse strapped black Velcro belts around my girth to monitor my contractions. I wasn't in labor, of course. A doctor told me my choices: "You can go home and wait, or we can induce you, break your water." I said, "I'm not leaving this hospital without two babies."

A short while later, a nurse came in the room and stuck a knitting needle–like instrument deep between my legs, a procedure that was oddly painless. The anesthesiologist appeared, a man who somehow knew my husband, and the two began to chitchat. I was nervous, edgy, aware that the pain of contractions would likely start soon, and although I had hoped to at least try for a "natural" labor without drugs, it took but a brief scowl from the nurse and I acquiesced. The epidural was administered. I lay back. Within minutes, I was the most comfortable I had been in months. We watched the midterm elections on TV. My husband napped. All was well, for a while.

Nurses and midwives came in to check on my dilation and seemed frustrated that I was not moving along quicker. Night arrived and still I did not sleep, but I was comfortable and tired, if increasingly fearful about all the possibilities of what lay ahead. Around ten o'clock, I was wheeled into a chilly operating room and hoisted by a handful of nurses and orderlies onto the operating table. I remember whiteness and a hard shine everywhere: the metal of lights, the metal of the table, and of two glass carts into which my babies would be placed. A midwife whom I'd never met, a doctor, several nurses, and random men (orderlies, maybe, and ultrasound technicians, too, if I had to guess) scurried around me and I was told to push. Although I was relaxed, I had very little strength, since I had not slept for so long. I pushed two or three times and the crowd between my legs frowned down at me. "You need to do better than that," someone said, and I pushed again. For ten minutes. Thirty minutes. An hour. I began to feel some pain, and again it was decided that I needed more drugs, so an anesthesiologist was summoned—about the sixth one I'd met at this point—and gave me enough to last the next half hour. "Push," the nurses demanded. "Do better." "Give it everything you've got." I pushed. I cried. I howled. I morphed into an entirely different species—part wolf, part immovable swine, part mewling kitten. I began to feel wildly ill-equipped for this whole mission. "Come on, get angry," someone ordered. I pushed again. I growled. I pushed more. "The head is there. You just need to push," the midwife commanded. Two hours had passed since I had first started pushing. The anesthesiologist returned several more times. Three hours. Four. At some point, it was determined that my daughter, who was lower and positioned to come out first, had jammed herself inside of me, using her elbow as a block above her head. If nothing else at this point, I felt vindicated and a little less incompetent. I may have asked for suction or a C-section, but my midwife wouldn't have it. Neither baby was breech; both were healthy. There was no real reason for surgery. A rust-haired nurse standing by my head brushed her dry lips against my ear as she said again and again, "Be a strong woman."

Now, I am a feminist. I consider myself an independent, strong-willed female, and so perhaps this is what prompted me to do the following. I sat partway up, for the first time in well over five hours, and announced to the crowd between my legs, "Please excuse me, but I need to say this." I turned to this well-meaning nurse and said, "Go fuck yourself." I collapsed backward as her mouth clapped shut.

More time passed. Someone said something about a head appearing and did I want to touch it? "No," I grunted—I was unable to move my arms or form any other word at this point—and I pushed more, six hours in total, to get the first baby out. And finally, finally, something large was pulled from me and whisked away. My baby girl, born at 4:14 a.m., was cleaned and wrapped in a blanket and placed on my chest. I said, "I've never been so glad to meet anyone." She looked pleased to meet me, too, if a little tired, but she was sweet and beautiful and far more human than I might have thought. So many books and people had warned us that most babies come out looking spotted or red, reptilian or skinny. But she was pleasantly filled out, weighing a healthy seven pounds, five ounces. The midwife nurses whooped at this. A twin rarely weighs much more than five pounds, they said.

My contractions had been measured by a loud, aquatic-sounding machine, and less than one second after my daughter pushed free, the hollow dreambeats began again. My husband took her and it was time, already, to get my son out. "Cough," the midwife said impatiently. "Just cough and he'll come out." I looked down at her. Who was she? Who was I? Where were we? The midwife returned and repeated, "Cough."

"I can't," I said.

"Try," she demanded. I issued forth the slightest, most feminine approximation of a cough. I believe I got more drugs and faux-coughed several more times.

Somehow, in some way, my son was born thirty-one minutes after his sister, crying and curled, probably terrified that he'd been left alone in that vast cave for so long. I held him and thought that he looked more vulnerable than his sister, adorable and alive and clearly frightened of this strange, new white and metal place. He weighed in at seven pounds, six ounces. News quickly spread through the hospital of the woman (the strong woman, damn it) who had given birth to nearly fifteen pounds of baby—and not by C-section.

I wish I could say that I felt only glee at these miracles. I certainly felt love as I held my children, each wrapped in a white blanket, and looked down at their faces for the first time. I felt enormous relief and pride and, perhaps more than anything, sheer disbelief that they had arrived now and were as healthy as could be. But I also felt enormous fatigue after more than twenty hours of labor and six and a half hours of pushing. I was in and out of consciousness. I had lost a good amount of blood and desperately needed sleep.

I was wheeled into a long hallway and toward a hospital room.

It was suggested that I receive a blood transfusion. I had torn slightly and the stitches needed to be resewn. I had to start breast-feeding immediately. Meanwhile, I felt about as animated and capable of any of this as a hand towel left out in a mud puddle. Someone else would have to get an IV full of new blood and stitches in her crotch and feed those babies. I did, however, feel capable of lying in my bed and holding them in their ill-fitting baby johnnies and tiny white caps. That I could do. And I could kiss their warm, wispy heads.

Many people—nurses, my family—came in and told me I looked terrible. They also cooed at the two babies, swaddled and lying snuggly next to each other in their glass-sided crib. I think I may have slept a while and made one or two lame attempts at breast-feeding. That evening, the babies were taken to the nursery for the night so that I could finally rest and my body could recover. My husband went home so that he, too, could get a decent night's sleep. But about halfway through the night, a frenzied nurse raced my babies in their glass crib back into my room. Apparently, they had been kicked out of the nursery for crying too much and waking all the other babies. Right on, I thought. Give them hell. But then it dawned on me that I alone would be on duty with them for the rest of the night. I was unable to sit up. I hadn't eaten in about three days. I still hadn't gotten that blood transfusion. I begged a nurse to help me, and she shrugged and reluctantly agreed. Thankfully, we all made it through that night.

I remember the surprise of how much was expected of me: I was to go home that next morning. I'd already had two nights in the hospital, more than was usually granted by insurance companies. Another midwife took pity on me and filled out paperwork that would allow me to stay another night. I would get that blood transfusion, and, with it, a flood of new energy. I practiced standing and walking, changed the babies' diapers. I ate something, I believe. And I lined up a crew of as many bodies as possible—my husband, nurses, family—to help me make it through the next night. And I—we—did. The babies spent another part of the night in the nursery and were returned to me washed and coiffed. Apparently, they had eased up their crying and other bad behavior. They now smelled of roses and their hair fluffed from their heads like the fur of new chicks.

That morning, we were sent off. Car seats? Check. Babies that are yours? Check of their wristbands. Breast pump, my clothes, their clothes, bottles, book-size maxi pads, blankets, flowers, toys, nose-suction bulbs—check, check, check. Ready? *I hope so.*

I waited in the hospital lobby with the twins in their enormous double snap-on stroller, my son wailing to the heavens, my daughter fast asleep, while my husband went off to get the car. I smiled at people who walked past me, their eyes wide. "I did it," I wanted to yell throughout the hospital. After so much, after everything. "I did it! Twins!" I grinned like a tired, proud idiot.

Three and a half years later, on a sunny April day, I was lying on our lawn between my children, next to our white fringe tree. We were "reading the clouds," or telling one another the animals that each cloud resembled: sheep, whale, dinosaur. Out of nowhere, my daughter said, "I wish I had a big brother." Of course, we had not told the twins about the first pregnancy. No one had, as far as I knew. I felt the strangest collision of shock and sadness and gratitude in my chest. I turned to look at her and touch her brown-gold hair and said the first thing that came to mind: "That would be nice."

What to Expect When You're Not Expecting

MARIE MYUNG-OK LEE

I didn't know what to expect while I was expecting, mostly because I didn't expect to ever *be* expecting. And yet here I was, in my ninth month, just beginning to learn about pain-relief options (there were options?) and that you could actually have someone other than a doctor deliver your baby.

In order to understand how I ended up this way, we need to reel the story all the way back to when I was nine, when I inherited an old typewriter from an elder brother. This event allowed me to type up one of my numerous horse stories, three-hole-punch it, and sell it to my parents for a nickel. I decided on the spot, a nine-year-old in rural Minnesota, that this was what I wanted to do: BECOME A WRITER, which meant I would (1) MOVE TO NEW YORK, (2) LIVE IN A GARRET APARTMENT, and (3) HAVE A CAT AND BOOKS FOR COMPANY. Because I'd be so busy pursuing my career, inherent in this list was the proviso: NEVER HAVE CHILDREN.

Thus, while my childhood friends played with their Baby Alives, eventually graduating to babysitting actual babies, I kept aloof, aided and abetted by the fact that my parents were Korean War refugees, plunked in the middle of midwestern nowhere due to circumstance and history. Ergo, we had zero relatives: no cousins, aunts, or uncles, no grandparents, no regular exposure to the cycle of life. I was often dispatched to study, or play the piano for guests, but never to change a diaper or amuse a baby cousin. This made it so much easier to concentrate on pursuing the artist's life, one without any familial responsibility. A high school English teacher noted my focus, monomaniacal even then, and allowed me to skip her class in favor of writing in the library. My senior year in high school was marked by publishing an essay in *Seventeen*, as well as by the first of my friends becoming pregnant.

After college I proceeded to New York to make a go of it. I acquired a stray cat, Arthur, both of us supported by my "day" job at Goldman Sachs. This was the age of Yuppies, and soon my Yuppie friends began having children in broods and packs. I was still partnered with my college boyfriend, Karl, who wanted and planned on kids. I presumed at some point he'd agree with me on the advantages of the kid-free life—no college tuitions to save for, and that most precious resource: time. Or, he'd move on to find someone more reproduction-friendly. But big life choices can be pushed to the periphery by the small urgencies of the day-to-day, and thus our twenties flew by, my fertility ignored thanks to birth-control pills.

At thirty, I had the cat, the apartment (nicer than a garret, thanks to Goldman Sachs), and I was finally hitting my stride. I'd also won a fellowship funding a yearlong research trip to Korea for my novel. And then, within the fissure of my leaving New York for Seoul, Karl's mother became ill with pancreatic cancer.

To make a long story short, the smugness I felt about being a young person, a Fulbright fellow happily writing into my future, was cut short when Karl's mother, only sixty-three, succumbed during one of my visits back home. The closeness I felt with Karl and his family in this time of crisis made me wonder if my usual modus operandi might be one I would grow out of, if being tucked cozily within the cell of a family might actually be something I'd want.

When I softened my stance on children, Reader, we married. After I came back from Korea, we stopped using birth control. I became pregnant right away, and we presumed everything else about creating a family would be just as easy. But I miscarried three months later. It was the miscarriage, or maybe the failure it represented, that made me want to try again, with gusto. After all, I'd achieved my childhood dream of becoming a writer despite everyone telling me it couldn't be done. And now that we'd moved to a much more financially sane situation, both returning to teach at our alma mater in a small, livable city, what better conditions could there be for having a child?

I redoubled my efforts, stopped drinking coffee, watched what I ate, and I was pregnant again. Then, seemingly days—and a shocking forty pounds—later, on the cusp of giving birth.

Again, since I'd presumed I'd never have children, I'd observed my friends' pregnancies with a kind of removed curiosity, like I do with my brother-in-law's job as an air-traffic controller, thinking, That is so cool, but also thinking, I can relax, knowing *I'll* never be called upon to do that.

So when asked about my thoughts on pain relief, I was clueless. To get up to speed, I turned to interviewing my sundry friends and various medical experts. I heard everything from "I felt like I was going to split in two!" to "I had a patient who felt some pressure and thought she was having a bowel movement. She delivered her own kid with no pain." People espoused breathing techniques, epidurals, the Bradley Method, the narcotic Stadol, doulas, a morphine drip. Each person's feedback took on the fervency and faith of a Moonie wedding; it was thus hard to know what was "normal." "You *have* to get an epidural." "Don't get an epidural; they cause C-sections." "Make sure you—"

As my last trimester dwindled, my confusion only grew. I'd switched to a midwife largely because I'd felt my male OB was inattentive and dismissive. Laura, my midwife, took the time to answer all our questions, no matter how paranoid or basic. When it came to pain relief, she was pretty catholic. The practice's only restriction was that if I should entertain even the slightest possibility of wanting an epidural, I couldn't use the hospital's cozy Alternative Birthing Center, which resembled a bedroom rather than the tiny dorm-like hospital labor room. So in order to have a birth that didn't use an institutional rubber-sheeted bed with a zillion beeping monitors, I'd have to have a *National Geographic*–type natural birth with very little medical equipment beside me—at best, a handheld Doppler device to check the baby's heartbeat from time to time, and *maybe* I'd be allowed a shot of narcotics if I became that desperate. It was a pretty big either/or.

In my third trimester, I also found myself hanging out with Deepak Chopra. (Who doesn't like to say that? Actually, we were both just taking part in the same lecture series.) Since he had begun his training as a neuroendrocrinologist specializing in *pain*, as well as being the alternative medicine guru we all know, well, *he* could decide! When I broached the topic over dinner, he gave me a long, pitying look. He didn't lecture me about an epidural versus narcotics or about dendrites, calcium channels, endorphins, the mind-body connection, et cetera, but instead declared that if I would just not "Westernize" (that is, fear) labor, I wouldn't feel any pain, like the African bushwoman who crawls behind a rock to give birth and emerges with her baby in a sling and still puts in the rest of the day's work chopping cassava and gathering firewood. It wasn't epidural versus no epidural; it was all in my Westernized mind, he insisted. If I didn't fear the pain, I wouldn't feel it. When I broached this with my friends who'd given birth, they'd all keeled over laughing. Only a man could say that with such aplomb, they said.

I thus arrived at the big questions of my labor ass-backward, more like a squinty, tentative anthropologist or like George Plimpton during his "participatory journalism" phase, where he'd write about boxing by observing from, well, the middle of the ring—with gloves on and a real boxer trying to hit him. Even after nine months,

I still felt like the observer, never like I was quite in it. But as my child's yet-unknown birth day drew inexorably closer and our midwife *and* doula (why not have more people on our side?) made us sit down and write out an actual birth plan, I was realizing that choosing one thing over another would be, basically, a referendum on what I believed, my earliest documented statement on parenting. Earth mother or high-tech urban mommy? Breast or bottle? Rooming in or nursery? Drugs or just say no?

The monopolistic high-rise women's hospital in our small state was built around the high-tech option. You'd be in a small room with a TV, hooked up to your drugs and a monitor that would record the fetus's vitals continuously; you'd be NPO (that is, nothing to eat or drink except maybe ice chips). When our prenatal class was given the tour, the last places we visited, almost like an afterthought, were the measly two rooms of the Alternative Birthing Center (one much smaller than the other). While both were appointed with homey touches, like a real bed, and the larger one had a Jacuzzi, they were still situated in the hospital's windowless basement, next to some kind of heavy hospital equipment that seemed to involve radiation. The regular delivery floor, it was stressed repeatedly, was by far the "safer" option, as opposed to the ABC, which, they implied, they kept only to placate the extreme hippy-dippy demographic. If something went wrong, our guide warned us, we'd have to depend on a balky elevator to get upstairs . . . and then who knew what could happen? Cue the ominous music: *dum . . . dum . . . dum . . .*

After that PSA, the only one of our group brave enough to declare her allegiance to the ABC was the gravida I referred to as "Yoga Lady": part-time yoga instructor, white woman with an acquired Hindi name. Even though a first-timer like the rest of us, she was sure she would never come within a mile of formula, pacifiers, cribs, or toxic birth drugs. During our last few meetings, she was a champ at calmly breathing through Braxton-Hicks practice contractions, while the rest of us doubled over and said, "Ugh!"

when they happened. Maybe there was something to the Yoga Mind.

I'd started my pregnancy on the opposite shore, as an M.D.'s daughter. I'd thus happily begun with the gray-haired male OB, had every clinical test and procedure and more, including a zillion ultrasounds, rubella titers, the newest "quad" blood tests, and a flu shot. My father was not just a doctor but a famous anesthesiologist—he had been one of the first anesthesiologists in the world capable of administering anesthesia medications during open-heart surgery. Thus, over the twelve years of my mother's fertility, she received what he proudly termed the "Cadillac of anesthesia drugs": saddle blocks (an epidural precursor), twilight anesthetics, major, *major* narcotics.

But now, what had been amusing family stories of birth—my older brother with his head dented and bruised by the forceps needed to drag his unresponsive body from my mother's womb; an overzealous helping of drugs, causing my sister not to gain consciousness for *two hours* postpartum—took on a very different cast. I ended up joining Yoga Lady in signing up for the ABC.

In a perfect dress rehearsal, in my eighth month, a mole on my back changed color and needed to be removed; I insisted on having it done without anesthesia. The dermatologist reluctantly complied, looking at me somewhat dubiously, but he cooled it with something, like using an ice cube for a home ear piercing, and it really wasn't that bad.

On the cusp of my due date, I was at a friend's house. We'd gone through pregnancy together, only her child was now on the outside. While balancing her newborn on my enormous dromedary hump, I contemplated how he looked impossibly tiny but also ridiculously large compared to my vagina, which contorted in spasms when I tried to merely insert a "junior" tampon. I asked my friend how her labor had gone. She replied she'd gotten through one set of the *hoo-hoo hee-hee* breathing we'd been taught in the prenatal class and then gave up and asked for an epidural, which, she said, was the best thing *ev-er*: She watched TV and joked with her husband for the rest of the labor, popping out her son with only a small tear a few hours later.

The fourteenth of January broke clear and cold. In fact, it was one of the coldest days ever recorded in Rhode Island history. The three-foot snowbanks outside our house suddenly solidified into ice sculptures. I remember thinking, Oh God, I hope I don't go into labor today. Two minutes later, I emerged from the bathroom, wondering why I'd just peed a bowlful of blood ("bloody show"— which is normally just a trickle, but as you'll see, I don't do anything halfway). I started having contractions right away.

The way we were taught, we had a bag packed: snacks, slippers, a tennis ball for back labor, two copies of the birth plan. We some- how got the car up the icy driveway and headed to the hospital, where we were to meet Ginny, a midwife. During our last prenatal visits, we'd rotated through the midwives so we could meet every- one, since we didn't know who'd actually be on call when the time came. We knew everyone *except* Ginny; she was part of a reab- sorption of health professionals resulting from the local Harvard Health HMO going belly-up. She greeted us grimly, her hair piled in a messy bun. She didn't know us from Adam, *plus*, she already had three other patients in labor. She actually seemed a little an- noyed to see us. I spent a few desultory minutes on the fetal moni- tor while she flew off, presumably to the ABC, and when she returned, she confirmed something I was keenly aware of: I was in labor. To punctuate the point, my water broke, dripping all over the sterile hospital floor. But Ginny insisted we go home, saying first labors are slow. We learned in retrospect that while first labors often are slow, it was hospital policy that you stayed in the hospital if your water broke there, because funny things could happen.

By the time we got home—a whole ten minutes later—I was racked with unbearable pain. It took forever to hump my bulk back up the iced-over steps to the house. Once there, all I wanted to do was roll like a weevil on the floor and howl. A hot shower, despite being sold to us as a miraculous analgesic, did absolutely squat. Karl, not knowing what else to do, made pancakes, which I couldn't fathom eating. Despite the edict not to call Ginny unless there was an emergency, it was clear I was about to lose it, so Karl called. It took forever for her to call us back. And when she did, she told us to come back in.

It was all I could do not to start screaming at the check-in desk, where the woman made us wait, and then, in the world's slowest Rhode Island drawl, took many minutes to insist that we resubmit all our insurance information, even though we'd just been at the hospital that morning. Ginny was called, but she was "busy," and also, both the ABC rooms were in use, so instead I'd be taken up to the regular labor floor. My contractions by then were insane, so unlike anything I'd ever seen in movies—including the movie they played in our prenatal class to show us what labor was supposed to be like. In a normal labor, a contraction comes on like a wave, then subsides. My contractions were piling up one on top of another into a single tsunami of pain. I tried to find some space between suppressing my screams to ask the nurse for a birthing ball—as if that would have helped. The nurse took one look at me (later she said it was the way I was grunting that made her realize) and said I needed to start pushing. I was having a "precipitous" birth, one that was too fast for me and possibly the baby. My gray rag socks had turned pink from the blood that was gushing out.

The rest was a jumble. I was hustled to a tiny delivery room, the halogen lights flipped on, rubber sheets out, people in what looked like blue hazmat suits with face shields wandering about. I remember hearing the male anesthesiologist coming in and telling not me, but Ginny, with some pity that I was too far gone for an epidural. Ginny had come in with her hair even more disheveled, that grim, annoyed look on her face, concurring with the nurse that indeed I had to get ready to push. I thought we would do one of the baby-friendly positions, maybe a squat to be aided by gravity, but she had me in the old OB's lithotomy position, flat on my back, while she attached a fetal monitor, stuck a hand up my vagina, and scratched the poor baby's head to see if it elicited a pain reaction.

Speaking of which, I had reached that threshold of pain where I realized if I had a gun, I would have shot myself just to make it stop. This kind of pain was unreal, unrelenting; it literally blinded me. I could hear only snatches of conversation. Karl said that in the excitement over my precipitous birth, the room became filled with personnel.

I did hear "That's *a lot* of blood." And "Uh-oh, the FH is dropping."

FH? FH? Fetal heart rate. FETAL HEART RATE!

I heard but didn't see Ginny saying it was very, very important for them to get the baby out NOW. Someone stuck an IV of Pitocin (ironically, to speed up the labor, as if it weren't already going at crazy warp speed) in my arm without asking. I pushed, and pushed again. Someone brought out the vacuum extractor. So much for the two-hour "transition" period that eases the labor to the pushing stage—I'd gone straight to the roughest and most painful work of pushing within minutes. The midwives had talked to us about using warm oil compresses to help the perineum stretch to let the baby out. Karl said Ginny emerged with a huge scalpel and, declaring more than asking, gave me a gigantic episiotomy (no-no number 3 on the birth plan), mumbling that there was no time for an anesthetic. I was in so much pain, I barely felt it.

J., a baby boy (we'd guessed a girl), propulsively shot out exactly at 3:00 p.m., a little more than an hour after we'd checked in. I had been pushing for *ten minutes*. I caught a glimpse of a purpled baby, intensively screeching, but Ginny, instead of putting him on my chest, as I expected, handed him off, and he was taken away. Midwives will routinely put a not-so-pink baby on the mother's chest (most of the time, they pink up right away), but, as it was later explained to us, being in the high-tech area, everyone was overly tense about brain damage from hypoxia and wanted to test J. six ways to Sunday.

I was dazed, feeling paralyzed. Karl and I were both crying from the trauma. We had just been through a war—and we had nothing to hold.

There was a clonk. Someone was trying to enter the already full-to-capacity room. It was our doula, finally. "What *happened*?" she said when she saw the mess, and about every kind of medical intervention short of a C-section and an appendectomy. And, at that time, even though I'd directed them *not to* (no-no number 5 on the birth plan), in some room somewhere, the staff was putting antibiotic eyedrops in J.'s eyes.

J. was returned to us, pinked up, blinking furiously through the drops, clearly making a mighty attempt to see me. I stared back at him, his tiny face, his corneas submerged in the viscous drops as if they were tears. This minuscule being seemed to be say-ing "Help meeeeee" with every bit of his blurry expression. For a minute, I was hit by a wave of anxiety: Could I do it? I'd already messed up his birth plan. But then in the next, I gathered him up and held on. He latched onto my breast like a pro. In the photo I have, his face is a picture of utter determination, and I was this beautiful creature's mother.

Labor is a metaphor for life. You can have your beliefs, your expectations, your plans, but when it comes, it just comes and does what it wants. Yoga Lady, it turned out, had had an interesting birth, as well: After thirty-six hours of "nonproductive" labor de-spite her preparatory inner toning exercises, she must have said whatever her version was of fuck it and not only agreed to a mor-phine drip but also opted to stay in the hospital, despite having gone to the trouble to get clearance for an early release so she could go home and thereby escape the "toxic" atmosphere and make her labor as close to a home birth as possible. Instead, she recounted at our reunion, she maxed out her hospital stay, thoroughly availing herself of the call button and various postpartum pain meds.

Thirteen years later, I still am trying to make sense of J.'s birth story. I joke that it was the most painful day of my life—and it definitely was. Nothing since has come close, both in terms of pain and emotional intensity. And the context in which J.'s birth should be seen is also still shrouded in a sense of ambiguity. Was this a case where crack medical personnel got him out before any real damage could occur? (He is also severely developmentally disabled, which may be, but likely isn't, related.) Or was all the to-do an over-reaction, the panic only intensifying my pain, our precious first minutes as a family squandered on useless tests and unnecessary eyedrops?

I can't help wondering, had I been with a midwife I knew and trusted or had the doula gotten there on time, whether I would have been able to be a more direct agent of my own labor. Maybe I could have refused to go back home after my water broke. And as the years have gone by, the intensity of parenting a special-needs child has made me a lot more patient, and a lot more chill—as well as quicker to speak up when necessary. To an often-judgmental outside world, I must speak for my child, who cannot communicate. Would this new confidence have helped me be more than just a passive, scared patient having things done to her? If I had been more relaxed, less fearful, could I have brought out my inner African bushwoman? Perhaps this is one of the subconscious reasons why my next novel is about an OB and the birthing industry. I have spent the last eight years steeped in that world and watched countless births, looking for an answer. I have as yet never seen a birth that even remotely resembled mine.

But what I do know for certain: That day I labored was itself an ending to a story. I stopped being a pregnant woman at three o'clock that afternoon. And right then, my son, J., started his own story, one that he adds to every day. And by doing this, he made me a mother, and so we are continuing this story, together.

The Twin

LAUREN GROFF

My baby grew at the center of me, his cells splitting into flesh, hardening into bone. As he grew, so did his imaginary twin, a baby made not of flesh but of sadness.

Before I even began to show, I was filled with wild pulses of anxiety. At night, I would roam the house in my bathrobe, checking the doors and windows for the twelfth time, the thirteenth, the fourteenth. During the day, unable to concentrate on my work, I would stay in bed, willing my eyes open to the sky outside the window. When I closed them, the nightmares would arrive. My imagination in my normal life runs to the exuberantly surreal, but these nightmares were far too real, the world as I knew it, but suddenly curdled. There were pandemics in these nightmares, people lying down one by one in the streets to die. There were droughts, the green places I love crisped brown, the lakes drying up, the fish beginning to stink. There were hurricanes, my Florida house smashed as if by an enormous fist. There was hunger.

As if to appease the darker twin, I ate; as if to sweeten his bitterness, I ate sweets: puddings and muffins and entire crisper drawers of fruit.

An image of me in those days: standing before the open refrigerator in my underwear on a hot March afternoon, belly only a little extended, sucking down slippery slices of mango, handfuls of grapes, pineapple that made my mouth burst out in constellations of blisters. At my four-month checkup, I weighed twenty pounds more than usual.

Whoa, said the midwife softly, then wrote the number in the folder.

My doctor was a small Greek man who spoke in a Muppet voice. My friend had recommended him, and I liked his bracing crispness, his efficiency when he did the exams. It meant that he saw a million women a day who were pregnant, that my pregnancy was no big deal, a matter of rote. When I was alone at home, this thing happening to my body felt far too horrifyingly specific, and there was comfort in the sea of round bodies in his waiting room, the calm women with the fat ankles and the toddlers gently misbehaving in the corner. I always left the doctor's office feeling reassured, practically jaunty.

And then the long, lonely walk to the car in the Florida humidity, and the darker twin would awaken and give me a kick, and before I even reached the car I would remember to be afraid.

Everything had slowly become perilous, the chemicals in my carrots, the plastic in my house, the water I drank, the forest fires that filled the air with smoke that spring and summer. Every single car crushed mine in my imagination just before it passed, and then the next one bore ominously down. I stopped driving.

And it is true: This world of ours is a frightening place. There is so much that can kill us suddenly, singly or en masse. We are tender creatures who are physically weak, our bodies easy to smash or bruise, our minds easy to warp. Being human means feeling pain. Having a baby means that you are bringing a person into uncertainty, into life, into an assurance of eventual death. Having a baby is an ethical decision, always. From within such deep sadness, the ethical decision became my moral failure, as if the filter that keeps the real horror of the world at a distance, so that I could function in my normal life, was gone, and the only thing between the baby and certain ruin was my increasingly stretched skin.

At six months, I would get out of bed for breakfast with my husband, wait until he left for work, then give in to the sadder twin and go back to bed. At seven months, I was forty pounds heavier than before pregnancy. At eight months, I sat in the examining room with the midwife for three hours, weeping so hard that I couldn't speak. She calmly patted my head and suggested drugs. I refused, fearing that they would harm the baby, the good, fleshly one who was already weighing in at eight pounds, with more to go. (A paradox: When I needed chemical intervention, I was in no position to make that decision. Friends, I should have had the drugs.)

By my due date, I was elephantine, seventy pounds overweight, unable to move well. It was a very hot August, the roads buckling, the vegetation dun brown, no hint of absolving rain in the air. I would go to the community pool to be briefly weightless for a few laps and cry in the water, which was almost like not crying at all.

An old man's sun-spotted hands on my belly in a wet black bathing suit: This is the only image I have of myself then.

The due date passed. My mother, who had come down to take care of us, and who is both the kindest and most anxious human being on the planet, began muttering to herself all over the house. I couldn't escape the roiling baby within or the thin hum of my mother's worried voice without. My father and sister came a few days later, having booked the flights with the expectation that there would be a baby to hold. We tried to wipe the strain off our faces when we came upon one another in the hallway.

On the seventh day past my due date, to jostle the baby out of me, I went for a three-mile run, which was more like a three-mile waddle with trotting intermissions. Nothing. On the tenth day, I started feeling queasy over lunch, and realized the queasiness was labor only that night, when my sister and I sat up to watch

Labyrinth and I had to run to the bathroom every two minutes to throw up. Even now, an unexpected David Bowie song will make me ill, which seems like a terrible waste. I tried to watch the movie again a year ago, but I felt the black clouds massing above my head with the first song and, in a panic, threw the DVD away.

That night was long and sweaty. I went to the hospital in the early morning, my husband's face taut with fear. I had been expecting a very localized, very precise pain, and I felt cheated when the pain was instead massive and everywhere: I didn't know how to fight something that was everywhere. I cried a lot, then grew angry with myself for crying, then angry at my body for not behaving. I was dilated only three centimeters for another fifteen hours. My mother fretted, pacing back and forth in the room. My husband's breath smelled horrid. I hated them both. I hated the baby. I hated myself. I would have erased the group of us from the world with my palms, like smudging away a drawing on a chalkboard, if I could have.

I had wanted a natural childbirth, but when the anesthesiologist came into the room with the epidural, I kissed his hands.

When, after more than thirty-six hours of active labor, the nurse said it was time to push, I was groggy and grateful and tried to be a good girl, my mom and husband holding my legs. They tell me I pushed for four hours. I can only ascribe my failure to progress as another sign of the bad twin, stopping things up. I vaguely remember my mother peering between my legs, then putting her finger in to feel for the baby's crown and, when she could barely touch it, shouting at the nurse. My mother became so gloriously angry, this marvel of a woman who will always have my back, that my husband was forced to gently eject her from the room.

That is when the Muppet doctor came in, gave a little clinical feel, and announced that my mother was right; the baby was caught on my hipbones, which never spread the way they were supposed to. He took a long look at the machine monitoring the baby and me.

Here is where things get unforgivable, though I have tried to forgive my doctor. Seen from the flip side, efficiency can also be criminal unkindness.

The baby comes out right now with a C-section, or it comes out in three days, in pieces, the doctor said.

Now! my husband and I shouted, and in a moment, we were in the operating room, and there were fifteen people wavering about like blue ghosts, and bright lights, and the anesthesiologist, and a curtain went up bisecting my torso, and everyone was volleying words like badminton birdies above me, and my body started to shake so hard that my shoulders and head were slamming down on the stainless-steel table, and the nurses, glorious nurses, were saying soft, sweet things to me, and finally my husband came in, crying a little above his mask, and the doctor told me he was making an incision. Everything became a bit more serious then.

There will be a little pressure here, the doctor said, and there was a huge amount of pressure on my midsection. I was sure I would never breathe again. And then there was a slow sucking sound.

They lifted something from inside my body, my child. Miracles are miracles because they are impossible to cage in words. The delivery of the flesh was a deliverance from the darkness; when the doctor lifted my baby out of me, they lifted my sadness with him. I cannot understand it. I bow with gratitude.

There was a gasp. The baby was so blue and his hands and feet so swollen that they looked like adult hands attached to a baby's body. My Greek Muppet doctor held him over the curtain, this screaming blue goblin, and shouted, He's perfect.

Then they were bent over the baby, administering his tests, and all I wanted was his small body on my shuddering one so that I could smell him and feel his warmth, suddenly external to mine. Nothing mattered; the world beyond the operating room was still as frightening as ever. There were still wars, there was still hunger, there were sudden invisible diseases everywhere, and no amount of checking the locks would hold them back.

At last, they brought my real baby to me, the puckered purple face, the extraordinary solidity of this person I had made, his searching tiny mouth, the bleeding laceration on his scalp from where it had rubbed against my bones. He still has a scar there, under his hair. It didn't matter then and still doesn't. The baby had arrived, and had banished his twin by arriving. He was well, at least for now. He was whole.

Blood and Chocolate

SARAH JEFFERIS

1. Warning: Live Sperm Inside

Every lesbian who has the mama bug wants healthy sperm, but I wanted articulate sperm. I didn't need a picture. I found a sperm bank that required donors to compose essays that expressed their opinions about families. And the donor we chose wrote about helping lesbians who couldn't have babies, providing them with a chance to move from sorrow to joy. My life before motherhood wasn't a constant place of sadness, but I had wanted to be pregnant since I was a teenager. To create someone inside my body seemed like the ultimate high, and the easiest way to repair what had always been broken. It would be like playing God, but without the hot mess of the cross. Or it would seal me closer to the divine. But in my early twenties, I believed I needed an actual man to make and raise a child. That wacky philosophy dressed up in Christianity knotted me to a lie of heterosexuality. Years later, falling in love with both poetry and a pastry chef named Tammy, the myth of the indispensable man cracked. Love between two women has the power to unravel all kinds of lies.

"Buckle up, little fellows," Tammy said as she secured the nitrogen tank in the back of our Volvo. She turned carefully out of the fertility clinic in Elmira, New York, bumping down the country road, past the quarter Laundromat and the feed store, to refill the tank at Natural Gas so our batch of six-hundred-dollar sperm wouldn't die. Rusty American trucks with gun racks honked and passed us on both sides. Walking up to the warehouse door, Tammy and I cradled the end of a silver tank the size of a keg, which was labeled *Warning: Live Sperm Inside.* I was afraid the Natural Gas employees would laugh at the sight of us. We would come to know them by name. But we didn't know that then.

Tammy and I dove into the ritual of intrauterine insemination (IUI) three times in six months. It took tank after tank, blood test after blood test, ultrasound after ultrasound to determine the best window of ovulation. I could have filled an album with my eggs' snapshots. Month after month felt like waiting for Godot. Like playing hopscotch blindfolded, counting and counting on one foot but not knowing if I was in the right square. I would have lined my eggs with red velvet and heart-shaped mirrors if that's what turned sperm on.

We worked with a fertility clinic that separated fast swimmers from their more tortoise-like cousins. After giving me the highest dose of Clomid, they inserted the sperm through a catheter into my uterus, and I lay back on the scratchy white paper with my legs in the air for a half hour. I had taken to visualizing myself nursing, and teaching a little girl how to write. I had taken to reciting nursery rhymes in my head. As if I could will myself pregnant through image and meter. As if I was inventing a new rhythm method. As if the sperm would hear my recitation and swim faster.

2. The Faulty Carriage

I didn't believe I could be a good mother. Becoming a mother meant I would be my mother, depressed and resentful. Tammy was nervous, too. Our immature mothers had been trapped by the illusions of southern Christianity, and shamed by intense poverty. We wanted to become the mothers we'd ached for as little girls. We had a vision: to create a family out of poetry and chocolate, metaphor and sugar.

And for a moment, the vision pronounced herself and possessed us together. A positive test.

The garbage disposal choked from shrimp and sun-gold tomatoes I couldn't stop craving. Days tripped over one another before the landlord fixed it. Then three, maybe four weeks later, summer knocked on the windows, but there was not yet a heartbeat inside my cluster of multiplying cells. The washer ran, leaked in our wet basement, clear water, and then brown. Mud? Blood? My blood. I doubled over with cramps and vomiting, could no longer see. *Miscarriage* was not the right word for the process. It wasn't my body releasing an unhealthy zygote. I believed it was my fault. That child—can I even say child if there wasn't a heartbeat?—that being must have realized my flesh didn't have a solid foundation, and evicted herself in self-defense.

The nurses counseled me to wait. To go to group. To try again in another season. I refused. I couldn't fail at making a family. I had to redeem the one I'd grown up in.

I conceived again, in and out of private grief, out of the blood of the lost one.

3. My Hard Pear

Being pregnant was like being on a seesaw between utter terror and complete awe. It was better than any drug I had tried in high school, back when escaping my body was my highest goal. But I didn't believe I could have a successful labor unless I could birth my daughter through my brain, like Athena, at home. I wanted to think her out. I trusted my head. My brain had not yet betrayed me. My plan included a water birth, and Maria Callas on CD, and no drugs. I would breathe deeply, lean against Tammy's legs, and invite our new daughter to appear. But near the end of the third trimester in the deep winter of Ithaca, I had all the signs of pre-eclampsia. My blood pressure rose and rose and rose, so often that the nurse in the doctor's office would call another nurse to take it again. They would tell me to lie down, leave me alone for what seemed like hours, and come back. My feet swelled. I couldn't see them because my breasts were a size F. I didn't even know size F existed. I wasn't a skinny woman to begin with, but I had gained fifty pounds, and topped the scales at three hundred.

So at thirty-six weeks, when Dr. Jamie Loehr told me I needed to begin cervical ripening in the hospital, I wasn't surprised. My cervix was a green hard pear. For three weeks, three times a week, Tammy and I would pack turkey sandwiches and check into the hospital. Jamie would slip the cervical ripener in and we'd wait and wait and wait for contractions. We'd watch reruns of *Judging Amy*, and talk about what super food Tammy would make, and not a damn thing would soften. Labor was a country I didn't have a passport for.

4. The Circus Act

Cervical ripening was a prologue to the medical initiation of birth, the Dantean circle of Pitocin. Wednesday afternoon, Jamie started the drip—the Pit—but my cervix was not on board. It had a mind of its own, but I blamed myself. I thought I was doing labor wrong. And I wanted to do it right. Not just right. Perfectly. I changed CDs. Maybe Yo-Yo Ma's cello sonata was putting her to sleep. Maybe she needed something louder, to wake her, to bring her out, something like "When I Grow Up," by Garbage. I refused an epidural and any pain medication. I asked Jamie not to bring in any nursing students to watch me (I wasn't an experiment) and requested that Tammy's aunt (who was a labor and delivery nurse) not be permitted in the room. None of Tammy's Baptist family could wrap their heads around us as a lesbian couple, and the idea we would bring a daughter into the picture was insane to them. It didn't matter that we had chosen to name our new one after Tammy's great-grandmother, Ilah. Late into the evening, I had Tammy, and our doula, Lauren, and our dear friend Maria, the brain scientist and stand-in-sister. All of these powerful feminists would call our little one out. But instead, there was more and more Pitocin.

Jamie broke my waters with a metal hook on Thursday morning, and it felt, though I trusted him, like a violation. It wasn't that it hurt. It was the insertion of an instrument. He sang "Singin' in the Rain," and still Ilah would not come. More Pitocin. He was willing to try anything in order to get me into active labor. He suggested tug-of-war, where I sat upright on the bed with my legs spread, my privacy evaporating. Jamie held a rope of blankets and I pulled and he pulled and then I was annoyed and let go. He flew into the wall and laughed. I tried yoga on the floor. I called on gravity.

I didn't get past five centimeters on Thursday. Pitocin contractions knocked me under like waves, one after the other, and I had forgotten how to swim. There was no time to breathe. All my prenatal yoga practice and meditation disappeared. I started to feel bad for my doula, who must have been missing her family. I felt bad for Tammy, who must have been sick of the hospital food and that hard half chair, half bed. I was keeping everyone from the real world. I rolled back and forth on a yoga ball, swearing, "Ah for fuck's sake, why can't I get this right?" Maria laughed. She told me I had to think about Ilah, and consider a C-section, that all of this was getting crazy.

The next morning, the fourth of February, happened to be Rosa Parks's ninety-second birthday, and I was determined to look my daughter in the eye. But Ilah's heartbeat was starting to feel the stress of the past three days of Pitocin. Jamie said I had to reach active labor within an hour or they would prep me for a C-section. He was a family doc, so he wouldn't be performing it, and I couldn't imagine trusting another man. Maybe Ilah heard him. Maybe she was afraid of the knife. The contractions came faster and faster and I started to puke grape liquid, a mixture of stomach acid and Recharge energy drink. The more I vomited, the more my cervix dilated. Tammy and Maria were experts at figuring when to hand me a bucket and when to hand me a washcloth. Lauren cheered me on.

I screamed for Tylenol, which made everyone laugh, and by this point, an epidural was my only option. I was terrified the anesthesiologist would paralyze me. He wanted me to be still, which was impossible because my contractions were overlapping each other. The moment he brought out the long needle, the color left Tammy's face. Jamie told me to look at Tammy, to focus on her, to let her be strong for me. He kept telling me I was not alone. He kept telling me I could do this. That Tammy and I could do this. In that moment of acknowledging our power as two women making a family, I began to let go. I had to forget that Jamie was watching; I had to forget he was in the room. This was about what Tammy and I could do together.

The epidural took the edge off, but I had to pee, and I wanted privacy. Privacy is funny to ask for in labor, but I had been vulnerable for so long, and I felt as if everyone had witnessed my inability to perform. I announced I was going to the bathroom, alone. But the nurse wheeled in a Porta-John. I was not about to pee in public or have my baby on a toilet. I thought I could hold it. I thought, Push baby out, hold pee in.

Tammy and I clasped the handles on either side of the Porta-John for balance. I pushed, to no avail. I panted and screamed, "Ilah, get out of me now." Then I shoved the Porta-John to the window, and clutched Tammy's wrists. We squatted and faced each other, gasping and pushing. "Ilah, Ilah, come out already. Ilah, we need you. Ilah, we're here for you." I'm sure I peed on the floor.

The nurses changed the mat beneath me. Jamie was in blue scrubs on the floor, shining a flashlight into my vagina. Another contraction, another push. It was 6:00 p.m.

"Time to get on the bed." He patted the sterile bed table.

"Uh, no fucking way." Then came this contraction that caused me to both vomit and piss myself. It was all so embarrassing. It was not supposed to happen like this. This was not in any of the books. No one had said if you struggle with feeling vulnerable, labor will be difficult. No one had said not to be alarmed by the pools of blood running down your legs. No one had said that in labor, you will go so far into your own spirit cave that you won't be able to see the door. No one had said that that deep self might scare you out of your pants and make you shit yourself. No one had said that if you have ever been violated, your body's memory will bring these moments to the surface and yank you in and out of the present. No one had said that your privacy evaporates, even as your need for it deepens. No one had said you might feel like a freak show, a circus act. I had to stop trying to protect myself. I had to forget myself and be in myself at the very same moment.

"Sarah, Ilah is finally coming, she's coming soon, and you cannot give birth on the hospital floor. Get on the bed."

I cursed him. I cursed that I couldn't get back on the bed by myself. Someone turned on Maria Callas.

"Four more pushes," he said.

I only needed one, and before Jamie had two gloves on he yelled, "I got a baby here." But she was quiet and still. Tammy's mouth dropped. Maria shook her head, rubbed Tammy's back. They looked shocked.

"Make her cry," I said, "please, for fuck's sake, make her fucking cry." I had birthed a baby with a brioche head, a little round head on top of her own head. Ilah was orange, ripe as a winter squash. When they placed her on my chest, and she pooped and cried, I thought she looked like a slippery fish with huge flipper feet. And I felt chosen by my little Aquarian. Tammy placed a beanie over Ilah's head and rocked her back and forth, telling her how much she adored her, measuring her three-inch feet and laughing. Maria held my hand as I squirmed through stitches and the mending of a second-degree tear. I was grateful for her, too.

5. The Little Bull

I wanted a second baby immediately. I would have taken Clomid with the stool softener they handed me on the way out of the hospital, prepping my eggs for another photo shoot. But by the time I finally convinced Tammy to try again, Ilah was three. Our second donor was an architect who wrote about the importance of different kinds of families. He believed that atypical families build stronger communities. I thought a community philosopher might make an easier baby to birth.

It was just as difficult to get pregnant with Frida, but my determination, desire, and luck saved me. And when I went for genetic testing, they told me my child had a one in nine chance of being born with Down syndrome. I wept. I hadn't worked this hard to create life, only to have to make the difficult choice of letting it go. I respect women who have babies with Down syndrome. But I knew my limits. I did not believe I had the resources within me to raise that kind of child. If the test results were positive, I would consider an abortion. We stopped talking about names.

On my thirty-seventh birthday, I had an amniocentesis. I didn't have to have it, but the only way to know for sure that this baby wasn't going to be born with a genetic issue was to have a huge needle inserted in my stomach. If I did the amnio, I was risking another miscarriage; if I didn't, I would worry and prep for six months for something that might or might not occur. Again, Tammy saw the needle and lost all color in her face, but she didn't let go of my hand. Two weeks later, after receiving negative results, we could name this little girl inside Frida. Because in the first year we met, Tammy and I had fallen in love over a Frida Kahlo exhibit at the Women's Museum in Washington, D.C. And also because Frida's paintings revealed that the other side of joy was blood.

Again, preeclampsia washed over my last trimester. Again, induction was necessary. Jamie Loehr had stopped delivering babies, a fact that all of Ithaca mourned, so I had chosen a group of midwives, some of whom I liked, and some of whom I didn't trust. On night one of Pitocin, a midwife told me I should spank my child for swimming away from the monitor. The next day, the contractions were so far apart, I sent Tammy away to pick up Ilah from preschool. Night two, there were twelve other babies born in eight hours. I was not even dilated three centimeters. I had to get off the labor and delivery floor.

I didn't care how many monitors I was hooked up to, how much Pitocin they were giving me. In my head, I sang, *Frida, Frida, I need you.* When I had a contraction, I leaned against the wall and moaned. My doula, Lauren, carried the IV pole. My massage therapist rubbed my lower back. Tammy pushed the elevator button and randomly selected a floor. I was going to walk this baby out. I shuffled in my elephant slippers. I would have had her on the front lawn if that had been where she wanted to appear. Clearly, I could not choose her birthday or her setting. She would come in her own time. She had her own clock. We weren't gone long before a head nurse came down to the front door of the hospital.

"What are you doing down here, Sarah?" she said, and her cherub print didn't match her sour tone.

"What the fuck does it look like?" I snapped, adjusting my satin pajamas. A button popped. I couldn't bend over to get it.

"You can't have your baby at the coffee kiosk," she said, shaking her head and steering my IV pole away from me as if it were a leash.

"I didn't sign any paper saying how long I"—and then came a contraction where I had to stop talking, try to breathe, and not dissolve into a dark, familiar well—"I-I-I would stay in pregnancy land upstairs."

"Sarah, come on. Do you want to lose this baby? Don't be irresponsible."

My doula clucked her tongue. Tammy looked like she was going to smack this nurse. Then another, stronger contraction where I squatted against the water fountain. The folks in the coffee line were starting to stare.

"I will not," I said, crisply, wiping away my sweaty head, "lose this baby."

In the elevator, my contractions slowed down. I wanted to spit on this nurse, to vomit on her shoes. I felt as if I were going to detention.

In the evening of the third day, I decided I had to write Frida out. While sitting on the yoga ball, I began a letter, asking her to please come out to meet us. I told her I was honored she had chosen me and Tammy for her family. I wanted to annunciate her with love, to speak her into being, to make her known, to meet her, to know this intimate stranger who was a part of me, and apart from me.

By then I was faint from the Pitocin and lack of food. They gave me oxygen. I had had enough. I told Tammy to get a knife and give me a C-section or to order me a fucking C-section immediately. Or I would do it myself. But there were five other women in labor at the time, so the midwife instructed me to rest with my legs in the air. I was in the most ridiculous position, working against gravity. I was to slow my labor down until they could prep the operating room. I wasn't supposed to be pushing. But I did anyway. Tammy turned on Johnny Cash's "Ring of Fire." Lauren called for the midwife to come quickly, and Frida slipped out within twenty minutes at 3:30 a.m. She was screaming, her eyes big, as if the journey down had been scarier than she'd expected, as if she was pissed off no one had told her, as if she would have preferred to stay inside. There was no brioche head, and not a hint of jaundice. I was filled with gratitude. She was my bull, my Taurus, colossal lips on a little face.

The next day, Tammy brought her chocolates and four-year-old Ilah back to the hospital. I had missed her in the three days I was stuck on this floor. Ilah immediately took off all her clothes, climbed into bed with me, and ate peanut butter from a jar with her finger. I was on my side, nursing Frida. Ilah leaned over and smeared peanut butter on her sister's face. Tammy laughed and laughed.

"My thighs are burning from all that squatting," Tammy said, sinking into a hard chair with a bonbon.

"Tell me about it. My entire being is burning," I said, adjusting the ice packs on my vulva.

Ilah said, "Hey, sissy, I waited so long for you. I'm so glad you're here." She clutched my face in her sticky hands and whispered, "Good job, Mama."

If, If, If

EDAN LEPUCKI

was born at home in Santa Monica. I was the third child, and in the photos, my sister Heidi, then two years old, watches the action from a family friend's lap, her gaze bemused and curious. My eldest sister, Lauren, then six, stands by the bed with a stethoscope around her neck. The light in these photos is honey-colored and soft, and my mother is focused yet relaxed, her hair limp, her glasses thick, her bathrobe hanging open, revealing her enormous belly and swollen nipples, her mass of pubic hair.

After my head emerged from my mother's body, I remained there for another forty-five minutes, stuck at the shoulders, both born and not born, until the midwives were able to wrestle me out. About twenty-four hours after my mother had felt the first contractions (and vacuumed the house and eaten a box of cannolis to prepare), I was fully born. The midwives put my placenta in a crystal punch bowl on the dining room table, and my father and his two friends gathered on the porch to sing the wedding-night ballad from *It's a Wonderful Life*. "I love you truly, truly dear . . ."

Ten years later, I watched my mother give birth, without drugs, to my sister in a hospital. A year and a half after that, I watched her birth my brother in the same fashion. Each time, she was quiet and calm, breathing deeply and closing her eyes, as if trying to recall a dream, or someone's phone number.

By the time I was pregnant myself, I couldn't wait to give birth. Many of the women I know are scared of labor pain, or nervous that they'll poop on the hospital table, or totally certain they'll beg for an epidural right away, but I was excited and ready for an unmedicated labor. (Well, okay, I was a bit anxious about the turd factor. Anyone with a shred of modesty is, right?) My mother and my sister Heidi had been excellent role models, and they taught me that although having a baby is a long and arduous process, the female body is capable. We are built to have babies. As soon as I found out I was going to be a mother, I readied my squats, I practiced my breathing. I'd pop my kid out in the hospital hallway if I had to. Get that epidural away from me!

I always figured I'd have a home birth someday, but my husband, Patrick, and I were living in a one-bedroom apartment when I got pregnant, our landlord in a nearby unit, and we worried he might balk if we decided to deliver on his property. Also, our insurance wouldn't cover a home birth, and we didn't have the few thousand dollars it would cost to hire a midwife. When we discovered our nearby hospital staffed midwives as well as ob-gyns, we figured it was the best option. My mother, who had returned to the hospital setting to deliver my younger siblings (because she was considerably older by then, and because she felt comfortable telling the nurses and doctors what medical interventions she did and didn't want), agreed it was a good idea. My sister's own hospital labor had also gone smoothly. "Heidi's delivery room had a view of the ocean," my mother reminded me. (Everyone in my family mentioned Heidi's ocean view whenever they talked about her labor.)

Patrick and I took a twelve-week Bradley Method class, where, along with nine other couples, we learned about the three stages of labor, about relaxation methods to use during contractions, about how and why medical induction, epidurals, and continuous fetal heart monitoring have led to an increase in cesareans in America, and about how to speak to nurses so that they won't make fun of your yoga ball. The Bradley Method is also called "husband-coached" natural childbirth, which means the birth partner plays an essential role. The days of the spouse who paces, clueless, in the waiting room are long gone; in these classes, Patrick learned how to time my contractions, how to keep me hydrated and focused, and how to stand between me and the medical staff so that I could labor in peace. According to the Bradley Method, the key to natural childbirth is breathing and relaxing; to this day, I use the exercises and techniques I learned in that room. Our teacher, Kate, taught us that the well-informed couple has a better birth experience, and she also assuaged my fears about evacuating my bowels in front of strangers. If it happens to you, she said, don't worry; the nurses have seen everything. *Everything.* This pep talk alone was worth the price of the course.

(Kate also assured Patrick that he didn't need to grow a mustache and wear skimpy shorts to the birth, as the fathers in the hippie birth videos we watched did. That was a relief—to both of us.)

I was the last of the moms in our Bradley class to go into labor. By then I was past my due date by a few days, and I felt like my child, a boy, would never arrive. A few weeks before, I'd gotten a crew cut that would have looked hip on a willowy model, but on my swollen face, atop my swollen body, I looked about as cool as, well, a pregnant woman with a crew cut.

Each day, I walked the one or two hills of our L.A. neighborhood, trying to make labor happen. If I didn't go into labor within two weeks of my due date, the hospital would want to induce. Patrick and I had been calling our baby Bean since the day we first saw his little lima-bean shape on the ultrasound, and as I walked, I'd think, Come on, Bean. Come on.

Finally, on the day after Father's Day, I awoke at dawn with cramps. They were mild and irregular enough that I sent Patrick to work a few hours later. "But what if there's traffic on the way back?" he'd asked. His office was only nine miles west, but the freeway was often clogged with cars, and it could take more than an hour to get home.

"Then I'll have my baby on the front porch," I replied.

As I negotiated early labor, I took a bath, checked my e-mail, and cuddled the dog. I kept track of the cramps, and once they became more regular, I called my in-laws, who were visiting for the birth, and asked them to bring me food. Like a marathon runner before the race, I knew I'd need the energy. I had always imagined downing a bowl of spaghetti Bolognese before the birth, meat sauce dripping down my chin like I was some kind of beautiful pregnant cavewoman. I settled on a turkey sandwich and fries.

In the next couple of hours, the contractions became more intense and closer together, and by the afternoon, Patrick was on his way home. By the time he arrived, I'd already taken another bath and I was working very hard on my breathing and relaxation. In the Bradley class, I'd been taught to keep my hands unclenched, my toes uncurled, and my brow smooth, and it was Patrick's job to make sure I remembered all this. He whispered to me about our long-ago trip to Santa Barbara and rolled a cold can of Diet Coke along my lower back, which ached terribly. As he did so, I imagined those winding roads of wine country, and then I visualized my uterus as a bag of muscles, working to open my cervix. My job was to get out of its way. My mom arrived soon after. This was her first labor where she wasn't the mother-to-be, and she was giddy but practical, her voice assured and gentle. Our goal was to check into the hospital as late as possible so that I could labor in comfort and familiarity. With my mom and Patrick, I labored on the bed, in the bath, and in the living room on the yoga ball.

By nightfall, I was in the shower, my cheek against the cold por-
celain wall, the water as hot as it would go. The contractions were
rippling over me, tightening at my lower back, squeezing. As
the shower's water fell over my back, I imagined the contractions
like a doorway filled with light that I simply needed to walk through.
I entered one glowing room, and then another and another.

At midnight, we went to the hospital. Before I got into the car,
I threw up on my neighbor's lawn. The speed bumps in the hospital parking lot made me whimper with pain.

The labor and delivery wing reminded me of being on an airplane: that canned air and light, everything plastic and metal, efficient women in uniforms asking if you needed anything. I was
thrilled to find out I was dilated four to five centimeters. The nurse
led me into a large hospital room with its own big bathroom, where
she asked me a bunch of intake questions. "Major concerns about
the labor?" she asked as I breathed in and out like a yoga teacher.
"Complications," I said, bending to steady myself against the bed.
"You want pain medication?" she asked, and I said no. "Don't ask
me again, thanks," I said, and my mother said, "She's doing great."
I was.

The hospital let me labor all night long without coming in for a
vaginal exam or to pressure us. We'd heard so many horror stories
about hospital births that Patrick and I were ready for a battle.
Thankfully, it never came; all the nurses, midwives, and doctors
had read our birth plan and were extremely respectful of our choices.
As I requested, I was placed on the fetal heart monitor only inter-
mittently, so I could move around freely most of the time; I knew
from my sister that the thing would drive me nuts. She was right;
I hated the monitor. (Even now, when I imagine the muffled
horror-movie drum of Bean's heartbeat on that monitor, and the
thick elastic band around me, I'm filled with dread.)

The next morning, twenty-four hours after my labor had begun,
and after a night of very strong and steady contractions, I was
checked to see how far I'd dilated. Five centimeters still. After all

that work. It was hard not to feel defeated, as I'd already thrown up twice and ridden through intense pain. Patrick and my mom held my hands, rubbed my back, and made sure I drank water. Their stamina amazed me; if they could do it, I could do it. Patrick told me my hair looked like Leonardo DiCaprio's, circa his stint on *Growing Pains*. This, too, kept me going.

My sister Lauren arrived and joined our little labor team. I began to walk the hospital halls, sometimes getting into a squat during a contraction. I was trying my hardest not to let my slow labor bring me down. In the Bradley class, Patrick and I had learned that most labors hit a plateau, where dilation seems to pause; hospitals call it "a failure to progress," turning a perfectly natural development into a flaw that needs to be fixed with medical intervention. It's why laboring at a hospital with a twenty-four-hour (or less!) time frame isn't helpful. I kept that plateau idea in my mind and tried to dismiss any notion of failure.

The nurses waved to me every time I passed their station, and whenever I heard a baby cry, I let that motivate me further. Otherwise, the hospital wing was eerily quiet and empty; I knew it meant that the other women were asleep in their beds, or watching TV, or scrolling through their Facebook feeds. They'd requested epidurals, and their labors looked nothing like mine. I felt both envious of their comfort, and also sad. If that sounds self-righteous, so be it. Feeling my body work to give birth to my child was unlike anything I'd ever experienced, and in the moment I couldn't understand why a mother wouldn't want that.

Midway through the afternoon, I was on the fetal monitor and getting into an upright squatting position for each contraction. Patrick was behind me, supporting my head, Lauren was next to me, rubbing my arm and breathing with me, and my mother had her hand on my lower belly, telling me to breathe into each wave of pain, to use that energy to open up. The contractions at that point were about five minutes long and barely a minute apart. My mother-in-law stopped in with Popsicles, and she took my other hand.

I was breathing so deeply and productively, the pain seemed to transform into something else, and I let it rush through and over me. I had tears in my eyes, but they were a comfort. Everyone was breathing with me and holding me, and I felt incredibly safe. I felt like I was dilating, that this baby was coming. It remains one of the most beautiful and important moments of my life, a moment when I was surrounded by love, and knew it, and accepted it.

Turns out, I wasn't dilating, and my baby wasn't coming. I was checked again a few hours later, and I was *still* only at five centimeters. I felt trapped inside of a demoralizing and exhausting practical joke.

And then Patrick ate a cheeseburger and I wept, the smell disgusted me so. "How could you?" I asked him.

Soon after, the midwife suggested we break my water (I'd had a trickle the night before, but still no big burst). We decided this was a good idea, since it's a natural way to advance labor. Once my water was broken, the contractions were even more intense. Also, at that point, I was so tired that between each contraction, I fell asleep, deeply, even if I was standing up, which lent the whole world a strange, hallucinogenic quality. I had to be monitored more often, which I resented. Thankfully, Bean's heart rate remained strong and regular throughout. I, however, was looking worse and worse. My blood pressure had begun to rise, and I had a very slight fever. My contractions were now eight minutes long, and I had less than a minute to recover before the next one rose over me like a steel wave.

What happens, you ask, when you're in labor for thirty-two hours and you haven't dilated past five centimeters? There are options, of course. One of them is to accept IV fluids and two rounds of narcotics, with the hope that some sleep will get your body back on track. If you take this route, you might remember a nurse coming in to offer you rabbits for your rabbit collection, but such memories should not be trusted.

Once the narcotic wore off, I was checked again. No dice—still five centimeters. At that point, I'd run through two hospital shifts and there were no midwives on duty. Two doctors came in, and we discussed next steps. The contractions had returned full force, my blood pressure was still very high, and my fever was a concern. They suggested I get an epidural (to continue to help me relax and rest, if that was indeed what was holding me back), and a dose of Pitocin to help spur more useful contractions. I really, really didn't want either of these measures, but I was going on thirty-five or so hours of labor, and my body was breaking down. Because the doctors, nurses, and midwives had been so supportive throughout the labor, I felt they had my best interest in mind; there wasn't any weird pressure from them, and I was grateful. So I relented.

Still, I remember asking Patrick and my mother, "Are you disappointed in me?" and, to my sister, "Will you talk shit about me behind my back?" The last thing I wanted was to be accused of weakness. *No*, they said. *Never.* So why did I feel so defeated?

To my delight, the anesthesiologist was very handsome and charming, and I'm pretty certain he fell in love with me on the spot: Was it my awesome crew cut that did it, or my by-then-legendary body odor, or the pimples that had sprouted all over my face in the last day and a half? Either way, he explained everything clearly and was very respectful of the plan I'd had, and the ways it had to be augmented.

At first, the epidural felt wonderful (when my mom, sister, and Patrick came back into the room, I said, "Fucking hippies!"), but soon I resented the way my legs and butt felt: heavy, dead. Also, because the baby had descended so far down, the drugs couldn't dull the contractions for long. Once I got the Pitocin, the pain was undeniable; it wasn't quite as bad as before, but it was still pretty horrific. I lay there for a couple of hours, trying my best to breathe, and hoping that these medical interventions would bring me what I wanted most: to be dilated ten centimeters and have the chance to push out my baby.

Unfortunately, I had barely progressed; the doctor even thought I was dilated four centimeters, not five. On top of that, my cervix had started to swell. This was beyond my "failure to progress" nightmare—I had been in labor for almost forty hours and I was successfully *regressing*.

Every option ended in a cesarean if I didn't dilate more in the next few hours. If I hadn't been so out of my mind with fatigue, I would have cried. I had labored well, exactly as I had imagined I would, but it didn't matter, my baby did not want to come out. I wanted to try to labor longer, on the chance that I would miraculously dilate, but my body couldn't take it anymore . . . and, really, nor could my mind.

Later, Patrick told me that after they wheeled me to the operating room, he went down the hallway and cried. He cried for me, for us, for the birth we wanted and didn't get. He cried because he knew I'd held on to this dream of a natural childbirth for so long. Since my own birth, maybe.

The cesarean was wild: the blood pressure cuffs; the way I lay supine, arms out like Jesus; the masked doctors and nurses, buzzing about; how I imagined what they were doing to my body even though all I felt was strange, rough pressure. Patrick arrived in his surgery moon suit, whispering to me and rubbing my face, and I was so happy we were together. When I heard our baby cry for the first time, relief flooded through me. They held him up, and I could not stop crying. He looked just like Patrick! He was red and wailing, and a few minutes later, I heard Patrick tell him, "I have a face, too, like yours; it just has a mask on it."

When they brought my baby to me, he stopped crying. We were like old friends. Patrick and I hadn't told anyone what we'd call Bean once he was born; we'd kept his name a secret for months. Now, though, he would be called Dixon. But he'd always be my Bean.

After my surgery, the doctor who performed it told my mother that Dixon had turned slightly transverse during labor, and so the side of his head was hitting my cervix, making it impossible for labor to progress.

I'm not sure why no one could figure out Bean's position during my labor; I still ask myself that question, almost two years later, and I wonder, if I had gone ahead and had a home birth, like my own had been, maybe things would have gone differently. After all, my mother's labor with me had been long and difficult, not without complications, but the midwives had been able to manage it. Sometimes I think about the photos of my own birth, of that gorgeous golden light, and how calm everyone seems, even when things must have been intense, and I feel a terrible longing, a kind of shame, even. Maybe it's my fault I ended up with a cesarean. Maybe somewhere along the line, I made a poor choice. If I had asked for a sonogram after hour thirty . . . If I hadn't squatted with such enthusiasm . . . If, if, if.

Something like 30 percent of women in the United States give birth via C-section, and that number is rising every day. I believe that many of these operations could be avoided. Was mine one of these? The truth is, I don't like to talk about my labor, mostly because I feel the need to explain the whole long story; otherwise, you might think I'm a clueless everywoman who let the doctors do what they did because I didn't have faith in my own body. Because I was weak, because I'm not in touch with my physical powers.

When my sister Heidi gave unmedicated birth to her second child, just as she did with her first, the labor was relatively short. Though I have no memory of it, I'm told that the first thing I said to her upon walking into her hospital room was "Fuck. You." I'm sure I meant it in jest, but that doesn't mean my words didn't come from a place of deep and complicated pain. Only eight months had passed since Bean's birth, and I was still struggling to accept my own labor. I would tell myself that I got three births in one—a natural one, a medicated one, and a surgical one—but the truth is, the first was the only one I wanted, that I still want.

If the female body is built to give birth, and if every other woman in my family can give birth naturally, then why did I have to meet my baby with an oxygen mask over my face, half my body so numb it became not my own?

The story of my son's birth has become a lament and a defense, when it should be a record of the moment when my life changed indelibly. It should be a story of triumph and love.

But the word *should* doesn't belong anywhere near childbirth. It's an unpredictable process, and different for every woman. In that sense, it's kind of like parenthood.

All the wondrous, messy, and challenging moments of mothering Bean remind me that there is so much I can't control, that my child arrived as he needed to, and that's what matters. He's here, I tell myself. He's here. He's here.

On Bean's birthday this year, I'll tell him how he came into the world. I'll show him one of the first photos ever taken of him: his pink old-man face swollen by the rough labor. "You look like a boxer, Beanie," I'll say. I'll put my finger to that picture's tiny face, press that tiny newborn nose.

Chances are, my son won't be listening. Not for long anyway. He'll run a race car across my thigh and ask for a slice of American cheese. "Now, Mama. Please now, Mama."

"Here you go, my silly boy," I'll say, and I'll give it to him.

This Life

ANN HOOD

The stories of my birth and my brother's birth are legendary in our family, mainly because my mother repeats them so often. Bring up the topic of pregnancy and she will launch into how, at twenty years old and alone while our Seabee father was away at sea, she went into labor, supervised by mean military nurses at the navy hospital in Newport, Rhode Island. "I didn't even know for sure how that baby was going to get out," she says jokingly, taking a drag on her cigarette and shaking her head. Skip was born in 1951, but the story of those Nurse Ratcheds laughing at her dumb questions and her fear of all things baby is as fresh to her now as it was on that November day.

It was five years before she'd even consider another baby, and only with conditions: no navy hospital and my father had to be with her. Luckily, my father relented, because that second baby was me. But all her planning could not stop the snowiest December on record, so snowy that my father missed the turn for the hospital and got lost, my mother cursing beside him and vowing never to have a baby again.

According to Mom, she'd been pregnant with me for ten months, not nine. And she was in labor with me for two days, arriving at the hospital on December 8 and giving birth at midnight on

December 9/10. At least this time she was tended by a handsome Dean Martin look-alike doctor, who held her hand and patiently listened to her complaints, which were numerous and included the story of my brother's birth. "I walked those halls for two days with Doctor Raccioppi in *agony*," she says. "Never again," she used to add when she was still young enough to do it again. She would grind out her cigarette extra hard to show she meant it. Apparently, even when I finally decided to be born, I got stuck in the birth canal and Doctor Raccioppi pulled out the forceps and yanked me out, leaving a mark on my forehead that still turns red when I cry or get too cold. "You tore me apart," my mother likes to remind me. "I couldn't walk for months."

When I was a teenager, if we saw a pregnant woman, my mother would nudge me and whisper, "That poor thing has no idea what she's in for." When some cousin or neighbor announced she was pregnant, my mother would mutter, "Good luck!" It's no wonder that having babies was not high on my list of things I was eager to do. In fact, unlike some women I knew, I seemed to have no biological clock. The sight of babies never made me swoon. The children of friends didn't make me long for some of my own. I managed to go through a first marriage with a man who felt the same way— not antibaby, just not babycentric.

But as these things happen, after my divorce I met a new man and fell in love. "I want to have a million babies with you," he said. "You do?" I said, baffled. *Babies?* With *me?* He spun a beautiful fantasy filled with golden-haired children and camping trips and days frolicking on Rhode Island beaches. Before I knew it, dazed and in love, I had moved from Manhattan to Providence. Months passed before I remembered that I didn't even like camping. But by then, it was too late to think about how I wasn't that crazy about babies. I had gotten pregnant the first time we tried and was throwing up all day, and nauseous when I wasn't throwing up. "Good luck," my mother told me. "They say you forget how much it hurts," she continued, leaning closer for emphasis, "but you never ever do."

I opened the Yellow Pages, not for ob-gyns, but for midwives. The story of my own birth, the story of my brother's, had convinced me that there had to be a better way. At that time, in Providence, Rhode Island, there was exactly one office of practicing midwives. As soon as I stopped throwing up long enough to dial the phone, I made an appointment, determined that my baby would have a birth story worth bragging about.

My husband, Lorne, came with a three-year-old daughter, and he did not embrace my plan to use midwives. His ex-wife had had all sorts of complications during her labor, complications I hardly paid attention to (high blood pressure, or a drop in blood pressure?). For me, pregnancy came with a certain amount of arrogance. I would not fall prey to my mother's drama, to an ex-wife's frailties, to what I saw as a culture overly obsessed with all things baby. Somehow, using a midwife fit my plan. The idea of a strong woman by my side, helping nature and me have this baby, was as no-fuss as my attitude toward the birth experience. Lorne did a slew of research and relented: Midwifery, which sounded archaic, actually did fit us better than obstetrics.

I was thirty-five years old, with a solid career as a writer and a strong sense of who I was and what I wanted. For years, I had watched women I knew give up too much when they had a baby. Smart, accomplished women got pregnant and overnight could talk only about the debate between disposable and reusable diapers, the importance of breast-feeding, and an endless number of topics that seemed to my nonpregnant self both indulgent and dull. Pregnancy didn't change that point of view. Baby topics were of interest in my private life, but throughout my pregnancy I continued to take ballet classes three times a week, finish a novel, go to Paris, and embark on a book tour at seven months.

My trio of midwives included Annie, a tall woman with a head of curly dark hair, who always seemed strong and capable and calm;

Ann, older and gray-haired, who looked grandmotherly and kind; and Dawn, a petite beauty with a cascade of rippling brown hair and a no-nonsense personality. Unlike women I knew who worried over which doctor would be on call when they went into labor, afraid of the gruff one or the one they hadn't even met yet, I trusted these women completely. They made sure that I had appointments with each of them equally, and I knew that whoever helped deliver my baby would be just fine. I also liked their proclivities toward noninvasive testing, their respect for my opinions, their intelligence and good humor.

These midwives' domain was the ABC (Alternative Birthing Center), a suite of rooms in the basement of Women and Infants Hospital in Providence. Upstairs was all beeping machines, bright lights, and impersonal hospital rooms. In contrast, the ABC looked like a combination Marriott and swanky spa. An enormous hot tub waited to soothe labor pains. A stereo waited to play your favorite music. There were dim lights and king-size beds and a fridge filled with snacks and beverages. It was close enough for medical intervention—"just in case"—but worlds away from the labor and delivery rooms above.

I returned from my book tour eight weeks from my delivery date and set about judging Barnes & Noble's Discover Award for first novels. Every day, a big box of books arrived on my doorstep and I settled in for an afternoon of reading and conference calls with the other judges. It was spring in New England. The dogwoods along our street bloomed pale pink and white. The daffodils and crocuses popped out of the dirt. Sunshine streamed in my windows. My baby rolled and kicked inside me, and I marveled at how easy all of this was.

And then it wasn't.

Ann, the matriarch of the group, measured my stomach and frowned.

She checked my chart and frowned more deeply.

"You're thirty-five weeks," she said, "but you're only measuring thirty-two."

I had started weekly visits now, and one of the hallmarks of those visits was the surprising math that my stomach measured the exact number of weeks pregnant I was.

"Last week you measured thirty-three," she said, reading Annie's notes.

"But Annie said that was probably because I'd been sick with that bad cold," I reminded Ann. "I didn't eat well for a few days."

"I see that," Ann said.

She studied the chart. She studied me. Then she smiled.

"You have had a fine pregnancy," she said finally. "This baby has a good strong heartbeat. You're healthy. I'm sure everything is fine."

But the next week, I measured thirty-two inches.

This time, without hesitation, Ann sent me for a sonogram. For the first time, I became uneasy. Even over the two weeks that I seemed to be shrinking rather than growing, I'd thought there was some logical reason. The bad cold. Even the fact that here I was at the end of my pregnancy only twenty-three pounds heavier than my usual weight. Maybe all the arabesques and pirouettes I did in ballet class had something to do with it. But the look on the technician's face as she slid the transducer back and forth over my gelled belly made me ask nervously, "Everything's okay, right?"

Back and forth again, and then again.

"I'll be right back with the doctor," she said without looking at Lorne or me.

She came back fast, a doctor in tow.

He took the transducer in his big hairy hands and slid it around, his dark eyes fixed on the monitor.

"Okay," he said finally with a vague accent, "you go to the hospital now and you have the baby."

"No, no, I have another month," I told him.

I hadn't packed my overnight bag with all the things on the list from the ABC. I hadn't done *anything* on that list. And I had my final conference call the next morning to pick the Discover Award winner.

"I can't have the baby today," I said.

The doctor patted my hand. "Yes, you are."

After he ordered the technician to let the emergency room know I was coming, he started to leave.

"Excuse me?" I called after him.

He paused.

"What's wrong with the baby?"

"He appears to be only somewhere between three and a half and four pounds," the doctor said brusquely. "His heartbeat's strong, so we need to get him out of there."

With that, he was gone, along with all of my beautiful dreams of a beautiful birthing experience.

The doctor who met us at the emergency room was an affable man with the look of an old high school football star. Casually, he asked me if I'd used cocaine during the pregnancy. "Low birth weight, you know," he added. Insulted, I said I hadn't even had a sip of wine in thirty-six weeks. He slapped me on the arm like we were pals and disappeared.

Twenty minutes later, a team of nurses arrived—at least I think they were nurses; ever since that ultrasound technician had introduced herself as Cheryl, no one had bothered to tell us any-thing else—and whisked me into a room with a tidy row of beds, each with its own set of machines.

"Could someone please call my midwife?" I kept asking. No one seemed to hear me as they set about slapping a blood pressure cuff on my arm, sticking a heart monitor on my stomach, and pok-ing an IV line in my vein.

"My midwife?" I asked the nurse closest to me.

"This isn't the time for a midwife," she said as if I were dense. "You're going to have a C-section—"

"Wait a minute!" I protested.

She patted my arm and told me the doctor would be in to explain everything. The arm patting was starting to piss me off. Condescending and dismissive, it seemed to be every medical person's method for personal contact. I missed the way my midwives looked me in the eye, shook my hand firmly, or even gave me a hug.

"Call my midwife!" I shouted to her disappearing back.

The beds were all separated by thin curtains, and the sound of moans mixed with the beeps of machines and the canned laughter of the different sitcoms playing on all the televisions. Lorne had gone to pack that hospital bag, so I settled in to wait—for him, for a doctor, for one of my midwives. What I got was another nurse (or technician), who wheeled in a bag of something and started a drip into my IV.

"Pitocin," she said after I asked.

"What does that do?" But it was too late. She was already on her way out.

I sighed and turned on the TV.

Soon enough, I learned that Pitocin would induce labor. The doctor returned with a plan. If I didn't deliver that night, he would do a C-section in the morning. When I asked if he'd talked to my midwife, he grinned and reminded me that a midwife couldn't do C-sections.

"You need a doc for that," he said before patting my arm and sauntering off.

As soon as he was gone, Lorne called the midwives. By now it was late, so he left a message with the answering service and we settled in to watch *Seinfeld*. Periodically someone checked me for dilation and other signs of labor, but my progress was slow. I sent Lorne home, having asked him to promise that he would come back first thing in the morning to help me block any unnecessary C-section. Then I dozed off.

A few hours later, the sound of a woman's angry voice woke me, and there at the foot of my bed stood beautiful Dawn, pointing her finger up at the doctor and reminding him whose patient I was. To say I felt relief at the sight of her is an understatement. She dismissed him and came and sat beside me, giving me a good strong hug before telling me that the situation was not dire but that the baby needed to be born. "The doctor thinks you're a coke addict," she said, shaking her head. "You who wouldn't even take cold medicine a couple of weeks ago." She told me that I should get a good night's sleep because I would need my energy the next day to give birth. "Annie's on duty," she said. "And I come in for the afternoon, so you'll have one of us."

Comforted for the first time since Cheryl, the sonogram technician, had scurried out of the room that morning, I fell into a dreamless sleep.

With my midwives in charge and the doctors kept at bay, I gave birth naturally at one o'clock the next afternoon to our four-and-a-half-pound son, Sam. Although it wasn't the perfect birth experience I had imagined, once the midwives stepped in, it came pretty damn close. No pain drugs, no drama, and a baby who had somehow tied a knot in his umbilical cord and therefore had stopped growing.

When I got pregnant the next time, there was no debate about who would deliver our baby. Annie had moved away and been replaced by a funny blue-eyed blonde named Jill. This time, my pregnancy was even smoother—except for a little morning sickness and a fall a month before my due date that sent me to the ER for observation. But my baby and I were fine and the next month passed uneventfully.

This time, labor began exactly a week early, progressed normally, and by four o'clock that afternoon, I was lounging in the hot tub at the ABC. An hour later, I moved to the king-size bed, and with my husband right there beside me, Simon and Garfunkel serenaded us as Grace was born, naturally and without drugs at 6:20 p.m. on September 24, the one-hundredth birthday of F. Scott Fitzgerald.

I was thirty-eight years old, and had two healthy children and a finished family. When I left the ABC with Grace close to my chest and Sam running beside us, I assumed this chapter of my life was over. There would be no more babies and no more midwives for me.

How we plan! And how hopeful and ignorant we are! With such certainty we move through life, making decisions—however impulsively—and moving steadily forward. A few years later, my life was very much as I had hoped, with the addition of two children, now ages eight and five. I still wasn't much of a baby person, but I was continuously surprised by how smitten I was by my own. My promise to myself not to change my life for them but to have them adapt to the way I lived had resulted in a quirky nomadic family. For two years, as I researched a book, we traveled through Mexico and Italy and France. A magazine assignment sent us all to Japan for a month. I imagined a lifetime of adventures like these. I imagined, as parents do, a lifetime with my children.

But on a glorious April morning, my plans were obliterated when my daughter Grace died suddenly from a virulent form of strep.

Months passed somehow. Grief blurs time, makes days seem both endless and astonishingly short. Somehow food gets eaten, homework gets done, seasons pass. One day, there was a knock on my door and my midwife Ann stood there. I had received sympathy notes from each of those women who had seen me through my pregnancies and births, but now Ann walked in, filled with compassion and purpose. How was I taking care of myself? she asked me. Had I had my annual mammogram? When I shook my head no, she picked up the phone and made me an appointment. She gave me vitamins and checked my blood pressure. Before she left, she told me that when she was young, her sister died suddenly and her mother wrote down everything about their life together— how they spent their days, what their favorite foods and songs were, everything. "Do that for Sam," she said. "Write it down while you remember every little detail and give it to him someday. He'll be grateful."

I did as she suggested. I wrote about the day Grace was born, about the ABC and Simon and Garfunkel singing "Feelin' Groovy" and how Sam had held her in his lap until we had to make him give her back to me. I wrote about how they'd invented games and slept side by side together every night, how they'd performed plays and sung duets. I wrote about how we used to sit on winter afternoons and work on jigsaw puzzles together while Nancy Griffith played in the background. I wrote and I wrote and I wrote. Then I put all those pages away in a manila envelope for someday.

That long-ago day when I opened the Yellow Pages and found the only midwife practice here in Rhode Island, I never would have imagined the impact these women would have on my life. How they would fight for my rights as a mother about to give birth. How they would share the frightening birth experience and the perfect one. How one of them would come to me in my grief and help me put things in order. All I knew then was that I wanted to continue living life my way.

Three years after Grace died, our family decided to adopt a baby girl from China—another unexpected event that I had never planned on. But during that fog of grief, those sad years, we knew we had to do something to bring joy back into our lives, to remind ourselves that we could take charge, in a way. One of the first people to visit Annabelle when we got back from China was my midwife Ann. She came with small, perfect hand-knit sweaters, some cable-stitched, some decorated with tiny rosettes. The next year, when I ran a sweater drive for Annabelle's orphanage back in Hunan, Ann showed up with a whole box of sweaters, all hand-made by her knitting circle.

I know now that for all of our careful planning, no matter how our birth experience turns out, we cannot prepare ourselves for anything or protect ourselves from disappointment and heartache. We cannot anticipate the sheer joy our children will bring, or the way our hearts can open and grow because of them. All we can do is choose the people whom we want beside us through whatever life holds, and take their hands and hold on tight.

Timely Born

LAN SAMANTHA CHANG

Years ago, I underwent abdominal surgery to remove benign tumors from my uterus. I was in my early thirties, and my first book, a collection of short stories, would be published in a few months. As my writing project that year I'd vowed to draft a second book, an ambitiously stretched novel in the form of an imaginary memoir of the Sino-Japanese War. My parents had lived through the war as children and I had always promised myself that I would try to write about it. I had spent the previous decade focused solely on the goal of learning to write fiction, and as a result of this relentless focus, my life was as clear and clean as it's ever been. I lived and worked in a one-room studio apartment in Menlo Park, California. I had no car, no mortgage, and no partner. My gynecologist described the growths in my uterus by comparing them to various fruits: I had one tumor the size of a grapefruit, one the size of an orange, one the size of a tangerine, one the size of a lemon, and so on. But despite these luscious comparisons, my womb was about as far from being fruitful as a womb could be.

To remove the tumors, the doctors made a four-inch incision in my abdomen. They then pulled out my enormous, misshapen uterus, cut several pounds of fibroid tissue from its walls, stitched up the many incisions, and tucked my uterus back into my abdomen. I had never been in the hospital before. I was afraid of being put to sleep and woke up feeling disturbed that I had been cut open. I lost a fair amount of blood and had to stay in the hospital for three days; it was months before I was able to make my usual hike into the foothills.

The myomectomy was a crude procedure and yet a hopeful one; it had been performed with the assumption that, someday, I might want to have a child. In my mother's era, women who developed so many large fibroids underwent hysterectomies. My surgery made it possible for me to complete a normal pregnancy. There was one caveat, the gynecologist said: Because of the size and number of tumors, the uterine wall had been cut through and stitched together. The contractions of labor could rupture the wall. If I ever decided to have a child, she said, I would have to deliver via a scheduled C-section.

"I probably won't have a child for a long time, if I do," I said.

The doctor, a Chinese American woman like myself, put down her pen and looked me in the eye. "You shouldn't wait," she said. "If you want a child, you should give yourself a year or two to get over this surgery and then you should have the child as soon as possible."

As it turned out, I didn't follow my gynecologist's advice. Over several years, my novel project took me from California to New Jersey, then to Iowa, Massachusetts, Wyoming, back to Massachusetts, and finally to Iowa again. Eventually I did acquire a car, a partner, and a mortgage, in that order. But it was six years before I married and another two years, when I was forty-one, before my daughter was conceived. I asked the doctors if it might be possible that my uterus had healed over time, making possible a natural birth. But the medical records of the procedure, if they still existed, were buried in microfiche archives somewhere in California. The doctors could not know for certain where the incision had been and if there was still risk of rupturing the uterine wall. My obstetrician in Iowa thought it best to go through with the planned C-section.

I went through my nine months of uneventful pregnancy without doing any research on the surgery I was to undergo. I felt curiously unafraid. I knew only what I'd learned from my tenth-grade English class: that my baby, like Macduff, would be "none of woman born." Macduff, the Thane of Fife, the hero of *Macbeth*, is able to slay Macbeth because he fulfills the witches' prophecy: Instead of having a natural birth, he was "from his mother's womb / Untimely ripped."

Cesarean sections had progressed a great deal since *Macbeth*. Whereas they had once almost certainly killed the mother, they were now often performed to save her. They had once been only "untimely"—in the case of a failed labor—but in my situation, the delivery would be entirely timely. In deciding upon this method, I was given the opportunity to pick the date of my daughter's birth. There would be no anticipation, no surprise about *when* it would happen. No Lamaze classes, no gush of water, no hours of terrible vulnerability, no question of how I would bear it. No envisioning of my own features stretching into that face I've seen so many times on so many screens—that animal face. I would be spared the transforming pain of birth.

Instead, I sewed white curtains for the baby's room. My husband, Rob, and I fussed over her name. I consulted my office about her date of birth: When would be a good time for me to leave work? The secretaries thoughtfully directed me to their copy of a large book that listed not only the luminaries born on every day of the year but a series of qualities a birthday would bestow upon its holder. I pored over the book. Did I really want my child to be "taken up with seeing or being seen in a social context"? Did I want to doom her forever, with a careless choice of her birthday, to being the kind of person who would make "an excellent shopper"? For a brief period, I wanted her birthday to match my good friend Nan's, but it turned out my obstetrician wouldn't be working that day. If I chose that day for my delivery, the procedure would have to be performed by a different obstetrician. I balked at this. I wanted as much as possible to proceed according to a plan.

I had begun to realize, however dimly, the absolute lack of control I was about to experience in having a child, in letting a child into my life. Without the experience of birth to be concerned about, I'd nonetheless become as anxious as any woman anticipating childbirth. I had wanted a child, had hoped and longed for a child, but I had no idea what having one would be like. For so many years, I had lived the solitary life of the writer because I felt a solace and pleasure in—and need for—being alone. My husband, a visual artist, understood this. My child could have no knowledge of this need at all; in fact, it would be her essential job to seek my attention, my company and love. She would be mine: and I, her mother, would be no longer alone.

Soon I would meet someone who would become one of the most important people in my life, yet I had no idea what she would be like. I knew a fair amount about the family in China, on my side. Had I not pondered their history, researched it, carefully imagined an elaborate fictional narrative stretching alongside it during the seven years I'd spent on my novel? But I knew almost nothing about my husband's family. According to his mother, his grandfather had emigrated from Austria, where it was rumored he'd gone to school with Adolf Hitler. He had come to the United States as a young man, and he claimed to have served in the cavalry that had gone into Mexico to search for Pancho Villa. These far-flung historical forces had gathered themselves up into my husband and me, and now they lay waiting inside me, still a part of me but soon to be brought forth and propelled into the future, as separate from me as they had ever been. Separate, and yet linked to me forever.

It was a perfectly uneventful delivery, designed to be uneventful. At seven thirty on the appointed morning, Rob and I arrived at the university hospital in Iowa City. We waited in a nondescript waiting room. The procedure would take place around ten o'clock. I changed into a hospital gown, fitting it around my belly. "Are you nervous?" I asked my husband. "Terrified," he said. "Are you afraid of the surgery?" he asked. I was not afraid, I understood now in the waiting room, because I had been through this surgery before. An incision in the abdomen. This time, though, there would be no general anesthetic, a quicker procedure, minimal blood loss, an easier repair of the uterus.

I clambered up on a table. I was wheeled into the operating room. The procedure took place behind a white curtain so that I could not see it; the local anesthetic was so powerful, I did not feel a thing below my waist. There was only a coolness, then a series of tugs. Rob held my hand. "Here she is," the doctor said. From behind the curtain, there came a small throat-clearing sound, followed by a series of cries that began reasonably and grew quickly into louder, longer, shriller screaming. Someone exclaimed, "This one has the force of life in her!"

Then, with no labor or work on any part from me, Tai Antonia was brought howling from behind the curtain. She was already clean and wrapped in a blanket. Things had gone according to plan, and now there was no prophecy that could tell us what her life would be.

What I recognized, viscerally, immediately, was her shrieking face, the eyes squinched shut, the mouth stretched open around a wail of fear and outrage: the specific shape of that crying face, familial and familiar. She was placed snugly into my arms. When I said hello to her, the crying stopped. My ability to comfort her was a surprise, was not at all what I had imagined. But of course she knew me and she knew my voice. I was what she knew of the world.

Ask Your Mother

JOANNA RAKOFF

At a certain point in my first pregnancy, my doctor—a taciturn South Asian woman in her fifties, whom I'd chosen because of her rumored sympathy for natural childbirth—asked me about my family. How long had my mother labored with me and my siblings? Did I have sisters? Had any of them given birth? What had their labors been like? "Fast, I think," I told my doctor, whose gaze remained steadfastly affixed to my chart. Her inability to make eye contact was beginning to make me wonder about these alleged noninterventionist inclinations. "Maybe very fast," I said, trying to remember the specifics of the birth of my eldest sister. I'd heard the story long ago, before it had dawned on me that I might actually give birth to a child of my own someday. My father, I knew, had been in Germany. This was in the fifties—my sister is eighteen years older than I—during the Korean War, and my father had enlisted in the air force. My mother could have gone with him, but the memory of the Holocaust was still too fresh, too vivid, and she hadn't wanted her child to be born on German soil. She'd stayed behind in New York.

"And your sister?" asked my doctor. My sister has three children, all of them grown. The first was born a full month early, I suddenly remembered. "*Four* weeks early?" my doctor repeated. I had succeeded in shocking her into looking at me directly. "How big was the baby?"

I thought about this. "Four or five pounds, I think." The doctor was shaking her head, seemingly overwhelmed with the possibility of a preemie. "But completely fine. Really. Fine."

"Four or five pounds is *not* completely fine," said my doctor, clutching my chart to her chest, hitting her consonants with angry precision. "Labor is genetic," she said, her hand on the doorknob. "If your mother was fast, you'll be fast. If your sister was early"— she paused here—"you may very well be early." She shook her head gravely. "Fast and early," she said with a sigh. "It will be fine." She seemed to be trying to convince herself as much as me. "We just have to be prepared."

"Okay," I said.

"Ask your mother," she said. "Ask your mother *how* fast. And ask your sister *how* early."

That night, after visiting the doctor, I got home, settled myself in bed with a glass of water perched on my stomach, and called my mother. "So, um, my doctor told me to ask what your births were like," I began.

"My *births*," said my mother.

"Like, um, how long you labored?"

"Labor?" she said, as if this were a concept she'd never heard of. "I didn't labor at all."

"Okay," I said, taking a deep breath. "Well, um, what happened with Amy?" This is my elder sister. There were two kids between us who died in a car accident before I was born. They are never mentioned. "I remember, I think, that it was fast."

"Fast?" my mother said. "Fast is an understatement. I didn't even have time to get my clothes off. I had to keep my knees together to keep the baby from coming out in the car."

"Wow." So much for no one gives birth in taxicabs. "So, what happened?"

"*What happened?*" she parroted. She seemed, these days, to be permanently angry with me, for reasons I couldn't fathom. Or was it just that the two generations between us impaired our ability to convey even the most basic information to each other?

"Well, I woke up in the middle of the night to go to the bathroom and my water broke while I was sitting on the toilet. It was very convenient, actually. I didn't have to clean anything up." Since my mother is a person who vacuums daily, I could see how she might have thought this rather felicitous. "As soon as my water broke, I felt something."

"Contractions?" I offered.

"Maybe," my mother admitted. "Kind of like when you have to go to the bathroom. I knew that baby wanted *out*." She laughed in a way that made me nervous. "Uncle Abe was supposed to drive me to the hospital—"

"I remember!" I interjected, for I did indeed remember, suddenly, having heard this story before, many times, actually. After they married, my parents had taken an apartment in the Bronx, next door to my father's favorite aunt and uncle.

"But it was the middle of the night, and he and Aunt Lillie had to work the next day. I didn't want to wake them up, so I waited a little bit. Well, that was a mistake. Finally, I went and knocked on their door. Aunt Lillie answered and I told her my water broke." She paused here. "Now, Aunt Lillie was the most wonderful person. We all loved her. But she and Uncle Abe never had any children. What did she know about having babies?"

"Nothing?" I ventured.

"Exactly," my mother said, a note of pleasure creeping into her voice. "*Nothing.* She told me it was too early, to go back home and have a cup of tea. But I knew that baby was coming. When it happens, you just *know*." This was comforting, after all the confusing rules we'd learned in birthing class about timing contractions and suchlike. "But Aunt Lillie was a stubborn lady, and there was no arguing with her. So I went back home and had a cup of tea, and by the time I was done, I knew the baby was coming right that second. I knocked on their door and Uncle Abe put on his clothes and we went down to the car. The hospital wasn't that far—we were just going to Columbia—but it felt like forever. I was *literally* holding my knees together to keep the baby in. And when we got to the hospital, I told them the baby was coming, but they didn't believe me, either. They put me on a gurney and left me in a hallway, and the baby started coming out. As I said, I didn't even have time to get my clothes off."

"You had the baby in a hallway?" I asked, stunned.

"I think they wheeled me into a room, but I was wearing my regular clothing. I just hiked my skirt up. I still remember what I was wearing. A plaid pencil skirt." I tried to picture a hugely pregnant woman in a pencil skirt, then told myself not to get caught up in the details.

"And you didn't have any pain medication?"

"Joanna, I gave birth *in my clothing*. There was no time. Of course not."

"Was it very painful?"

"No, there was no pain at all. People always talk about pain, but I never felt any." No pain? No pain *at all*? From what I'd heard, this wasn't within the realm of possibility.

"How long did you push for?" I asked my mother.

My mother sighed in exasperation. "I didn't push. The baby just shot out of me."

This all sounded very strange. Impossible, even. In birthing class, we'd learned about what seemed like every possible scenario. There had been no footnote, no P.S., in which we learned that some people deliver their babies painlessly, without any effort on their part, in an hour or less. Was it possible that our birthing teacher was *wrong*? That these thirty-hour labors were caused by a sort of mass hysteria on the part of my endemically anxious generation? Or was it, perhaps, the opposite, that my mother and I—and my sister, too, presumably—were of some sort of superior race, built for birthing, a race that had evolved so highly as to eliminate the unnecessary pain of labor?

To my surprise, my doctor said the latter might be true. "That sounds like propulsive labor," she told me. "It's unusual, but a certain percentage of women have a predisposition for it. Did your sister have it, too?"

"Propulsive labor," I repeated. "My sister. I don't know." I hadn't called my sister, because, I suppose, the information gathered from my mother seemed to trump anything my sister might potentially impart. I had already, I see now, decided to believe my mother, decided that my body would behave in the manner she described, that my baby would want out, too.

"Ask her," instructed the doctor. "Regardless, as soon as your water breaks, you need to call me and get to the hospital. Just in case. But ask your sister. Today."

That night, I called my sister. "Fast?" she said. "Yeah, let's see, with Jessie"—her eldest, the baby born four weeks early, in Mexico—"it was definitely fast."

My heart beat a little faster. "Like an hour?"

"An *hour*?" My sister laughed. "I don't think anyone gives birth in an hour, Jo. An *hour*?"

"Mom said you were born in an hour. She said you shot right out of her. That she didn't even have to push."

"Really? I've never heard that." She paused. "Mom exaggerates sometimes. You know how Mom is. I don't think anyone gives birth in an hour." She paused again. "I don't know. Maybe." My sister, as it happens, is a nurse, with several graduate degrees. But my mother has a singular knack for making everyone around her doubt themselves.

"The doctor said it could really happen. It's called 'propulsive labor.'"

"Yeah, I've heard of that," my sister said skeptically. "It just seems *weird* that I've never heard this before."

"So," I began, trying to tamp down disappointment. "This didn't happen to you?"

Again, my sister laughed. "Let's see, with Jessie, I went into labor around midnight. And I think she was born around four or five. So pretty quick."

"And was there any pain? Mom said there was no pain at all."

My sister almost choked, she laughed so hard. "Mom said there was no pain? Are you sure she wasn't zonked out on Demerol?"

"She said they didn't give her any pain medication. There was no time; you were coming out too quickly. She said you were almost born in a hallway."

"Wow," she said. "I guess I must have known that at some point. I thought Jessie came fast, but apparently not." She had stopped laughing and her voice turned darker. "You know Mom," she said. "You can't compete with Mom."

"Tell me something I don't know," I said.

And yet my mother was beginning to soften toward me. She called daily with cheerful questions about cribs and strollers and blankets. She sent box after box filled with tiny clothing that I—being superstitious—banished to our building's storage space. We'd not experienced such generosity from her in years.

And I, in return, I chose to believe her. I wanted to believe her.

Reader, you are probably, by this point, chortling to yourself over my idiocy. You will think I'm being too kind to myself if I insist that my doctor shared in, even *encouraged*, my delusions. But the truth is, she did. Two weeks before my due date, I went in for a checkup and was told I was 100 percent effaced and dilated three centimeters. "This is just what I expected, based on your mother," my OB said. She snapped her gloves off. "You could go into labor at any moment. But it will very likely be in the next three days."

But three days came and went, then four, five, and six. On the seventh, I was back in her office again. "Three and a half centimeters," she said. "I thought you would have had the baby by now." She gave me a hard look. "I think, for you, it's going to be zero to sixty, if you know what I mean." I nodded. "Don't travel. Take it easy. It could be any minute."

"Is it . . . okay for me to walk around like this?" I asked. It seemed somehow unsanitary, as though something might drop out of me or seep into me.

"Sure," she said. "Orthodox Jewish women, on their twelfth child, they walk around like this for months. But stay close to home."

On my due date, I returned again. The doctor frowned as she checked me. "Still three and a half. I thought you'd be further along by now. If you don't go into labor in the next week, I'm going to induce you."

I'd thought women could go two weeks past their due date before being induced.

"Sometimes," my doctor said. "But you've been three centimeters for two weeks, maybe longer. You might never get past three centimeters. This might be it."

"What about my mother?" I asked.

She shrugged. "I don't know. I'm confused by this. But you're fully effaced. You can't walk around like this forever. There's a risk of infection." Two weeks ago, she'd told me I could indeed walk around like this. I was now as confused as she purported herself to be. I squeezed my feet back into my clogs and wandered out into the freezing air.

The next afternoon as I scrubbed a coffee stain off my desk, I found myself standing in a pool of water. For a few minutes, I stared at the puddle in wonder. Then I called Evan, who raced home from work. Together, we called the doctor.

"Get to the hospital *now*," she shouted. "You have a family history of propulsive labor. Get to the hospital NOW. Do you want to have this baby in a taxicab?"

As soon as I hung up the phone, as if on cue, a hammer began pounding away at my tailbone, a hammer lined, perhaps, with sharp teeth. The world became foggy. Somehow, as I clutched a pillow to my chest, Evan guided me out of our apartment and into a car from the local car service. Sometime later, I woke from a sort of fever dream with the realization that we had been in this car for a very, very long time. Out the window, I saw brilliant lights, enormous billboards, throngs of people. The driver had decided to drive through Times Square at dinnertime on a Thursday night. We were stuck in stopped traffic. "Are we on Forty-second Street?" I asked Evan. He nodded. "It's just before curtain at all the theaters. What is wrong with him?" My voice had risen to a scream now. "Oh my God, what is wrong with him? Does he not realize I'm in labor? Forty-second Street? Who would do that? This is completely insane. There has to be another route. I have to get out of this car!"

"She's about to have a baby," I heard Evan say to the driver. "You have to forgive her. She's not herself."

I am myself, I thought, but then, suddenly, I wasn't. When the car pulled up to the hospital, I opened the door and almost fell out. Evan grabbed my arm and slowly we made our way inside, the hammer beating out its awful tattoo on my spine, my hips, my everything. At labor and delivery, we were directed to the waiting room. A moment later, a nurse appeared at the entryway and motioned for me to follow her to the unit's main desk. Clutching my pillow, doubled over at the waist, I attempted to do so. It was perhaps eight feet from the waiting room to the desk. Halfway there, I nearly crumpled to the floor. Instead, I let out a long, low moan. "See, I really think she's in active labor," Evan told the nurse.

The nurse glanced at us tensely. "We're completely full tonight," she explained. "I don't even have a nurse for the triage station."

"What are we supposed to do?" asked Evan. This was our hospital, the hospital we'd toured and with which we'd filed reams and reams of paperwork, the hospital with which my doctor was affiliated. We'd spent an hour battling midtown traffic so that I might benefit from their enlightened nurses and lactation consultants, so that I might deliver in their birthing center, laboring in a whirlpool, free from the institutional pressure for monitors and epidurals. We'd never thought for a second that it might be *full* when I went into labor.

"My mother had propulsive labor," I told the nurse, tears suddenly streaming down my face. I was bent over the front desk, and I could see that both the nurse and Evan were horrified and trying to find a delicate way to tell me to get up, but I could not get up. "She gave birth in a hallway. My doctor told me to come to the hospital as soon as my water broke."

"Who's your doctor?" asked the nurse. Evan told her and we watched as her face turned businesslike and serious. My stern doctor, I would realize later, was not the sort of practitioner to tell a patient to get to the hospital early unless she *really* thought that patient needed to get to the hospital early. "Okay," she said. "Let me page her." She handed me a hospital gown and a pair of paper booties.

"It hurts so much," I told the nurse, the words seeming to leave my mouth through a thick fog. Time had slowed down and the world had receded. There was me, my eyes smarting from the fluorescent lights of the triage room, and there was the unspeakable pain that threatened—it really felt this way—to shatter my body. Nothing else. Was this the normal pain of labor? It felt worse, so much worse than anything for which we'd been prepared. Was there something wrong—with the baby? Or with me? Or did the pain seem so extreme because I hadn't believed there'd really be any pain? How could my mother have told me that there was no pain? Had she simply told me what she believed to be the truth? Or was she trying to set me up for heartache and disappointment?

Somehow, I ended up in a delivery room, frighteningly cluttered with medical equipment. We were assigned a nurse, a formidable black-haired woman in her late forties, who sat me down on the edge of the bed, put her hands on my shoulders, and said, "Listen, the baby's coming and you're in a lot of pain, but you have to calm down and keep quiet."

I nodded, head bowed like a cowed child. "Where's Dr. Paka?" I asked again.

"The resident's coming in to check you," she said. "I'll go see if I can find out what's going on with Dr. Paka."

The nurse never returned. It was seven o'clock, the chaotic hour when hospital shifts change over. Which meant Dr. Paka, too, had left—left without even stopping in to see me. Her partner, Dr. Francis, whom I'd never met, would be delivering the baby, but she was currently tending to four other women at once, one of whom was delivering twins. We were informed of this by a male resident, who stuck his hands between my legs without so much as introducing himself. "Four centimeters," he said, a bemused expression on his face. He was blandly handsome in the manner of a television actor and his manner, too, was briskly efficient, a cliché of the all-business medical student destined to be shocked into humanity over the season's thirteen episodes. "You have a long way to go. Let's get you an epidural."

"She doesn't want an epidural," said Evan.

"If she's having this much trouble handling the pain at four centimeters, she's not going to be able to cope when we get to ten," the resident replied.

"I don't want an epidural," I said, and the strength of this reply somehow gave me the will to calm down, to lie back on the brace of pillows and breathe, just as we'd been told to do in birthing class. The handsome resident disappeared and I breathed more deeply, while Evan held my hand, until pressure roused me. A sandy-haired woman—beautifully coiffed, immaculately made up, slender under her lab coat—sat on the edge of my bed, smiling. I didn't know who she was, but in the ugly, antiseptic world of my hospital room, she struck me as a friend. Indeed, when she smiled and took my hand, the pain receded a bit.

"Joanne," she said, and I excused her mispronunciation of my name. "Joanne, you are in so much pain. I have two children, and I know this pain. This pain is not going to stop. Let us make it go away. We can just make it go away." For a moment, I didn't realize she was talking about an epidural. I thought, perhaps, she had magic powers or knew of some heretofore-unmentioned alternative procedure, an ayurvedic pain release ritual maybe. Then the reality sunk in. It was just as our birthing teacher had told us. Lying there, untethered to any of the monitors and IV racks and who knows what around me, I was a problem. I was a risk and an annoyance. "You don't need to suffer. The pain doesn't make you a better person. Trust me. Let us make the pain go away."

There was a moment in which I almost said yes, but then I remembered what I'd learned in birthing class: The epidural was a Pandora's box that would lead to Pitocin, to a C-section, to things I didn't want. And then—*then*—I remembered my mother: The baby would be out soon. There was no need for pain medication. "I don't want an epidural," I told her.

"Okay," she said, her voice growing harder. She had not been a friend at all, of course. "But if you don't get one now, and you decide you want one later, it may be too late." She had already dropped my hand by this point. It lay freezing on my thigh.

After another visit or two from the handsome, condescending resident—he never told me his name—a small woman with lush ringlets springing from her head came bounding into the room. "I'm Dr. Francis," she said. "I'm Dr. Paka's partner. I'm sorry it took me so long to get here. I just delivered *four* babies." She smiled. "This is *some* night." I was, at this point, crouched on the floor in a position akin to child's pose in yoga: my seat to my heels. "What's going on here?" Dr. Francis asked. "You're in a lot of pain." I nodded, to the extent I was able. "Let me see what I can do." She knelt down on the floor behind me and put her hands on my lower back. "It hurts right here?" she asked. I nodded again. "You're having back labor," she said. "Definitely. Do you know what back labor is?" I nodded. "The baby's facing the wrong way. The back of his skull is against your pelvis. It's *banging* into your pelvis. Oh my God, it's so painful. It's the most painful thing in the world. It's so much worse than regular labor." As she said this, she put pressure on my lower back and magically the pain disappeared. I groaned and collapsed, and she laughed. "That's better, right? Back labor, God. It's the worst. But pressure can help."

Soon a nurse popped her head in the door. "She's ready to push," she said. The "she" wasn't me. Dr. Francis left and Evan tried to replicate her magic, without success. An hour went by, then another.

Instead of Dr. Francis, the handsome resident returned and checked me again. "She's only seven centimeters." He sighed, glaring at me as if I'd done something wrong, then turned on his heel and walked out. On the bed, I squirmed and moaned, trying to get myself into a position that wasn't all fire and rage. How could I only be seven centimeters? The resident, I thought, was right to be disappointed in me. I was disappointed in myself, in my body. I was not my mother's daughter, apparently. I was not, as my mother used to tell me in childhood, "like Mary Poppins, practically perfect in every way."

"Evan," I said. "I can't take it anymore. I want an epidural."

Suddenly, everyone loved me. A team of residents and nurses hooked me up to an IV drip of saline, a blood pressure cuff, a fetal monitor, all of them jovial and calm. This, they understood, they could handle. I was complying, admitting defeat, succumbing to my body's inferiority to the miracle of modern medicine.

And then we waited, and waited, and waited. There was just one anesthesiologist on call, and the night unusually busy. "If you'd decided earlier, it would have been much easier," the handsome resident informed me.

"Okay, okay," Evan told him. "We get it."

"I can't take any more," I whispered.

"I think she's in transition," Evan told a nurse. "Could she be?"

But before anyone could answer, a cart crashed through the doorway. "Hello, hello!" cried a smiling African man. "Ah, I am sorry it took me so long. But I am here to take your pain away. It will only take a second." There was a prick—the lidocaine going into the small of my back—and then: nothing. To this day, Evan speaks of that moment with wonder. "All the pain just went out of your face," he says. "In an *instant*."

But that release was not without repercussions. Just as I'd learned it might, my labor stopped. This was, a resident explained, a good thing. "Get some rest," she said chirpily. "Save your energy for pushing. Go to sleep." It was one or two in the morning by now, the hospital dark and hushed but for the beeping of the monitors and an occasional scream. I fell into a strange, broken sleep, woken every ten or fifteen minutes by a blood pressure cuff squeezing my arm. Eventually, Dr. Francis returned and fiddled with the monitors. "We've got to get this going. Let's give her some Pitocin." More bags were hung on the IV stands. I tried to sit up but couldn't, my legs a deadweight. The handsome resident returned and checked me again. "You're dilated," he said flatly. "It's time to push." Then he disappeared. Alone in the room, except for Evan and a nurse on either side of me, I watched the monitor. When a certain line crested, I was supposed to push, but what did pushing mean? I could feel nothing below my waist. For an hour, then almost two, we stayed like this, a frieze of confusion.

"I just can't feel anything," I told them finally. "When does the epidural wear off?" We had been told, in birthing class, that the epidural would be turned off when it was time to push.

The nurse raised her eyebrows at me. "The epidural's still on," she said.

Softly, I began to cry.

"Could we have it turned off?" Evan asked.

The nurse looked at us as if we were crazy. "Let me see," she said testily, and disappeared.

Soon, the handsome resident walked his brisk walk into the room. "We can dial the epidural down," he told Evan, ignoring me. "But she has a really low threshold for pain, so I wouldn't recommend that."

I didn't have a low threshold for pain. As a child, I'd broken my collarbone jumping off my bed, and kept it a secret for three days. I'd run through knee blowouts and walked off a back injury after being extracted from a crushed car by the Jaws of Life.

"Can we just try?" Evan asked. I had, apparently, become invisible.

"She's been pushing for two hours," he said. "That's long enough. I think we should do a C-section. She's just not strong enough to push the baby out."

"Could she just try a little longer?" asked Evan.

"*The baby isn't coming down*," he said slowly, as if we were mentally deficient. "*We have to do a C-section.*"

"No," I said weakly. "Why?"

"You're not strong enough," he said, and strode out of the room.

A moment later, Dr. Francis raced in, stretching her arms above her head and brushing the sleep out of her eyes. During my hours of futile pushing, she'd taken a catnap. "What's going on in here?" she asked.

"He said I'm not strong enough to push, but he won't turn the epidural off and I can't feel anything," I cried, pushing back tears. "He said I need a C-section, but I don't want a C-section. I don't *need* one. I can push this baby out. I just need to be able to feel something."

Dr. Francis rubbed her hands together. "Listen," she said, "you don't need a C-section. You're strong and you can get this baby out." She gestured to the nurse. "Turn the epidural all the way off.

Just dial it all the way down, okay?" She pulled on her gloves with a snap. "I can see the head!" she said, then gave a sort of low growl. "He didn't even check you!" She popped her head up and looked me in the eye. "Listen, the baby turned. That's why this is taking so long. The baby's the right way now. While you were sleeping, the baby turned. Good baby!" The feeling began to return to my legs. When Dr. Francis told me to push, I could feel something, could roughly discern what she meant. "Okay, this is great," she cried. "You're so close. Let's get this baby out."

Twenty minutes later, the head that had caused me so much pain emerged, followed by a body that seemed to just keep coming. A boy. "Wow, this baby is *big*," cried Dr. Francis. "No wonder you were in so much pain. Back labor with a baby this size. I can't believe how long you went without the epidural." Placed on my chest, he took up the whole of my body, his beautiful almond-shaped eyes opening and closing, his cheeks trembling for air. "She was having back labor," Dr. Francis told the various people assembled in the room. "With a baby this big. Can you imagine? Look at how tiny she is!" The assembled murmured their assent, as if the entirety of my sojourn in this room hadn't been characterized by a somewhat different sentiment. Dr. Handsome was nowhere to be seen. "Back labor," Dr. Francis told the pediatrician, who was pounding on the baby's chest now to clear his lungs. "This is a nine-pound baby," she said to me. "You delivered a nine-pound baby. You got that baby out."

I got that baby out, I did, though Dr. Francis used a vacuum to help me, and though my mother seemed to take the twelve hours I labored as a personal affront.

What was my mother trying to tell me with her story? I can't believe she would lie to me, not about something so fundamental: the birth of a child. So I have to believe what she told me is true, or a version of the truth. That my sister—and my ghost siblings, and

I—entered the world without agony, without labor, without the normal human trappings, the usual mess of life. Or, at least, that this was what she wished for us, and for herself, for the lives that lay shining ahead of us, an existence in which joy is not intrinsically linked to pain and grief. That's how it seems to me now at least. Someday, someday, I'll ask her.

my 1st ds was born on tues at slr!

SUSAN BURTON

As much as I wanted a birth, I wanted a birth story. Oh, that's not exactly right. Obviously I wanted the baby more. But it's fair to say that I was anticipating the birth story. It was part of what I would take home with me. It was something I would be wheeled out of the hospital with, along with the formula samples and the sitz bath. But it was more precious than these free handouts, more like the diamond bands some women got from their husbands as "push gifts." I didn't want a reward for pushing out my baby. I wanted the story of pushing him.

I was introduced to the idea of a birth story on an online parenting bulletin board called UrbanBaby—this was several months before a big article about the site appeared in *The New York Times*. After that, a lot of women on the board became very invested in wanting the newbies to know that they'd been there when it was still cool. I felt superior, too, but I had no way to share it, because I was too nervous to post. The single time I had gotten up the courage to do so, I had written

does anybody else ever worry that ub can trace our
posts, like by the ip address, or something?

And somebody responded with a dismissive

```
of course
```

And some other people, whom I believed were naïve, maintained that UrbanBaby was completely anonymous.

It didn't seem anonymous to me. There was the Hong Kong poster, who was always on in the middle of the night. There was the Apple poster, who, any time anyone posted asking for

```
good names for a dd?
```

would respond with the infamous name of Gwyneth Paltrow's dear daughter. Then there was a woman I couldn't characterize, except for the fact that she had responded to the post

```
name of your secret crush in the 90s
```

with the name of a man who had also been my secret crush in the nineties. This man was not famous, and when I saw his name on the screen, I seized in regret and alarm, like I had typed this in when I was drunk; except for the fact I was never drunk, because I was pregnant.

I was pregnant with my first child, and I was writing a book that was basically due on the same day he was. I spent most of my days in my office, which was a room in our Brooklyn apartment that the former owners had used as a nursery. The room was painted yellow, with a border of white curlicues. Finishing the book on time was a practical necessity as well a professional one. But I couldn't stop myself from clicking, frequently, over to UrbanBaby. People complained that many of the posters were vapid or snarky, and while this was true, others were thoughtful and kind. I found it comforting that for every worry I had—about my thyroid medication, about the rumor that my OB was secretly antiabortion, about the assessment that I was measuring "small for dates"—there was always at least one other like-minded worrier.

But what I liked best on UrbanBaby were birth stories. I especially liked ones by women who had delivered at St. Luke's–Roosevelt, where I would be giving birth. But I wasn't picky. I read all of them. Women would post the stories as soon as they came home from the hospital. Sometimes they would even write them while they were still on the maternity ward, or in the hours after a home birth on what was now the family bed. They would thumb in their birth stories on their BlackBerries. They would begin with something like this

```
these stories really always helped me, so i wanted
to post mine, too. so, here goes. whew! i started
laboring monday at around noon. at first i thought
it was just braxton-hicks
```

and go on from there.

A big part of the stories involved your birth plan being derailed. You failed to progress and had to have a C-section, or you were given Pitocin when you'd been set on natural birth. Natural birth was what I wanted. Actually, you were supposed to call it "unmedicated birth," because birth was, by definition, natural.

My mother thought it was weird that natural birth was the exception rather than the rule. "Everybody had a natural birth when I had you," she claimed. But while this may have been true among her young, progressive cohort, natural birth definitely wasn't the norm in 1973. My husband was born two weeks before me to parents a decade older than mine. During my pregnancy, we learned that his mother's doctor had scheduled the delivery around his golf game, and, as I understood it, had put her to sleep for it. I wondered if it was "twilight sleep," the amnesiac state induced by an anesthetic that was once commonly administered to women during childbirth. These "chemically silenced" women were denied their own birth stories, which future feminists tried to reclaim.

But on UrbanBaby, the birth stories weren't political, at least not overtly. Sometimes they were so full of drug names and numbers and times

```
i had cervadil overnight, starting at 7pm. pitocin
started at 8am
```

that it was like reading a medical chart. Our twenty-first-century pregnancies were all about information: about fertility monitors and triple screens and sonograms. Our data *was* our story, from beginning to end.

Yet an activist would argue that even the simple act of telling a birth story is political, in that it demystifies birth. And the Urban-Baby stories did this for me. They made the unknowable concrete. I liked the strings of facts, the sequencing of events. This-then, this-then, over and over again. Reading these stories in my yellow room was a rehearsal. It was a way of imagining myself into something, and on the other side of it, too: What wonder would I feel when it was over, when I had my own baby in my arms, when I became a mother at the end?

When my water broke on a hot April afternoon as I sat at my desk, I was conscious both that labor was starting and that this was my birth story's opening scene. That was a Monday. On Thursday, I came home from the hospital with my baby and my husband and my mother. I took a shower with the bathroom door open in case I needed help. Then, with Nick asleep in my mother's arms, I went into the office and sat down at my computer. Now was the moment to do it.

```
my 1st ds was born on tues at slr!
```

But even though I had my first line, I didn't type anything in.

Partly it was because I didn't have time. I had messages on my voice mail from the lawyer for the publishing house. The manuscript was being legally vetted, even though I was still rewriting large chunks of it. I was angry at myself for not having finished; now the work would have to get done while Nick slept or nursed.

But something else was holding me back, too. Because really, how much time would composing my birth story have taken? Especially given that over the next couple days, I continued to write it in my head, in UrbanBaby form, the way I would later think in tweets.

```
i was trying for an unmedicated birth on the reg-
ular l&d floor.

i was still only at 5cm, and it had now been 24
hours since my water had broken.

when it was time to push, ds was out in less than
20 minutes.
```

Eventually so much time passed that it was too late to post it, in the way that it's sometimes too late to send a thank-you note.

```
i hope these details help someone! all my best
to everyone who's still expecting, and thanks to
everyone who came before me on here.
```

When, in June, the book was finally done, I sat down at my computer to write a private, richly detailed account of Nick's birth.

I started with a walk my husband and I had taken on the Sunday before. We'd been holding hands on a wooden bridge in Prospect Park. I wrote down everything I could remember about that afternoon and that evening, and the next morning and afternoon and the next walk. Then I stopped writing. Labor was about to start. The story, the real story, was about to begin, but I held myself at a distance from the monitor instead of myopically leaning in. Then I saved the document and stood up from my desk before even getting to the moment my water broke in my chair.

Several months later, we had friends over for dinner: my high school prom date and his girlfriend, Edith, who was pregnant with their first child. I thought Edith might be a vegetarian, and though I'd been a vegetarian during the years the boy and I had gone to high school together, in a town where the most popular bumper sticker was I EAT TOFU AND I VOTE, I became terrified that I wouldn't know what to cook for her, so with Nick in the baby carrier, I bought a heavy, expensive Deborah Madison cookbook and made a pasta dish from its pages. The panicked episode was emblematic of the kind that had characterized my early months as a mother. But by the end of the dinner that night, as I sat at our little cherrywood table, surrounded by my past and my present, Nick sleeping in his crib on the other side of the French doors, I felt fortunate and serene.

Edith reached across the table and put her hand on my arm. "Sometime I'd really love to hear your birth story," she said.

Oh, how I ached to tell her then! She had said "sometime," meaning the future, but I wanted to stop the conversation at the table, break in, and say, "Okay, I'll tell you right now; this is what happened." But I didn't.

I was unable to tell the story I had wanted so badly to. Can you see that even now I'm not telling it here? It's not like the details I'm withholding are traumatic or shameful. But I feel tender toward the story, and I'm keeping it near. Cradling it, something I can no longer do with Nick, an eight-year-old with permanent teeth, a blond bowl cut, and long, thin, soccer-playing legs that once kicked inside me.

What happens to a story if you don't tell it? The story stays perfect. It stays intact.

I came to understand another reason why the UrbanBaby birth

stories took the form that they did: all those numbers, times, facts. Data was a language that helped you get down what was harder to express, like:

The park's full, pink blossoms. That Monday, so hot in my dark corduroys, but I didn't want to buy spring maternity clothes, because I wasn't going to be pregnant much longer. The way the water broke. A knock inside me, and then a spreading warmth. The exact spot of polished wood floor I was standing in when I called my husband at work. A silver cell phone that snapped shut like a clam. Our bedspread with ferns marking my face. How at 2:00 or 3:00 a.m., the same radio programs I'd heard earlier in the day played again. The dreamlike repetition. But the pain, and throwing up from it after one spoonful of raspberry sorbet. The labor doula and the paper cups of coffee, how easy it was for her and my husband, a normal April morning on Fifth Street. The birth canal that is the Brooklyn Battery Tunnel. Pulling into the hospital circle at noon in the Volvo we had leased because we needed a safe car now that we were going to be parents. My water breaking again in the revolving door. The sunny labor and delivery room, and how at home my OBs were here. They seemed looser. Was this the real thing to them, and all the visits in the little warren of offices the secondary piece of it? How I labored so long, all three OBs rotated in: the smart doctor my age from Northwestern; the intimidating, decisive, older doctor; the smart doctor my age from U of M. The decisive doctor: "It's been more than twenty-four hours since your water broke, and you're only at five centimeters. I'm sorry, but I have to give Pitocin. And I will not give Pitocin without the epidural. It's cruel." Lying on my side, turning to the anesthesiologist. "Are you sure the dose is adjusted, because I am, like, really small. I am way smaller than most women. My prepregnancy weight was ninety-one and a half pounds. Now I weigh one hundred and eight." And then the calm. The orange light through the slatted blinds. My husband and the labor doula talking softly. The warmth of the microwaved blanket. The release when my catheter was emptied. How the IV fluids I hadn't wanted were better than ice chips. The pressure of pushing, the fierceness with which you had to try, a kind of bursting trying from childhood. And Nick. "My baby," I said, "my baby." How he nursed right away. Holding him in the wheelchair, a nurse peering down. "He doesn't even need an ID bracelet. He looks just like you." The swell of pride, the rightness of our resemblance. That night, Nick awake in the bassinet next to me. Not crying, just wide-eyed. Just watchful.

That's a detail that Nick knows. How he was still and awake his first night of life. My tiny, vigilant observer. There was something so incredible, and characteristic, about Nick in that moment. On alert. Tense but composed. Not shrinking from his surroundings; not burying himself in his mother; just keeping to himself, taking everything in.

Nick seems a little proud whenever I tell him this. He usually wants to go over what his younger brother, Will, did in his first hours of life. "He only wanted to sleep on top of you, Mommy, right?"

"Right, sweetie."

"But I stayed awake with you, and looked around, the first night."

"That's right, love. Not the whole night. Maybe even just, like, a few minutes. But it was unusual. It was really special."

This kind of telling I've never shrunk from; this kind of telling has always felt right.

As much as I wanted a birth story, I wanted a child to share it with.

The Broken I

RACHEL JAMISON WEBSTER

there is an amazon in us.
she is the secret we do not
have to learn.
the strength that opens us
beyond ourselves.
birth is our birthright.
we smile our mysterious smile.
—Lucille Clifton, "female"

My face has changed since I had my baby six weeks ago. I hold my calmly nursing daughter, and I smile—but there is something broken, stunned in one eye. I don't notice it until I see photographs, and then I feel a little sad missing the girl I was. She is gone now, and I am not sure who the new self is and what new outlooks will emerge through the fissure. I saw the look again tonight, in a photo e-mailed by a friend who just had a baby. Like me, she had a long labor that she insisted on doing without painkillers. Her one eye stares out at me, as if to say, *I didn't know it was like this. Nothing said it was this terrible, except maybe the Bible, and I thought that was just a man writing about the "woman's curse" to keep us down. No one told me.*

But looking at the babies in these photos—babies whose mothers were lucky and stubborn enough to have them naturally—I think, These babies look like angels. Their countenances are deeply peaceful. They sleep as if in unbroken memory of the other side.

And I get a reminder of why I chose a natural labor. Since those days, I have delighted in my healthy, beautiful daughter, but I have also wondered if I was crazy to give birth without painkillers. Where had my insistence come from? Had I behaved like some kind of martyr? Had I been playing out some old generational guilt by making myself suffer unnecessarily?

An eye can stare outward as if it knows—and can hardly believe—it is no longer its own eye. The "I" has split, the body has opened into the truth of its own death, the truth of its own birth, and the new person who's emerged is whole. Is separate. I wanted my daughter to be free of her birth. I wanted this birth—which was her first experience of a death, being the death of her life in the womb—to be as gentle as possible. I wanted it to proceed wholly in the rhythms of our shared body, so that she could begin her life in continuity with the unfolding and connection she had known before.

I cried when I saw the video taken just after my daughter was born. She was relaxed, but her head was disfigured from being in the birth canal for so long. My eyes were bugged out and my face was contorted because of extended pushing. In the first hour of my daughter's life, I nursed her, the nurse cleaned her and weighed her, her father held her tiny hands and sang her a song he'd written, and my mother held her and rocked her. And, through all of this, my midwife was still stitching up a jagged tear in my labia. Three days later, my family was watching the birth on film and celebrating, but I wanted to yell "It was terrible! It was the worst day of my life!" But of course, "worst" was way too small a word, and an egocentric smallness in me really did die during labor. It was the most powerful day of my life, the most transformative day. It was a day that I would not trade, but one that I will not simplify or romanticize, either.

My pregnancy had not transpired under simple circumstances. I had conceived my baby accidentally with a man I loved deeply but had not known long, before my painful divorce with my ex had even been finalized. I did not have health insurance or a steady job. We had moved twice in six months and did not know where we would live or how we would support ourselves. I had weathered judgment and fear from others. My family has a history of mental and physical handicaps, at least one of which was due to a mishandled labor, and so I had to resist worry every day, to train my body and mind to be calm. And yet, somehow, through all of this, I had a healthy, deeply joyful pregnancy. I was convinced of my baby's strength and of her desire to be here. I was also convinced of my own health and of my own authority in the birthing process, and my stubbornness on this point surprised everyone—especially me.

The first stages of labor were triumphant, even ecstatic for me. I experienced mild contractions for three weeks and learned to breathe and stretch through them, to trust the rhythms of my body and marvel at the swells of clarity and emotion that these surges brought forth. I walked a mile or two every day along Lake Michigan, amid apple trees, lilacs and peonies just beginning to bloom, and the perfumes and the sights were so tender, so miraculously alive, that I would weep. I felt porous, strummed by the nerves of the earth—my body registered the movement of the grass, the stirring of the leaves. I could feel a friend who was hurting or rejoicing across the country, and I would call and drop into the moment midconversation. I felt connected to everyone I loved, especially to other women, and I felt—and still feel—awed to be a portal through which another would enter her life.

My baby was due on the summer solstice. That morning, I knew I was in labor. I drove myself to my checkup, excited and chatty, and my midwife was surprised to find me dilated five centimeters. Because I was managing, breathing through the contractions and resting between them, she allowed me to go home to get my partner, Richard, and my mother, who had come into town to help. I walked along the beach before going back to the hospital, and I continued dilating at a steady pace. At the hospital, I rocked and leaned on the bed while my water broke around my feet. I squatted, swayed my hips, and did every yoga pose I knew of. Then, when that got unbearable, I got into the tub while Richard sat beside me and played guitar.

I sang with him until my singing turned to screaming. At first, I was afraid of scaring the other women in the hospital, and then the noises I made became involuntary. At one point, I heard another woman screaming down the hall. My midwife apologized for her, and I nearly snapped at her—I liked it! The woman and I were connected in our labor; we were connected to all the other women who were laboring at that moment across the world. I needed to know that what seemed impossible was possible, and so I thought of them, and of all the women I knew who had given birth naturally. Then I had the idea that the baby needed to hear my voice in order to come out, that somehow she would travel out of me on the sound of her mother's power. And so I tried to cut the fear out of my screams and make them strong. This went on for hours, and at one point I realized that I sounded like a baby myself, wailing inconsolably as the contractions hit one on top of the other. I wondered if I was crying through my own birth again. Maybe, I thought, I am crying for my own mother, who had not screamed because she'd been alone in her hospital room, spinal-tapped and flat on her back when they pulled me out with forceps.

Then, after screaming and squatting my way to full ten-centimeter dilation, my labor just stopped. The halt was probably due to sheer physical exhaustion, compounded by the fact that I had not eaten for hours and the hospital thermostat had malfunctioned, leaving us in a frigid fifty-degree room. In any case, my stopped labor materialized as fear, a feeling of not knowing how to move forward. I suddenly could not picture my baby or see the other side, in which my pregnancy would be over and I would be a mother. I had gotten used to braving the waves of contractions, but now that it was time to push through the pain, I had no instinctive urge to do so. I had no idea how to invite pain to the site where pain—it suddenly seemed—had so often been inflicted.

My vagina had been the port of suffering, and in the middle of my labor, I remembered it—sexual abuse as a girl, disrespectful sex as an adult, jarring pelvic exams. My own instances of pain began coming at me, but violations I had not experienced firsthand came to me, too, in rapid Technicolor flashes. I seemed to be traveling with women through time and place. My mother had been abused, and her mother and hers, and there was an ache at this site as old as the world.

Meanwhile, my halting contractions were making my mother increasingly nervous, and even my midwife was worried. "This is not a normal labor," she kept saying.

"Nothing about this pregnancy has been normal," I said back.

"You should have the urge to push," she said again and again. But the urge—a physical need as undeniable as the need to scream— was nowhere. All the books I had read described "bearing down" as an instinct that didn't really need explaining, but I had never understood it. Leaning against the bed, I asked my midwife to tell me again how to do it, and she was baffled. "It's an urge," she said, "like needing to pee."

But I couldn't locate it. I thought of a different group of women then—women closer to me, less generalized—many of my close friends, who had also set out to have natural births and whose labors had stopped right where mine had, just before the pushing stage. All of them had had cesareans. And I realized that all but one of them had been sexually abused.

Our vaginas are sites of magnificent power, but they often become wounds of powerlessness. Ideally, they introduce us to our own sexual and creative instincts, but in reality, they often host the loss of our agency. And so I wonder if this absence of instinct to push, to birth, may simply be evidence of another instinct—one related to our very survival.

After my daughter was born, I discussed my labor's stages with a midwife who works with women from all over the world. She said that many women from Third World countries experience a halt in labor exactly where I did, because they are afraid to die. After all, in their countries a significant number of women still die in childbirth. They know this as fact and experience, and their labors force them to push through their mortality—literally, in a way we may deeply intuit.

Now, a fear of birth seems natural and well-founded to me, as elemental as our fear of death. And I can see that our society's medicalized, frantic resistance to death is mirrored in our medicalized, systematic avoidance of natural birth. One hour of prime-time television in this country can show dozens of shootings and violent deaths, and yet most of us do not know how to be really present with a person who is dying. Similarly, we can treat birth as a dramatic medical emergency, but few of us—women or doctors—have the patience and faith in nature to ride out the natural and individual process of birth. We are afraid of the dangers, but we are also afraid of the mystery. And we have less practice in our society trusting what comes *out* of women as much as what goes *in*—whether it is a tampon, an antidepressant, an epidural, or a shot of Botox. In our culture, we are taught that we need to be augmented to be desirable, feminine rather than female. And real female power is nothing less than the power to risk death to bring forth new life.

I was surprised by the ferocious femaleness I felt in labor, my trust in my own authority to bring in my daughter, and even in the midst of agonizing pain, it thrilled me. I felt utter clarity about how we both needed to experience birth, and while I was laboring, I protected that space like some kind of ancient, natural woman. Had my daughter showed any sign of distress, I would have been grateful for medical intervention. But I had a patient baby with a steady heartbeat, and a partner who trusted me. He got us moved to a warmer room and deflected doctors in order to buy me some time until the sun came up. Finally, I agreed to take Pitocin just as a new midwife was beginning her shift. After hours of being told that my labor was "not normal," I looked deep into this woman's eyes—a woman I had never met—and asked her if she thought I could have my baby vaginally.

"Yes," she said simply and calmly.

Then she showed me how to work with my contractions, which, despite the Pitocin, were still weak and fatigued. On each contraction, I held my breath, pushed, and did a sit-up, while Richard and my mother pulled back my legs. Exhausted, I thought every push would have to be my last. But I pushed for five hours, and finally, our daughter was born. With her, a knowledge of my own strength—and my mother's and her mother's—was born, as well.

Just before her death, I saw the poet Lucille Clifton accept the Ruth Lilly Poetry Prize. Two of her daughters and a granddaughter attended the ceremony. After her glowing introduction, her granddaughter chirped out, "Grandma!" And Lucille Clifton said, "That's the best introduction of all." Throughout the evening, Clifton read poems, told stories, and made us laugh and feel. Like a true mother, she expressed love, indignation, and sorrow about the state of our time and society. Afterward, I said how wonderful I thought she was. My friend agreed, and said, "Where does she get the authority?"

She gets it from her life, I thought, from the experience she's lived through her body. She was sexually abused by her father. She birthed and raised six children. She lost a breast to cancer, she lost her beloved husband to death, and she writes about all of this with fearless beauty. Seeing her, I was starstruck, and I realized that this is something I see through the new cut in my eye. Women who experience their own authority, who know that authority, and who use it to become mothers in whatever way they must. There is a brokenness, I know now, that can open us to others, a self that can split into something more whole.

Thirty Hours

1. Like every other good thing that had ever happened in my life, it seemed impossible: impossible that I would be able to bring a child into the world.

2. This story begins—as so many do—with my own mother. Not to throw her under the bus or anything, but mothering wasn't her forte. She was good at other things: collecting art, fund-raising, gardening. Recently I was asked to contribute to a book of essays by women writers about lessons their mother had taught them. I had to decline. The only thing I could come up with was a tip about being extra careful when driving on wet leaves. You can lose control of your car on a patch of wet leaves just as easily as if it were a sheet of ice. My mother taught me that.

3. I have been plagued by terrible anxiety all my life. It is always in the room with me. At times, it sleeps in the corner. At other times, it is like a loud, unruly drunk, upending the table, causing all the good china and delicate glassware to crash to the floor. The thought of childbirth terrified me. *Theoretically*, I wanted children, of course. I wanted them

in the way that I wanted to go to medical school, or live in Morocco, or hike Kilimanjaro. Which is to say, childbirth, for me, felt like overreaching. Like asking for too much. It was an exotic and deeply ambitious thing, possible for some people but not for me. It was hubris to think otherwise. If I could have blinked and had children, I would have. But the process, I was quite sure, would kill me.

4. But then I met my husband, and it seemed clear to me that he should be a father. I saw him with friends' kids—holding their little hands, reading books to them with a simplicity and ease that startled me. He was okay with the idea of not having children, but I wasn't okay with the idea of his not having children. I loved him enough to take the leap. Still, I was definitely not in a rush. Thirty-four, thirty-five, thirty-six. Ticktock.

5. During this time, my anxiety surged. Finally, a doctor put me on an antidepressant. Very simple stuff. Millions of people take these things, I know. But I was such an anxious mess that I was quite certain the medicine itself would kill me due to a freak allergic reaction. My throat would close up, and I would break out in hives. I would die trying to cure myself.

6. Two weeks after going on the antidepressant, I had a symptom. My thumb. It began to twitch. I watched as my thumb began to hammer back and forth like a woodpecker. We were at our tiny, ramshackle beach cottage. I wondered if I should go to the emergency room. Instead, I called the doctor. He sounded more perplexed than alarmed. He'd never heard of anything quite like that before. He suggested that I wean myself off the medication. That we'd try another. But that twitching thumb led me in a different

direction altogether. I realized that I wasn't in control—not of my body, not of my well-being, not of my future. That anything could happen, and likely would. I was reminded of one of my favorite cartoons, in which thought bubbles float up from a closed casket: *It's just a panic attack.* I was tired of panicking. I was exhausted by my own terror. I turned to my husband. Let's make a baby, I said.

7. A twitching thumb, a bizarre reaction, a tiny yellow pill, an afternoon at a beach cottage. The randomness staggers me. I got pregnant that afternoon, during our one and only try. I was thirty-six years old.

8. The day before I gave birth to my son, my husband and I walked the streets of the Upper West Side. I was having contractions but hadn't dilated one little bit. Was I in labor? Wasn't I? I was told to keep walking. From Ninety-second and Broadway, where we lived, we walked the side streets. We paced Broadway. I was enormous, and my ankles were swollen. With every step, I could feel my baby's head knocking against my pelvis, as if politely inquiring as to whether it was finally time to come out.

9. In the late afternoon, after walking the span of the Upper West Side, stopping on occasion to hold on to the top of a fire hydrant, doubled over with a contraction; after three cups of raspberry leaf tea, which, according to my bible, *What to Expect When You're Expecting*, was a natural way to induce labor; after what had already been sixteen hours of *something* going on, we went to the hospital. I figured by now I was probably dilated four, five, maybe six centimeters.

10. I should mention that during my pregnancy, my anxiety vanished so completely that I couldn't recall what it had

felt like all the years I had been consumed by it. Perhaps it was the hormones. I was a happy pregnant woman. Peaceful, even. If my anxiety had its origins in a need to control every aspect of my destiny—hell, of the entire universe's destiny—that control-freak aspect of my nature had subsided. I had always been one of those passengers, on airplanes, who felt they had to spend every single moment of the flight telepathically communicating with the pilot in order to keep the plane aloft. Now I understood myself to be a passenger on the flight of my life, a passenger in the Boeing 767 of my own body.

11. The hospital, the paper gown, the monitors. They were all ready for me, but I, apparently, wasn't ready for them. According to the nurse on duty, I was dilated zero centimeters. Zero. How could that be?

12. My husband is a filmmaker, and he will often say that the story of how a movie gets made is different every single time. The same is true for childbirth, I think. Oh, the mechanism all looks pretty much the same, and there are only so many variations on the theme. But the inner life of a woman about to give birth is a world textured and complex and all its own. I was far from alone that day. My ancestors surrounded me, an invisible huddle, as I lumbered back into my own bed and waited for my cervix to cooperate. My father, dead thirteen years at the time. My mother, who'd given birth to me by planned cesarean section in the same hospital that had just sent me home with the advice to take a bath and drink a glass of wine. My parents, my parents' parents, and their parents—the men small and scrawny, the women squat and big-bosomed—rooting for the newest generation, their voices at once foreign and familiar. They were singing a language I have never known,

an ode to the survival of the genetic code that had managed to link peasant farmers in a dusty eastern European shtetl to two artists in an air-conditioned two-bedroom apartment on the Upper West Side at the dawn of the twenty-first century.

13. And now it is midnight. We've returned to the hospital of my birth, and this time they're not sending me home. The contractions have left me weakened. The pretty doctor, her long brown hair tucked into a blue bonnet, gloves covering her long fingers, breaks my water. There's no going back.

14. Pitocin. Epidural. Two things I'd been told to avoid at all costs by my granola-crunchy mommy friends, who have urged birth plans and doulas and acupuncturists and evening primrose oil, who have contemplated, if not actually gone through, home births themselves, who believe in a combination of positive thinking, choreographed breathing, dim lights, the right sound track, and, oh, an available Jacuzzi in case a water birth is an option.

15. And sixteen, seventeen, all the way through twenty. The hours have slowed. My much older half sister arrives at the hospital. She and my husband have always gotten along well, and now is no exception. By my bedside, they are engrossed in a conversation about a puppy she's planning to buy. A rare breed, a very large breed. She shares pictures with me, when I'm not in the middle of a contraction. The dog has a very big head, which makes me think about what's going on in my body. I've seen on sonograms that my baby also has a big head. As does my husband. As do I. We're a big-headed family. How is this baby ever going to come out? This breed of dog has a French name and is known for being

both smart and temperamental—not particularly good with kids. My half sister never had children and never will. She's not married. She's a psychoanalyst. I'm not sure, really, how she feels about what's happening. Or whether she's analyzed the idea that this puppy might be a child substitute.

21. Some people, when they call to mind their families, think of large, noisy gatherings, shared meals, the wafting scent of dumplings, marinara sauce, latkes, a ham roasting in the oven. They think of football games; gin and tonics on summer patios; Mom reapplying sunscreen; Grandpa in a cardigan, smoking his pipe. I am romanticizing this, I know. When I think of my family, I see a large and fractured piece of ice. I picture the kind of news footage that demonstrates the effects of global warming, in which a once-solid glacier loosens, breaks off from the point at which it connects with the rest, and slowly melts, until it disappears completely.

22. By this point, I become aware that—induced labor and Pitocin aside—my birth has become *medicalized*. This is a word my granola-crunchy mommy friends use disparagingly. It is the opposite of the soft lights, the Jacuzzi, the birth plan. I am being given oxygen. A mask covers my nose and mouth, and a scalp test is being administered to my baby—a pinprick, they assure me, that he cannot feel—to assess his level of comfort or distress. The Pitocin hasn't done its job, and I am still dilated only five centimeters. I watch my contractions on the monitor but feel nothing at all. The labor room nurses come in every half hour or so to check the computer readout of my baby's heart rate. The doctor pokes her head in. *Let's give it a little more time*, she says, frowning at the readout. But I—the queen of worry—am not worried.

23. I should mention that it is spring. Outside of this shabby but excellent hospital, the cherry trees and dogwoods in Central Park have begun to bloom. It is dawn. Runners circle the reservoir. Dogs are being walked. In apartments and town houses all around us, children stir. Parents shower. Men tighten their ties. Women dab cream beneath their eyes. Coffee is brewing. Oh, the humanity—the teeming fullness of it all! Every single one of these people had a mother who brought them into the world, just as I am doing now. I close my eyes.

24. My son is now fourteen. He's just about as tall as I am. He is quick to hug me, and equally quick to fight me about some random thing. His feet are huge. His voice is deepening every day. He looks adults in the eye, and greets them warmly, unlike some of his friends, who—forgive me—are Neanderthals. He says please and thank you to waitresses. He loves little kids, and is good with them. He plays a mean ukulele, and can pick out any tune on the piano and learn it by ear. He calls his father by his first name, and me, "Mr. Mom." He is a beautiful boy. I write this knowing it may embarrass him. He has sandy blond hair that falls over his very blue eyes, an elegant, delicate chin, a strong Roman nose. His backhand is killer.

25. Did I hear the doctor say *I don't like the looks of this*? I don't remember. I may be making that up. I did hear an announcement over the PA system in the labor unit, something about a code (red? yellow?) and prepping the operating room and a certain room number that I didn't realize was mine. I did have the sudden awareness that there were quite a lot of people surrounding my bed, people who hadn't been there before. That my bed was on wheels—it had now become a stretcher—and my husband was being

told to scrub up so he could go with me. Somewhere, the word: *emergency*.

26. My ancestors flanked the stretcher as we sped down the hall. *Kayn ein hora. Gai gezunterhait. Baruch Hashem.* My mother, who had given birth to me in this ward thirty-six years earlier, who perhaps even had her C-section in the very same operating room into which I was being wheeled, my infant cry as I was lifted out of her bloody belly, who was now in her apartment on West Eighty-sixth Street— toasting her corn muffin, opening her front door to collect *The New York Times*—unaware that I was in labor. My husband's eyes, above his surgical mask, were frightened and trying not to let me know it.

27. *Knock me out*, I said to the anesthesiologist. My whole body was ice-cold and shaking hard. The ancestors stood by. My heart rate was setting off all kinds of alarm bells. I wasn't afraid that the surgery would kill me or my baby. I was afraid that I—my panic back in full force, like a gal- loping stallion—would implode. How naïve of me to think it might actually have gone away for good! All that stored- up terror was now going to do me in; payback for nine blissful pregnant months of peace. Inside me, a voice whis- pered, *Impossible*. I was bisected by a sheet and couldn't see what was going on in my lower half, which was probably a good thing. Were they cutting me open? I had no idea. *I can't do that*, said the anesthesiologist. *After the baby is out.*

28. Later, perhaps the next day, a friend called my hospital room. She was the mother of two. She congratulated me, and then simply said, *Tell me about it. Tell me the whole story of the birth*. With my perfect newborn son cradled in my arms, I began to tell her the story of the thirty hours,

and before I knew it, I was sobbing. Big, ugly, snot-filled sobs. *I'm sorry!* I gasped. *I don't know what's gotten into me. I didn't mean to fall apart like that.*

29. Our son's raspy cry broke the world open. From the other side of the sheet that separated my top half from my bottom, I watched my husband's face as he was handed his boy. The ancestors rose and cheered, formed a circle, and began to dance a hora around the operating room. My body, though. My poor heart would not stop racing. *Please*, I looked up at the doctor, who was still standing just behind my head as they stitched me up. *I can hardly breathe.* He tried to tell me that I was okay now. That it had all gone well. That my baby had a perfect Apgar score, ten fingers, and ten toes.

30. In a black-and-white photo that my husband took that day, my son and I are lying side by side. He, swaddled, his head in a little cap, is turned to me. I, bloated, beatific, am turned toward him. My hair is fanned out across the pillow, my eyes are wet, and I am smiling. I'm stoned, of course. The morphine tricked my heart back into a normal, even placid rhythm. But no, that isn't it. I am looking at my son. *Impossible*, the familiar whispering voice again. From deep within myself, a quiet response. *No. No, it isn't.*

The Rest of Life

GINA ZUCKER

prepared for the birth of my baby in the ways that women of a natural-leaning persuasion prepare for this most sacred of days. I swallowed raw food vitamins the size of beetles. I practiced prenatal yoga. I read books (*Ina May's Guide to Childbirth,* natch). I signed up for childbirth-education classes at a place called Birthday Presence, taught by instructors who screened videos of women birthing their own babies in tubs of water, and who warned us about the "cascade of interventions" pushed by the medical community on unwitting laboring women. I researched hospitals, settling on one with an in-house birthing center, a Jacuzzi tub, and a double bed so my husband could sleep in with me and our newborn. I secured a highly sought-after midwife, known for her magic hands in the delivery room. I tried (and failed) to meditate. I needed to get in the zone for this birth I was planning, one without drugs or medical procedures, one in which I *pushed my baby out* all by myself, with the guidance of a midwife and a doula, squatting and swaying like a peasant in the fields, bellowing uninhibitedly, coaxing my child into the world through waves of pain, which, one learns in the natural-childbirth classes, is not pain, but *sensation,* your body's way of doing what it must to accomplish its miraculous task.

I was immersed in this culture. I lived in a community of like-minded progressives, where people shopped for hemp milk at a socialist-modeled food co-op and the local parenting Listserv popped out questions such as "How do I capsulize my placenta?" My friends who already had children encouraged me to go the natural route. A researcher-journalist by training, I took their advice and ran, or, rather, waddled, deep into my project: creating the perfect natural birth experience.

Long after the birth itself was over, I was reminded of how I'd planned my wedding day. I was so fixated on the event that I gave little thought to what came next: being married to my husband for the rest of my life. The details I'd obsessed over for months became beside the point afterward. Likewise, what followed birth (life with my new daughter) mattered so much more than whether or not I'd used a hypnobirthing pool. Hearing her cry for the first time was a little like saying "I do" on my wedding day. The big push was over. Now the rest of life had begun.

But I didn't know that when I went into labor. I also didn't know the meaning of true pain. I was told once by an eye doctor that the worst pain a man can feel is a scratched cornea. There is no comparison, he said, except one: the pain of childbirth. "That pain is of an altogether different persuasion. A man can never know that pain." I'm not sure how he could know this, as a man, but he is likely right. If joy is the conclusion of birth, pain is the plot. At least it was for me. With my daughter, I had what those in the field call "back labor," which means my eight-pound-four-ounce baby was facing sunny-side up rather than down or sideways, a position that puts increasing pressure on the mother's spinal nerves. So when my contractions began, each of them felt like a bomb slowly exploding in my lower back and radiating throughout my body. There was no riding the wave of *sensation*, like the childbirth instructor and the doula and the Ina May Gaskin book said. Do tsunami victims ride the wave of sensation? No, they run the other way, screaming. With back labor, there is no space between contractions, no counting minutes to time whether they're coming fast enough to go to the hospital. They come one after the other, with no break between, an unending cascade of agony.

Yet I had a goal. I did not waver from it, except for screaming a few times that I couldn't do this. Room three of the Saint Luke's–Roosevelt Birthing Center was like an Obama convention that day in December, with cries of "Yes you can!" rising to the ceiling as I bore down. My husband, midwife, nurse, and doula seemed to think I had some kind of supernatural ability to push this thing, this watermelon, out of my body. Mainly, I did not want to die with a watermelon inside me. At least, I figured, I would die trying to get it out.

Toward the end of my twenty-four hours of natural labor, I felt the watermelon move forward and then, sickeningly, back again. I felt the "ring of fire," the name they give the sensation of the baby's head crowning, but since I was more tired than I have ever been in my life and believed that I was dying, I didn't know that the baby's head was almost out. When someone (the doula?) asked, insanely, if I wanted to look in a mirror to see the baby's head, or reach down and touch the baby's hair, I shook my head. I was *dying*. Dying people do not want to look in mirrors and rub hair. I pushed and cried, "I can't." "Yes you can!" the room said. They were all wrong, but I pushed because they told me to, and because I did want my baby to survive, even if I didn't, and then things went *whoosh* and I heard a baby squalling. I was drained of all feeling but relief. I could barely hold my infant daughter in my arms. All I could think in that moment was, *Thank God it's over. Thank God that watermelon is gone. I will not do this again.*

I did it again, three years later. By then I'd registered that although I'd had the childbirth I wanted, it had nothing on the vastness of parenthood, just as weddings have nothing on marriage. In those early days after my child was born, I would lie in bed, replaying the labor in my mind, marveling at my strength, my power, my courage. Was it really *me* who'd done this thing? But the high was short-lived. My daughter couldn't latch and therefore couldn't breast-feed; I had to pump every three hours to coax my breasts to make milk; I produced nowhere near enough to nourish the baby and had to supplement her with formula and count every ounce she consumed so she wouldn't lose more weight. I discovered that on top of pumping and trying to teach my baby to breast-feed, I couldn't handle cloth diapers, cosleeping, or wearing my infant in a sling at all times—those tenets of attachment parenting I assumed I'd adopt along with exclusive breast-feeding. I learned my daughter had eczema, allergies, and asthma. She might have come into the world au naturel, but within weeks she was drinking Similac from plastic bottles, peeing and pooping into disposable diapers, and getting slathered in steroidal creams.

I couldn't orchestrate this—I was just surviving and trying to get my baby to breast-feed. I did things I'd never imagined would be part of having a baby, like taking her to craniosacral therapy sessions and using a finger feeder twice a day to improve her latch. I took drugs purchased from New Zealand to boost my milk supply.

After that, after experiencing the sleeplessness of motherhood, and potty training, sickness, and love that made me feel more deeply alive and afraid and joyful than anything ever had, I realized this small person had taught me most of what really matters, and that my life would never again be just my own. So when I found out I was pregnant again, I thought, If I can be a mother, I can sure as heck squeeze out another baby with no painkillers. The hours just after childbirth were a lot of fun, too, as I recalled. The oxytocin high. Everyone swooning over the perfect newborn. The take-out food shared with my husband while the baby slept, swaddled, in the bassinet. Replaying the birth in my head; hearing the doula say I was "a rock star," that she was never worried about me, that I gave myself over to the experience completely and "let go of control" without losing my wits.

In spite of the pain, or in part because of it, having a natural childbirth had been incredibly empowering. It was until that point in my life the bravest, most challenging thing I'd ever done, like hiking my version of the Pacific Crest Trail, or sailing solo across the ocean. It was big. Doing it had made me stronger, different, more capable.

The due date for my son's birth was February 6, but I felt cocky. "I'm thinking the end of January," I told anybody who asked. "My daughter was nine days early, so I assume this guy will be, too . . . He's already so big!" I would confidently pat my swollen abdomen. Privately, I became less sure of myself. A blizzard dumped two feet of snow on New York City, causing chaos that seemed to mirror the emotions churning inside me. I got nervous about logistics: child care for our daughter, driving in snow from Brooklyn to the hospital in Manhattan. I'd been reviewing the literature, the positions, the breathing techniques, planning to give birth in the same birthing center where my daughter had been born. I knew the folly of having certain plans, but I wanted to prove to myself that I could do it again.

Everyone warns you that a second baby comes much faster than the first, that there is no time to waste in getting to the hospital once contractions start. As the end of January approached, I began to feel anxious; every twinge seemed like a potential contraction. I checked the weather forecasts obsessively. The overnight suitcase was packed. I had the pump, the bottles, the formula, and the milk-supply pills ready in case this baby also had trouble nursing. I watched my daughter vigilantly, terrified she might come down with a cold that would trigger her asthma at the same time I went into labor. I tried to remind myself that no matter how carefully I prepared, I could not control this experience.

January ended, February began, and still no baby. The deadline for qualifying for childbirth in the birthing center was six days past the estimated due date. Anything later than that and I'd go to the labor and delivery floor, and a more traditional hospital setting. I told myself I was okay with that. But my desire for a natural childbirth stayed strong. I couldn't be a perfect mom, wife, writer, but I could push out babies like a rock star.

"We'll do a membrane sweep," said the midwife three days after my due date. "If it works, you'll be in labor by this afternoon." She did something that felt like a vigorous internal exam and then I went home and waited. Nothing happened. I went to a flurry of acupuncture appointments. I trudged through the snow. I picked up my thirty-eight-pound daughter and swung her around. The baby seemed to become heavier with each passing hour. My hips ached when I lay down. Standing made me pant. Instead of "getting in the zone," I was scarfing bagels, teaching, cleaning, waddling around frantically (if a waddle can be frantic), and arranging playdates. Then my daughter got a cold and started to cough, and the coughing became asthmatic. I always became panicked when my daughter had asthma, ever since the first episode when she was ten months old and had to be hospitalized. It had happened, one of the things I dreaded most: My daughter was sick, and I wouldn't be able to take care of her.

My husband tried to reassure me. His mother and my mother were both present. They knew what to do. They would make sure our daughter was safe. I had to trust them. It was time to have the baby, one way or another.

I went back to the midwife's office. "If you want, I can meet you at the birthing center this afternoon and we can try some things to get labor going," she told me. At 2:30 p.m., I met her at the birthing center. My mother, who'd come to town a week earlier in anticipation of the baby's arrival, accompanied me. My doula met us there. My husband headed home from his job to take our daughter to his mother's house and pick up the suitcase and the car.

Although I wasn't technically in labor, my midwife somehow got me checked into room three, the same room where my daughter had been born. This seemed like a good omen. The nurse measured the baby's heart rate. "Eat some sugar," she commanded. Apparently the baby was asleep. This did not seem like a good omen. I ate a Luna bar and we tried again. "Better," said the nurse. I sent my mother home. It was going to be a long afternoon. I was going to need to let go of control, something that is difficult for me to do with my mother around.

"Let's do stairs," said the midwife. For half an hour, I marched up and down several flights of stairs in the hospital, wearing my hospital gown and socks, as the midwife and doula trailed behind, trying to keep up. My adrenaline had taken over. "Drink this," said my midwife, presenting me with a cup of dark herbal tincture, blue cohosh, that was supposed to inspire contractions. We did laps around the hospital hallways. Next I downed a cup of black cohosh, a stronger version of the blue. I did some more stairs and some more laps. "Anything?" asked my midwife hopefully. I shook my head. My husband arrived. He walked with me. I drank more herbs.

After two hours of herbs and exercise, my midwife said, "Let's try an enema." "Oh, *let's*," I said. She gave me the enema, and while it certainly accomplished its ordinary purpose, it did not start labor. "Why don't we take a break," said my doula, sensing my frustration. "Why don't you sit on the bed with Russ and he can do nipple stim on you and you can read these trashy magazines I bought for you." "Nipple stim": nipple stimulation, another "natural" technique that is supposed to start labor. I gazed longingly at the pile of *People*, *Star*, and *Us*. I leaned against my husband, who tried to massage my decidedly unstimulated nipples under the hospital gown while I attempted conversation with our doula, who sat at the foot of the double bed. "Um," I said after a minute. The doula looked at me. I shook my head. "I don't think we're doing this." I patted my husband's arm and he removed his hands.

Labor did not start. The celebrity magazines went unread. The midwife came back in the room. "You don't respond to the nipple stim at all, do you?" she asked. I shook my head, feeling close to tears. What was wrong with me? What was wrong with my nipples? "Maybe we should talk about what's holding you back," said my doula. "Are you worried about Mia?" Suddenly I started to cry. As hokey as it sounded, I wondered if my concerns about my daughter were holding back labor in some way. I'd heard that when pregnant women are sick, their bodies won't go into labor until they are well enough to handle it. What if my psychological state was keeping the baby from being born?

Admitting my fears about Mia made me feel much lighter and suddenly I knew—somehow, someway—everything was going to work out. I would have a baby tonight. When my midwife said that she could break my water manually, that nine times out of ten the rush of hormones released by this act starts labor, but that if it didn't work, we'd have to go up to labor and delivery and start Pitocin, I said, "Do it."

A little after 7:00 p.m., the midwife stuck something inside me and I felt a rush of warm liquid, not unlike pee. "Usually you'll feel something like a contraction within the hour, maybe sooner," said the midwife. My husband, who hadn't eaten, ran out to get some food. I began to pace the halls again. Within ten minutes, I felt something shift in my groin and the twinges of cramping. "Great," the midwife said. "That's a good sign." My doula took over while the midwife went to look in on another woman, who was deep in the pain of labor. My cramps became more intense, and pretty soon I was having contractions mere moments apart—it felt almost like the wave of contractions brought on by back labor with my daughter. It was as though now that I'd acknowledged my worries about my first child, who'd come early and been born before I knew the fear of motherhood, this new baby, who'd been late, was free to be born. By the time my husband returned, I was swaying back and forth from foot to foot, moaning, as my doula leaned over me and squeezed my hips.

"Things changed while you were out," the doula said to my husband.

"I can see that," said my husband.

"Squeeze my hips!" I shouted. Someone squeezed my hips. "Harder!" There is something about having pressure bearing down on your hips that helps to counteract the pain of those hips being stretched apart to make room for a baby. I had learned this technique in my first childbirth class. Of all the pain-management tricks, I liked the hip squeeze the most, and also getting in the Jacuzzi and having my husband spray my back with the handheld shower nozzle. "That's too hard!" I yelled, assuming my husband had taken over the hip squeezing at this point. "I want Shara!" Shara was my doula. "It is Shara," she said. Shara is very strong, one of the reasons why she is a great doula. Plus, she has thick skin, which is essential. A woman in labor is a rude woman.

"I want to get in the tub," I announced. Hands rushed to assist me into the Jacuzzi basin. Hot water hit my lower back, offering a fleeting reprieve. "Keep doing that!" I commanded. Moments later, I felt an uncontrollable need to push. It was only an hour or so after the midwife had broken my water. I had never felt the urge to push with my daughter's birth; the midwife and the nurse had had to instruct me to lie down on my back, pull up my knees, and count as I pushed for as long and hard as I could. It was a tremendous effort of physical and mental concentration, and I was never sure I was pushing at the right moment. This was different. I felt something moving down. "I'm pushing," I said. At the same moment, the midwife walked back into room three.

"She's pushing?"

"That's the first time she's said that," said Shara.

"Gina, when you're done with the next contraction, I'd like you to get out of the tub and onto the bed, okay?"

"Water on my back!" I yelled. My husband sprayed.

They got me onto the bed. I was on my hands and knees, naked, dripping, and draped in towels. I pressed my face into the pillow and felt myself push. And push again. It was all happening so fast. Too fast. The baby was getting ahead of me.

My midwife checked my cervix to make sure it was fully dilated. A little lip of cervix was stuck over the baby's head, and she moved it out of the way. Somewhere in the recesses of my mind, it occurred to me that it was a good thing I had such a skilled midwife; otherwise, I could have been pushing in vain, and pain, for who knows how long.

Shara pressed my lower back as another contraction seized me. "Don't do that!" I screamed in her face.

"Okay," she said kindly. I put my face back in the pillow. I pushed. I felt that watermelon feeling. That burning. That sensation that I might burst open if something didn't give soon.

"Gina, I need you to hold off pushing for just a minute, okay?" said my midwife.

I wondered why.

"There's a little bit of cord—" I heard the nurse start to say, but the midwife cut her off with a curt "No."

"Oh no," I cried. If the umbilical cord was visible at this point, that couldn't be a good thing. It wasn't supposed to come out before the baby; if it did, this could cause severe bleeding and danger for the baby. I stopped pushing, felt the baby move back.

The midwife's hands were doing something. "It's okay," she said. "Keep breathing and push now."

"I can't do this!" I heard myself groaning. It was what I'd said when I was pushing out my daughter, and my husband said to me now what he'd said to me then, back before Obama was president, back before we were parents: "Yes you can. You're almost there." I pushed long and hard, heard my voice carrying on through the length of the push and beyond, wavering a little. And I felt the baby leave my body. A flood of ecstasy surged through me (the blessed oxytocin that gets you through those first months of sleeplessness and endless feedings without committing mass murder). I had done it! I had pushed the baby out! Later, my father told me that the photographs taken of me just after this birth, with my son lying on my chest and me smiling at the camera, reminded him of when I was a girl and had just accomplished something. "Look what I did!"

I was not tired this time. I heard the bellows of the first-time mom in the room next to mine. She was still laboring. I felt for her. Then I saw the nurse put my baby on the small gurney beside my bed, where she suctioned out his lungs. He coughed but did not cry. He looked blue. He was silent. Later, they told me that the umbilical cord had been wrapped tightly around his neck but that my midwife had managed to lift it off before any damage was done. Again, her quiet skill had probably saved my baby's life. He was a bit stunned. The active labor had been very fast—only an hour and forty-five minutes from the time the midwife broke my water to the time of my baby's delivery. Not a lot of time for him to acclimate to the transition from womb to world.

I learned other things later, about how life changed in good and hard ways when you had more than one child, about how having a boy was different from having a girl, about how much love one is capable of feeling, that it is possible to love your children the same amount and yet so differently. But now, I was focused on my newborn baby lying there, a shade of blue that made my blood cold. "What's wrong with him?" My voice was shrill. Please don't leave me now, I thought.

"He's fine." The nurse smiled. She slapped the bottoms of his feet (something I likely would have forbidden in my birth plan, if I'd still had one) and I heard my son's voice, louder than mine.

Live from the NICU

SARAH A. STRICKLEY

1. A Medical Wilderness

The first time I refer to myself as a mother, I'm standing fog-headed and locked outside a hospital door at four in the morning. The voice coming from the call box asks me to identify myself, and I say I'm my daughter's mother. Her name is the password that opens the door. As I walk to the elevator, I think about whether I feel like a mother now and whether that means I feel like my mother or her mother. My thoughts are marbles in a rolling jar. My excuse: It's late. I'm hurrying to relieve my husband, who has just spent four hours wedged in a pink vinyl recliner next to my daughter, who is a few days old and four weeks early.

Once I'm upstairs, I supply a numbered code: 81626. This gets me past the first impediment and then I identify myself by a name I don't actually use. Perhaps the system can't quite account for mothers who don't take their husbands' names in marriage, or perhaps any such complexity is one complexity too many for the NICU. Another door opens and I'm obliged to remove my wedding rings and scrub my hands for a full fifteen seconds with a pump-foamed antibacterial soap. Then I douse myself from the elbows down with a spray that evaporates on my skin with a light singe.

An interior door leads to a large room where beds and incubators are huddled around architectural posts, which are made to look like trees, complete with birdhouses in the cherry molding. We're off to the side in a private room because we're a readmit and a threat to the sensitive systems of the babies who have never left the hospital. Most of these babies are so tiny, they're often invisible in their incubators, little heaps of clothes and swaddling into which wires and tubes run. When I see a pair of eyes through the plastic, I feel pinioned, as though sighted by a deer in the woods, as though I've wandered into a medical wilderness that is strangely, vigorously alive.

2. Hurricane Prego

I knew I was pregnant, but three negative home pregnancy tests conspired to convince me otherwise. The fourth, a pricey digital wand, was the charm. PREGNANT, it said. No blurry cruciforms to discern, no blops to decipher. By that time, I was fully ready to find out I was pregnant, but where I expected a slow easing into the waters of pregnancy, I found instead hurricane gale forces. I was immediately ill, unable to eat or drink. I lost weight. Fatigue closed upon me like blackout drapery; a restlessness that began in my spine kicked my legs awake at night. Despite all this, I was massively, unequivocally happy. Cloud-nined. I muddled along in a state of bemused bewilderment.

For every new-to-me pregnancy-related phenomenon in my life, there was a long thread leading me into the maze of the Internet. A search for "pregnant with sprained coccyx" delivered the news that I was not the only one who'd ever bruised a tailbone while sneezing during week twenty-seven of pregnancy. I also had company when pregnancy-induced migraines sent pinwheels spinning through my peripheral vision. Early on, I had the idea that the Internet is the oracle of our times—its powers of inscrutability are derived from its capacity to say too much rather than too little—and yet I kept asking it questions: "How do I avoid having a C-section in Texas?"

For all the strangeness and blind groping, there was also an abundance of wonder and joy. Why do I so often fail to catalog the marvels? The daily revelations in the mirror, the ultrasounds that elicited the impossible-to-anticipate joy of witnessing a little girl waving her arms in my uterus, the sensation of a profoundly intimate accompaniment. Why don't I tell you about the long walks I liked to take with the dog? They were an opportunity to sense others sighting my pregnancy. I felt this distinctly: I was both more abundantly there and hidden enough to disarm the habitual weaponry of manners. I was more and less myself as a pregnant woman.

3. Feel Like a *Natural* Woman

When the word *natural* is directed at the choices women make with regard to childbirth, it often manages to relegate all manner of births as artificial, while maintaining an air of guiltless, guileless remove. "Can there be any question that when a woman labors without pain medication she is laboring as millions of women before her have labored—*naturally*?" the purists ask. It's difficult to argue with the whole of human history when it's presented as a default setting with which we'd be reckless fools to tamper.

I was aware how insidious the use of the word *natural* could be, and yet I found myself persuaded enough by it to read a library of books on the topic and watch all of the requisite documentaries. I decided that I'd like to avoid medical intervention, in part because I feared a cascading sequence that would result in a C-section. I felt confident and safe in my decision until I learned that the hospital where I was scheduled to deliver had a C-section rate of 46 percent. Whether I liked it or not, I'd have only about a fifty-fifty shot of escaping the knife.

When my husband and I toured the hospital, we were introduced to the hypermedicalized boutique style of birthing, wherein the whole of human history is presented as a default setting with which we'd be fools *not* to tamper. The highlights included shrimp cocktail, mani/pedis, vaginal-rejuvenation therapy. When I asked if natural childbirth could be accommodated, the answer was yes, but there were provisos. Rather than a birth *plan*, a birth *wish* was recommended for mothers who desired a *nonmedical birth*. It was about this time that I began asking the Internet whether or not it was insane to move across the country while very pregnant. We were already slated for relocation to Cincinnati; the question was how to time it.

I managed to find a group of midwives attached to a hospital and arrange an in-person visit. It would be an odd transition—from cinema-style ultrasounds in a lavishly decorated Houston highrise to a little Cincinnati clinic with no tech and nary a framed photo on the wall—but there was comfort to be found in the numbers. The midwives boasted a C-section rate of less than 10 percent. The trade-off was clear: I'd be more confident in my sense that I'd get my birth *wish*, but the lack of decorative flourishes would throw the stainless-steel realities of birthing into stark relief. I took the left turn.

4. The Early Bird Gets Stuck in Triage

Pregnancy is like a drivetrain with an independent intelligence. Every moment of it is an opportunity for discovery because so little of it can be mapped or directed. Our cross-country move was drawn out. When we finally landed in our new apartment in Ohio, I was eight months along, carrying a buoyant beach ball. Then a heat wave hit and the baby was a sinking cannonball.

An irregular pattern of contractions unfurled about thirty-four weeks into the pregnancy. Too early. The midwife on call told me to take a hot bath, drink water, sleep. In the bath, my husband and I watched as our baby slid from one side of my body to the other, a slow stretching journey. In a few hours, the contractions subsided and we went about our business. I sweated through my maternity dresses at work and my husband painted used furniture for the nursery. The oracle of the Internet assured us that modern technology made many of the complications surrounding preterm labor a thing of the past. Don't worry, we told ourselves. Relax.

Two weeks later, the contractions revved again. This time, the midwife on call told me to place a heating pad on my back and take a few Tylenol tablets. I slept for about four nonchalant hours—a feat I now find difficult to explain—and when I woke, I knew there was cause for alarm, or, at a minimum, action. There was no stopping labor with a simple home remedy this time. Had there ever been? Labor is an interstitial fugue; it's a being and a becoming. I stood in the shower, consumed by its momentum, and knew myself as utterly unprepared to undergo this thing.

We arrived at the hospital at seven in the morning and the nurses in triage were not keen to admit me. It was too early; they couldn't be sure it was real labor. I then found myself in the awkward position of auditioning for admittance. I had to stay on my feet and walk around the maze of the hospital for an hour. I managed thirty minutes before the contractions were so painful and intense and frequent that I had to prop myself on an errant hospital bed in a hallway to stay on my feet. A man in a loose white tank top drew soda from a straw while observing me at close range. While doubled in pain, I could see the hair rimming the side of his areola.

By the time I made it to the labor suite, my contractions were cascading so quickly that I didn't have a chance to try out the fun birthing toys I'd been schooled to employ: the rice-filled sock, the aromatherapy, the soothing iTunes playlist. My birth *wish* was to avoid medical interventions if at all possible. The best and only strategy I had for coping with the pain of labor was sitting on a birthing ball and holding my husband's hands. I thought that would be enough. Then the anesthesiologist arrived and introduced herself with a handshake I was unable to return. She left some equipment and IV bags just in case I changed my mind.

Throughout the pregnancy, I'd wondered what labor would feel like, whether I would manage to endure it, how I would hold up. Would I make a fool of myself or prove myself weak? The presence of the anesthesiologist's equipment was both a comfort and a terror for this reason. This is a test, it said. Are you passing or failing?

5. Alone in the Room

When I closed my eyes, I envisioned a red, glowing cup. In my mind, I endeavored not to drop the cup as the heat around it grew. I realize in retrospect that this visualization was likely a result of my sense that I wasn't ready to deliver this baby. As it turns out, the desire to withhold is precisely the opposite of the desire to release required of the birthing process. By four in the afternoon, I was wavering. I didn't know if I could maintain the suspension. I knew the IV and epidural were stationed somewhere nearby.

When I announced my ambivalence, the midwife emerged, pronounced me "dilated enough" at nine centimeters, and began preparations for the pushing phase. Having passed the first test, I was eager to get cracking with phase two. I expected instinct to kick in, but instead, I was confounded. I didn't know what pushing meant or how it was supposed to happen. When I screamed out in pain, the midwife told me to get ahold of myself. Stunned, I settled into a quiet seethe of resentment until she and the nurse began to force back my legs. In my most panicked moment, I tried to kick them both away. I tried to flee labor. The problem was that my mind was corralled inside the idea that we could go back to the purgatory of triage and say this wasn't real labor after all: Can we please go home and try this another time?

When the nurse suggested I get on my knees and face the back of the hospital bed with my head and arms flung over the top, I made no argument. With my legs stabilized, I realized what pushing meant and resolved to get the baby out—as though I was only conceding to the wishes of the hospital staff. Once my daughter's head began to emerge, I was repositioned on my back and went through a series of unproductive pushes. This was the ring of fire the oracle of the Internet had warned about, and we were caught inside it. Soon my contractions dissipated, and the nurse and midwife were counting off nonexistent waves. I didn't bother telling them they were wrong. They were witnessing their own ideas of what was meant to happen. I was in another room altogether.

I suppose we're always alone in our pain, but we are rarely positioned appropriately to view the isolation accurately. Most of the choices with which we are presented in childbirth are secondary to the one most important in practice: We must be prepared to labor alone, even in the company of others, even with the brilliantly blinding help of loved ones. Perhaps the debates regarding childbirth are so heated because in the end it's one woman's experience, not a shared cultural phenomenon. It's you and your pain; it's you and it's your baby.

I don't know why the push that delivered her was the one that brought her into the world. It didn't feel different from the others, but there she was. In less than two days, we were wheeled into the sun together. In less than a week, we were headed back from whence we'd come.

6. What Hope Sounds Like

This is a Catholic hospital, which means that Jesus, the Pope, and a bevy of bishops feature heavily in the decor. In the morning, a light sermon is transmitted through the intercom at a volume so low, its origin in the room is difficult to discern. There is no specific diagnosis for what has gone wrong with our baby. She's what they call "late preterm," a category of early babies particularly confounding for their appearance of health and vigor, which masks underlying problems with feeding and breathing. We are told that Cincinnati has an unusually high rate of premature birth—the very highest in the country, in fact. No one knows why this is so, but what it means is that Cincinnati also has an unusually high infant mortality rate. Ten babies out of every one thousand born alive in Cincinnati die within one year. In my attempt to avoid the statistical likelihood of a medicalized birth in Texas, I have inadvertently subjected my child to perilous postpartum odds.

The oracle of the Internet tells us we're in good hands at the NICU. Smiling "graduates" gather annually for happy reunions with staff. I'm encouraged by a series of lactation consultants to attach myself to a pump for several hours a day so that I can feed my baby *naturally*. That word again. There is no less *natural* a process than extracting breast milk in this way—we're talking about a machine, after all—but it's something I can do for her and there's a chance she may return to my breast once we're released. The pumping sessions are painful, time-consuming, and often depressing because they are opportunities to revisit my failures as a new mom: I must rely on a staff of highly trained technicians to do the job of teaching my baby how to nourish herself.

Every three hours, a nurse pulls a carefully measured cylinder of my breast milk from the fridge, marks the time, and stands by as my husband or I attempt to coax our little sleeper into feeding. If the baby is unable to consume the allotted amount in the allotted time, she will be tube-fed, an uncomfortable procedure and a big step backward. And so it is under considerable duress that we experience these feedings. We attempt to appear serene for her benefit, but the internal roil must reach her. She must sense it in the tendons taut in my thighs, my twitching hand. In our worst moments, we evade the gross invasion of the tube by pouring a few milliliters of milk into the sink behind the nurse's back; in our best moments, we're able to coach our baby through the bottle in record time.

Through the windows of our dimmed private room, we watch nurses dash to attend to the final moments of the babies who don't make it. We also play witness to the reality that the longer your baby manages to stay alive and stay in the NICU, the less likely you are to manage to be there with her. The daily demands of work and life finally intrude and the best you can do is send tubes of breast milk to the hospital with love from work or home. But you can't do that if your supply tanks, which will inevitably happen if you allow more than a few hours to pass between sessions on the hospital-grade pump, which is called, incredibly, a Symphony. I have two: one at home and one at the hospital. I pump and pump and pump. Like it's a song I'm singing, a symphony in situ. *Whoosh, whoosh, whoosh.*

By the time I surmount every obstacle between hospital parking garage and our little corner of the NICU, thirty minutes have passed. I arrive, to find my daughter sleeping soundly in her bassinet. As I watch the numbers on the oversize clock count down our next feeding, I attach myself to the Symphony. It's all I can do. In this small time, there is comfort at least in the *whoosh* of the pump, sounding my hopes, my fears, my God, my love. My dear baby girl, I am here while you sleep. Do you hear my song? Someday soon, we will leave this place and find out what it means to be mother, to be daughter, to be ourselves in the wide world.

Twice Delivered

JANE ROPER

When I found out I was pregnant with twins, I was—to put it mildly—terrified.

The reasons were legion, but to name just a few: I was afraid that I might love one baby more than the other. Afraid that I wouldn't have the energy or time or simple logistical ability to bond with them in the way that mothers bond with a single baby. Even afraid that I might resent them because they weren't the single, one-at-a-time children I had always imagined and hoped for.

More than anything, though, I feared the upheaval that twins might cause in our lives. While I was eager to be a mother, I intended to be a mother who continued to pursue her professional ambitions—namely, writing. But as the primary breadwinner in our family, I would also have to continue my day job as an advertising copywriter. Could I do that, be a responsible and loving mother of twins, *and* continue to persevere as a writer? It seemed highly unlikely.

There were medical and physical concerns, too. With twins come elevated risks for miscarriage, preterm labor, gestational diabetes, and preeclampsia. And then there was the delivery itself. Before finding out I was pregnant with twins, the prospect of giving birth had never worried me. It would be hard, but people did it all the time, right? Giving birth to two babies, on the other hand, was a whole different story. And it wasn't the story I'd ever imagined or hoped for in all my family-making fantasies.

Nothing about having twins was.

Luckily, my pregnancy was easy and routine. And it seemed safe to hope that my delivery would be routine, too. As routine as pushing out two babies in a row ever is, at least.

My water broke two days after Christmas, shortly before midnight. I was just shy of thirty-seven weeks pregnant at that point—a week past what's considered term for twins—and was dying to deliver. I had exactly three maternity tops that fit over my zeppelin-size belly, my pelvis felt like it was about to crack, and I occasionally experienced bizarre shooting pains, like someone was sticking a needle up through my cervix. (Who knew you could feel things in your cervix?)

Meanwhile, I couldn't manage to get comfy in bed, even with all manner of pregnancy pillows and folded blankets, and had excruciating heartburn almost every night around 1:00 a.m., regardless of what or how little I'd eaten hours earlier at dinner. Plus, I had a persistent pain beneath one of my right ribs (somebody's foot?) and the middle right side of my back (somebody else's elbow?).

For a week, I'd been taking measures to get things moving, enlisting all of the folk remedies for labor induction: warm baths, brisk walks (as brisk as was possible for someone of my girth), raspberry-leaf tea, and spicy foods. I even tried sex, though it was about the last thing I felt like doing. Having to wear sweatpants and schlubby extra-large maternity sweaters, being constantly achy and feeling exhausted all the time doesn't exactly get one's libido fired up. Or one's husband's.

But at last, my body had decided to pull the trigger. Halle-freakin'-lujah.

We headed for the hospital immediately, as we'd been told to do if my water broke. No waiting around counting the minutes between contractions for us bearers of twins. And it was a good thing, because the frequency of my contractions accelerated quickly. These babies were coming fast and furious.

More than 50 percent of twins are delivered via C-section, but mine were both head-down, in ideal position for a vaginal birth, and I was determined to deliver them that way. I'm not generally squeamish, but I found the idea of someone cutting through my skin and muscles a tad unsavory. I also wasn't keen on the whole epidural thing, having had an extremely painful experience with a botched spinal tap a few years earlier. Plus, overachiever that I am, I wanted to get through the birth without drugs if I could.

I'd discussed all of this with my obstetrician, and he was supportive, though he urged me to keep an open mind. "There's only so much you can control," he told me. "Just be prepared to go with the flow." I assured him that I would.

But from the minute we arrived at the hospital, it seemed that every doctor, nurse, and anesthesiologist on duty assumed that, as a prospective mother of twins, I'd go under the knife and, in the meantime, drug myself to the hilt. When I protested that I'd like to try to have a drug-free birth, they all but said, "Sure, lady, whatever you say."

The on-call obstetrician, an awkward, skittish little man who must have been out sick the day they taught bedside manner in medical school, admitted that he'd never actually delivered twins in the traditional manner, only via C-section. And he didn't do breech extractions, so if I managed to give birth to the first baby vaginally and then the second baby turned feetfirst, we'd have to go to a C-section for her.

He then informed me that I could get my epidural whenever I wanted. "It's pretty much standard procedure for twins," he said.

I informed him that, actually, it was my decision. (Meanwhile, I should note, my contractions, which had started almost immediately after my water broke, were becoming stronger and more frequent. So I really wasn't in the mood to be going tête-à-tête with the medical industry.)

The doctor then informed me—as if I didn't already know—
that if I didn't have an epidural, and I ended up having to have a
C-section, they'd have to use a general anesthetic. "And you don't
want that, do you?"

At which point my husband, Alastair, asked him when his shift
ended.

That shut him up. But I was already feeling defeated and dispir-
ited. All I wanted—just like any other mother-to-be—was to have
some sense of control over how my labor and birth were going to
go. Was that entirely off the table for me just because I happened
to be having two babies at once? Did I not even have the right to
hope for a routine, possibly even drug-free birth? For the rest of
my life, I was going to be a mother of twins—an experience completely different from that of 97 percent of other mothers in the
world. Couldn't I just have this one, last normal thing?

I thought, at least, the labor nurses would be on my side. They'd
be supportive, help me manage the pain, and coach me through
the contractions, just like in the videos we'd watched in our birthing class. (The same birthing class where—sigh—the instructor
kept stopping to look at us and say, "This actually doesn't apply to
you, since you're having twins.")

But the nurse on call, though friendly enough, wasn't actually
that helpful. My contractions were coming one on top of the other
by the time we got into the labor and delivery room, but the nurse
didn't have much in the way of encouragement or advice to offer.
Just, "Try to relax as much as you can." She was more focused (and
I suppose I can't fault her for this) on getting the fetal monitors
strapped onto my belly and getting a trace on the girls' heartbeats,
which wasn't easy to do. I had to lie on the bed as still as possible
while this was happening—no small challenge when you feel like
someone has affixed a large vise to your lower back and abdomen
and is steadily, mercilessly tightening it.

I was getting scared. I knew labor was going to hurt, but I
hadn't realized just how much. When my mother told me about

her (drug-free) labors with my brother and me, she described it as feeling like "extra-strong menstrual cramps." She remembered it as being not so much painful as "hard work." I had hoped that, through the power of genetics, it would be the same for me.

Perhaps my mother has a higher pain tolerance, or a highly selective memory. Either way, I clearly wasn't having the same kind of labor she recalled. Then again, she gave birth to only one baby at a time. And yet I still felt like maybe I just wasn't managing the pain the right way. Or maybe I just wasn't strong enough.

For the next hour or so, Alastair valiantly rubbed my back and shoulders, fed me ice chips, endured my cursing, and even managed to make me laugh a few times. He also periodically helped disentangle me from the tubing of the contraction and fetal heart rate monitors and pull the damned hospital johnny back up onto my shoulders when it slipped off.

Prelabor, I'd had visions of managing the pain by assuming wolf-woman primitive squatting poses and channeling lunar energy and whatnot, but on account of all the crap hooked onto me, this proved impossible. I began to understand why the people in earthy-crunchy natural childbirth books I'd read were all naked. I would have killed to be naked.

It was right after I puked that Alastair gently suggested that maybe I should get the epidural. "We can do whatever you want," he said. "But it could be a few more hours of this, and I just worry that when you get to the pushing part, you'll be totally exhausted." At the most recent cervical check, I'd been dilated only three and a half centimeters. But my contractions were already only a few seconds apart, and the pain was constant and knife-sharp in my lower back.

Feeling another wave of nausea coming on, I agreed that he was probably right, secretly relieved that he'd been the one to make the suggestion. This way, I could tell myself that it hadn't been *my* idea; I'd just gone along with it. (And God, did I ever want to go along with it.)

The epidural was fucking amazing. Suddenly, the contractions felt like gentle cramps, nothing more. I felt infinitely less anxious. I even got an hour or so of sleep. I woke up praising modern technology, the medical establishment, and the merciful (and not bad-looking) anesthesiologist who had so gently and expertly administered the blessed spinal drip.

And then, somewhere around 7:30 a.m., I started feeling an undeniable urge to push. When the doctor came in—a different one now, a very competent-seeming young woman, thank God—I asked if there was anything I should be doing to resist this urge. She thrust her arm elbow-deep into me and reported that I was fully dilated. Push away. Now I was excited: We were on the homestretch. We were gonna get these babies *born*!

This part of the process was actually quite satisfying. And surprisingly comical: I had to assume all manner of absurd contortions—lying on my side, getting on all fours, semisquatting, and holding on to a bar over the bed—while gritting my teeth and straining every muscle in my body and making, I'm sure, completely ridiculous noises. And the doctor kept saying, "Push into your rectum! All right, there in your rectum! Like you're having a bowel movement!"

While all this was going on, what seemed like the entire maternity ward's medical staff was parading in and out of the room, introducing themselves, some of them even extending a hand for me to shake:

"Hi! We're Babs and Carol, the pediatric nurses who'll be at the birth!"

"Hey there, I'm Fred, the pediatrician for Baby A, and this is Barney, the pediatrician for Baby B!"

"Greetings! I'm Ollie, the anesthesiologist, and this is my assistant, Stanley!"

"Like, hi, nice to meet you. We're Madison and Addison, the first-year medical students who'll be watching this whole random thing, right?"

"Hello! I'm Jim, the orderly who will be mopping the blood and amniotic fluid up off the floor after you give birth!"

We'd been warned ahead of time that because I was having twins, there would be a staff the size of a softball team at the delivery, but after the fifth or sixth person came in to say howdy and make chitchat, I looked over at Alastair and we exchanged expressions, as if to say, Dude, what's with the Welcome Wagon? We're trying to give birth here!

Meanwhile, the OB was still urging me to push everything into my rectum, and I could have sworn her thumb was up my butt. Given that I was about to pass two children through my vagina, the whole thing was surprisingly ass-focused.

Then, things got dicey. And my anxiety took an uptick again: Baby A's heartbeat was dipping with each push, leading the doctor to suspect that her umbilical cord was being compressed. Meanwhile, she wasn't making any downward progress. All my hard work wasn't actually accomplishing anything.

The doctor told us she'd try some suction and if that didn't work, we'd have to go to a C-section. Hearing the dreaded C word, I summoned all of my primal, wolf-woman, moon-goddess strength. I sent silent messages to my baby: *Come on. You can do this. We can do this.* I gave a few colossal pushes (into my rectum), and did it: I got things moving. I was so proud of myself—and of my little girl.

In fact, I still tell her the story today: how she was having trouble, and things weren't looking good, but we did it. Together, we did it.

Now, I was wheeled into the operating room (which really *is* standard procedure for twin births, in case an emergency C-section is needed) for the grand finale.

More pushing, some Pitocin when I was bleeding a bit too much, a small episiotomy, which I didn't even feel, and lots of excited shouting from Alastair and the docs alike: *We can see the head! You're almost there! One more big push! Here she comes!*

And finally, at 9:28 a.m., nine hours after my labor had begun,

Baby A, soon to be known as Elsa, was born. She was held up for me to see, then whisked quickly away to transitional care for oxygen and monitoring, as the difficulty of her birth had left her a bit worse for wear. Meanwhile, the doctors were prodding my belly to get Baby B, Clio, into position. I braced myself for another long round of pushing, but the child popped out like a champagne cork. She had a good healthy cry and seemed royally peeved to have been evicted from her penthouse in the womb. Time of birth: 9:37 a.m.

In the years ahead, one of the things I would hear most frequently when people learned that I had twins was, "I don't know how you do it"—often accompanied by incredulous head shaking. (Ask any parent of twins, and they'll tell you they've heard the same.)

"I just do it," I always reply. "You would, too."

And when I talk to women who are expecting twins and are as frightened as I was about giving birth and beyond, I tell them more or less the same thing: Don't worry. You'll do it.

You won't always do it as gracefully as you might like. And there will be multitudes of occasions when things don't go the way you've planned—whether it's how you'll give birth or, say, how you'll manage to get the rest of your grocery shopping done when you forget to bring a snack for your whiny twin toddlers. (Answer: Take a package of Fig Newtons off the shelves, subtly open it, and start feeding it to your children as you go.) But if you accept this—if you take my obstetrician's advice and remember that some things are beyond your control, and you're better off "going with the flow"—then there's not a whole lot to fear.

What seemed like mere minutes after giving birth to my girls, I was back in our labor room with Alastair, babes in our arms, looking out the window at a panoramic view of the Charles River. It had just started snowing. And we had just become a family of four. I was exhausted, exhilarated, and a little bit disoriented. I knew we faced difficult weeks (months, years) ahead, taking care of these two little babies. But I wasn't afraid anymore. I didn't know how I'd done it. But I had.

Lucky

HEIDI JULAVITS

My first child was born in a sparsely populated Maine county, where the nearest hospital is considered more hindrance than help in matters of mortality prevention. Many of the doctors who work at this hospital give birth at home. So do many of my friends. Despite compelling evidence against the hospital, however, my husband wanted to go to the hospital. "If something happens to you or the baby, everyone will blame me," he said. This might sound paranoid, but it's actually just true, and a fine-enough reason to choose a bad hospital over a good home. Birth makes people blame other people. Even when nobody dies, there is blame galore. You should have waited to go to the hospital. You should have gone earlier. You should have said no to this and yes to that. I hope you're happy with your healthy baby, but you fucked up, you seriously fucked up!

We said no to home birth and yes to the hospital. When we arrived, we were told that the only available room was a large supply closet. The outlets in the supply closet were so distantly and inconveniently located that whenever the nurse tried to measure my daughter's heartbeat with the electric heart monitor, the plug was yanked from the socket. He repeatedly attempted and failed to angle the monitor on my stomach without dislodging the plug.

Finally, he gave up. "I'm sure she's fine," the nurse said. Throughout my labor, random people came in to peruse the shelves of the supply closet for gauze or whatever. I was never offered an epidural because this hospital didn't stock epidurals. For pain relief, they typically administered an analgesic that was popular in the eighties. Neither was this offered. My daughter, when born, cried. This was considered so unusual that the doctor asked if I had taken any weird drugs during labor, like weirder, I guess, than the eighties-era analgesic no one had given me. (To be fair to this doctor, there's an OxyContin problem in this part of Maine, and the people who end up giving birth in hospitals tend to be drug addicts uneducated about their baby's health—otherwise, duh, they would stay at home—which precipitates signs on the hospital walls such as PLEASE DO NOT SMOKE DURING YOUR ULTRASOUND.) The doctor could not tell me how to breast-feed because she didn't have any children and had never breast-fed, and so (according to her) possessed no information on this topic. She'd spent the entirety of my labor in the hallway, reading a Sue Grafton novel.

When I was finally moved to a proper room, I found a pair of gigantic bloody underpants on the bathroom floor.

My husband said, "I guess we should have stayed home."

For our second child, we stayed home. Home, now, was Manhattan. In Manhattan, even nonprescription drug–addicted, folic acid–supplementing, multiple Ph.D. investment banker types gave birth in hospitals. This rendered our home birth decision controversial in the eyes of some people I'll just call My Father. Again to be fair, my father, a lawyer, used to work as the in-house legal counsel for a hospital. He'd been privy to home birth situations that had not turned out prettily. And he believed that we were being negligent and selfish by refusing to go to a perfectly amazing hospital, even though, as I kept pointing out to him, we lived just two blocks from a hospital, and given that hospitals in New York were the size of many city blocks, our apartment nominally counted as being "in the hospital."

But I'd heard horror stories about New York hospitals, even the reputedly good ones. In the entirety of Manhattan, there existed basically five rooms in which a person like me (that is, someone who wants a doctor within paging distance while she floats in a tub by candlelight) might want to give birth, and in order to gain entrance to these precious rooms in the city's only birthing center, you had to (a) put your name on the wait list before you'd had your first period and (b) when in labor, be admitted via the hospital's triage unit, which involved hanging out in hallways with bloody-faced drunks until you'd dilated the acceptable number of centimeters (I believe the number was six).

So this time, we said no to the hospital. We not only decided to have our son (he was a son) at home but also to do his birth on the cheap. The first time around—I forgot to mention—we'd had a doula. Her name wasn't Hyacinth Sky, but it basically was. Birth, as I've said, inspires a lot of blame, but it also inspires unspeakable indebtedness. No one is ever as unspeakably indebted to any other human as a woman is to the person who helps her get her baby out. This was and is my feeling about Hyacinth Sky. But because New York doulas cost thousands of unreimbursable dollars, we decided to forgo the doula. I knew what happened during birth. This and then this and then this. We'd hired a home birth midwife, so why did we also need to hire a doula?

Why indeed? I will tell you why. You probably already know about the doula—that is, that many people claim that the word comes from the Greek for slave and that she (usually she's a she, unless he's a character in a Sam Lipsyte story) "supports" the laboring woman, not just with back massages and fruit juice but by calling the labor like it's a soccer game ("The next contraction's going to be a doozy") and doling out lots of savvy baby-getting-out tricks that have, within the medical community at least, gone the way of the iron lung.

A midwife, we figured, would be similarly skilled and savvy, and too much skillful savvy in one apartment might just end in a rumble. We chose our midwife for her midwifery chops and not her soothing hippie vibe. She was tough and funny and matter-of-fact, and I felt the need to act equally tough and funny and matter-of-fact around her. This worked fabulously as a prenatal dynamic; our encounters were wry and witty, and didn't even happen very often (I was out of town for a third of my pregnancy). But when I went into labor and when the midwife showed up at the apartment, and when she proclaimed me to be barely three centimeters dilated, and when she broke out an accordion file on our dining room table and started paying bills, I realized I couldn't have her in my home. I gave her permission to leave and to go to another birth that was happening concomitantly in Brooklyn, which she clearly wanted to attend, given that this other woman, she'd told me, was much further along than I was.

And then we were alone. And I was relieved.

It was roughly 10:00 p.m.

I paced the dark house; I did circles around our living room. Our daughter had been outsourced to a grandparent that morning, so I could range freely and not feel the pressure (as I had with the midwife) to be the kind of personality that syncs magically with labor. I felt pretty wimpy because, according to the midwife, I had many hours to go (I'm a long laborer—my first labor lasted more than twenty-seven hours), but I was in quite a bit of pain. By 1:30 a.m., I couldn't imagine that the pain could get worse, but that's usually the way it is with pain. When you're in a lot, you can't imagine being in more of it, but that doesn't preclude the possibility that you will be. How had I done this the last time? I was very confused. I'd been awake at this point for almost twenty-four hours, having contractions every eight to ten minutes for the first fifteen of those hours, after which the intervals decreased to between one and four minutes, without any emerging pattern, save to somewhat resemble water torture. Without a doula, we had no one to explain the pain. Pain, when explained, can be much less painful.

Because I am stoic—I've since learned I'm less stoic than I thought I was, but at this point I was still a self-professed stoic—I did not tell my husband when I was struck by the most profoundly overwhelming sense of being trapped, in my body and in this patternless state that was not perceptibly moving toward closure. There was no predicting the next contraction; there was no one breaking down the plays, no one except my husband, who, despite his lack of training, was not completely unhelpful. He sat in a nearby chair and sped-read a book called *The Birth Partner* (our son was two weeks early); this book was written specifically for the nonlaboring party. At the end of each chapter was a section called "What You Might Be Feeling." Between contractions, he'd ask, "Do you want to know what I might be feeling?"

But mostly I felt trapped because I knew I could not be moved. Even if I decided to go to a hospital, how would I get there? I couldn't ride in a cab in this state. I couldn't even make it to my lobby. There was no way out of this apartment. There was no way out of this situation I'd chosen for myself (the first choice: getting pregnant). None of these feelings was particularly remarkable; what was remarkable was that it was the first time I'd felt any of them. How had I managed to give birth before without being scared? I'd been tired, very tired, but never once frightened. I'd never once despaired. The first birth proved a challenging athletic event, but I didn't have to press my face against the cold glass of the self. Now my face was crushed against the glass, and the glass was about to shatter, my face disfigured by the combustible black gas that comprises, or did that night, my soul.

Because I was so focused on keeping my head together, on not totally fucking losing it, I didn't panic or even really react when it became clear that I was much closer to the end than anyone had thought. Thankfully, my husband was more attuned to the essential tools one needs when a labor is drawing to a close, tools like, for example, a midwife (props to *The Birth Partner*). He called the midwife. "I think we might need you," he said. We're both very polite and don't like to inconvenience people, especially people we're paying. The midwife said she was almost done delivering the other baby. He hung up. Things got rapidly more intense. He called her back. "Just in case this happens before you get here," he said, "is there anything I need to know?" The midwife said she was weighing the other baby. She promised to get in her car soon and drive over. He called the midwife again. She wasn't in her car yet, but soon, soon! Finally, she was in her car. Then she was on Fifty-third Street. Then she was parking outside our building. Then she was in our apartment. Then, roughly one minute later, she was holding my son.

Afterward, like immediately afterward, before we went to sleep that night, I felt compelled to reflect on the many things that might have gone wrong. We'd seriously fucked up, hadn't we? The midwife, when she'd arrived, had acted as though this were a totally normal birth situation for her, but beneath her bravado she seemed a little sheepish. She never billed us, which seemed an admission of regret or wrongdoing on somebody's part (hers). We never told my father what had happened, which seemed another admission of regret and wrongdoing (ours). In the weeks following my son's birth, during which I continued my postgame analyses, my husband stopped participating. He didn't see the use in running the many alternate scenarios in which a tragedy might have occurred; his take was, we had this incredible experience together, let's let it stay incredible. It wasn't what we'd wanted or intended, but he was trying to see the upside. Not too many couples get to have a baby (minus the final minute) alone, just the two of them, with no doctors or nurses or midwives or doulas or taxi drivers standing around. It was like we'd been on an episode of *The Bachelor* and we'd rappelled down the face of a skyscraper, but without the camera crew.

And we did have an incredible experience. My husband was my Hyacinth Sky; my indebtedness to him is unspeakable. But I still feel guilty. Whenever I tell the story of my son's birth, I always preface it by saying, "We were just really stupid and really lucky." But this is less how I honestly feel, and more a preemptive maneuver. If I tell people I was stupid and lucky, those people might judge me less harshly. Or they might tell me I was smart and deserving, and that luck had nothing to do with it. But luck has everything to do with it. Everyone relies on luck when a baby is born; most everyone who has an alive baby should be considered lucky. Am I luckier than other lucky people because my son didn't die? Maybe I am. I'm happy to give luck credit at every turn because luck is my only god. But were I to have a third child, I would probably try to rely on luck a bit less. I'd still have my baby at home, but I'd hire a doula to interpret my pain for me.

After my daughter was born, I'd felt an "I can do anything" rush. After my son's birth, I felt traumatized. I obsessed over death. Not just my son's but mine. I understood not just that I would die but that I would *have a death*—just as I had had labors—and that there were many different ways this death might transpire. Would it happen quickly, and would I stay strong? Or would it be endless and painful, and would I, in the process, become unrecognizable to myself as myself? Before the night my son was born, I believed I would never be undone by my own body. I would remain me until the end. Now I know otherwise. I can be undone. I might be.

California Grown

SARAH SHUN-LIEN BYNUM

She was long and thin. She came fast at first, but then things got complicated.

Last memory of my life before: Jennifer Garner on the TV screen, doing kung fu moves against a backdrop of generically Asian mountains, tossing her opponents through the air. Dana had rented it. I fell asleep. Why not something better in those final moments? Something with Kate Winslet or Cate Blanchett. Or a documentary?

Sunday, early. Early! Wobbling out of the bed and into the bathroom, surprised to be awake. Then calling out to Dana from the shower, "I think this might be it." My hand flat against the wet tile wall, holding up my weight.

Wrapped in a towel, still wet. Still surprised. How was I supposed to bake cookies for the nurses? Or take a long walk around the neighborhood and go to a matinee? I could barely catch my breath long enough to brush my hair.

Dana handed me the receiver. "How are you doing, sweetheart?" The voice of Renee, our doula, reaching me through the phone. I told her: I'm fine, I'm good, I just got out of the shower, it started a little while ago, I'm so sorry to wake you up this early, and on a weekend, I'm fine, I'm just feeling a little—I thrust the telephone back at Dana. Couldn't talk anymore.

Out the door, into the car. Dana, shockingly, unwashed. His steering perfect as he backed out of the narrow driveway. "Renee timed you when you were talking on the phone." According to her watch, my contractions were two and a half minutes apart.

The quiet and emptiness of Los Angeles on a Sunday morning. Even on Wilshire the traffic was sparse. I braced myself against the dashboard and the car door and let Dana drive down the deserted streets as fast as he wanted, the streets still new to us, the car also new.

At the emergency entrance, someone politely asked if I would like a wheelchair. A wheelchair? Why not! It wasn't easy remaining upright. But the cramping didn't feel altogether unfamiliar. I'd lived through painful periods before. Terrible cases of the runs. This was kind of like that. Only the frequency, the intensity, felt different.

Admitting room, delivery room. Bathroom adjoining delivery room. Shuffling from room to room, doubled over. Renee had arrived by then. Briefly limp with happiness upon seeing her, but then pulled away again, everything clenching, pulled away by what was happening in my body.

Ocean waves is how I'd heard it described. But instead of waves, I saw a long hallway with a dark, tiny room at the end. A room no bigger than a box, and I pushed my arms and legs hard against the walls of that box. With each contraction, I was sucked down the length of the hall and into that small, isolated, box-like room.

Some concern: I wasn't progressing. Dilation stalled at five centimeters. They broke my water. They gave me Pitocin. The fetal monitor showed that the baby was in distress. I was too far away to understand completely. What kind of distress? Where did the meconium come from? When asked, at last, if I would like an epidural, I nodded. Oh yes. I looked at Renee: Is that okay?

A needle in my lower spine, and then I was back. Back in the delivery room. Back with Dana and Renee and the daylight glowing along the edges of the hospital blinds. So grateful that the lights were off overhead. Turning my head to the side and vomiting neatly into a plastic dish held up to my chin. Sucking ice chips. Smiling. Entirely delighted to have returned. What had Gurmukh, my Kundalini yoga teacher, been talking about? Epidurals were wonderful! Miraculous! Yet a part of me had believed otherwise. The part that had faithfully attended prenatal yoga classes and held hands with other pregnant women as we danced in a large, uneven circle. The part that had welled up with feeling when Gurmukh struck the gong and its reverberations passed through me, the part that sang weepily, open-throated, "I see the light in you; you see the light in me." Meanwhile, the other part of me looked on in complete astonishment. How did I end up teary and chanting in Southern California? Only a few weeks earlier, I had been taking the subway to work from Brooklyn to Manhattan, practical and distracted, barely registering the pregnancy, my one concession the swallowing of a huge, bad-tasting capsule of prenatal vitamins every morning.

I moved to Los Angeles at the same point that I moved into my last trimester, and in both cases it was as if I had relocated to another country. I could no longer ignore the drama of the physical changes I was going through, and this resulted in a new preoccupation, to the exclusion of nearly everything else, with the well-being of the person taking shape inside of me. I found myself sitting cross-legged on a little sheepskin rug and listening attentively as Gurmukh, radiant in her white turban, extolled the joys of natural childbirth. She told us that drugs would cloud our thinking, dull our feelings, and prevent us from being fully present at the moment of first connection with our child. Which had made a lot of sense to me in the soothing, dim interiors of Golden Bridge. But now, on a hospital bed, devouring my ice chips, I inwardly shrugged. Why not avail myself of the latest advances in medical knowledge? California was the birthplace of fruit smoothies and the Esalen Institute, but it had also given us iPods, right? And major pharmaceutical companies. I felt safe and calm and free of pain, cradled in the embrace of local contradictions: under the care of a midwife and a doula, yet surrounded by all the technologies and resources of a state-of-the-art teaching hospital.

I noticed then for the first time that the technology arrayed behind my hospital bed was beeping rapidly. Dana, at the foot of the bed, tried to maintain eye contact with me, but his gaze kept drifting above my head and fixing on the monitors. I could tell from his expression that things had continued to go awry. The baby's vital signs were erratic. After every contraction, her heart rate fell. Dana stood there, trying not to appear stricken, and I felt suddenly how alone we were. There were no family members or friends outside in the waiting room. Almost everyone we knew lived more than three thousand miles away. We had wanted it this way; the choice was deliberate. Wasn't going it alone essential to the appeal of heading west? Just the two of us, starting out for territory unknown. It was in that spirit our daughter's name had first occurred to me: Willa. After Willa Cather, of course, chronicler of the frontier. *O Pioneers!* Isn't it a wonderful title? I hadn't actually read the novel, but how I loved her for throwing in that ecstatic, admiring exclamation point! At the foot of the bed, Renee touched Dana's arm and leaned up to say something in his ear. The nurses began to come and go more quickly. There was talk of the OR, its availability. There was further talk of fetal distress, and now, more specifically, of the umbilical cord being wrapped around the baby. Renee knelt beside the bed and told me that I needed to prepare myself for the possibility of a C-section.

I began crying then, out of disappointment and out of fear; I had never had surgery before and I was scared of being operated on, scared of the anesthesia, the incision, the long recovery. But even though I was crying, I still felt safe. I knew that if Renee said a C-section might be necessary, I could trust that this was really the case. And I realize in retrospect that while the sybarite in me had wanted a doula for the Reiki and the unlimited massages, what Renee had actually given me was the ability to accept this news with relative serenity, or at least without the suspicion that I was being coerced. All throughout my pregnancy I'd heard stories of peremptory OBs insisting on cesareans in order to make their afternoon tee times, but I knew that someone's impatience wasn't pushing me toward the operating room. I didn't feel like I was in the hands of a faceless medical establishment. I was in the hands of Renee and the nurses and the midwife, Ann, women of wide experience who wanted to make sure that my child and I were going to be okay. I felt this, and I cried, and, worn-out, I fell asleep.

I slept for hours—from the early afternoon into the night. Asleep, I was spared most of the anxiety that followed. Dana has had to provide all the details of that long afternoon. And because of this difference in our experiences, he says that we will always regard our daughter a little differently. Here is what he told me: that with each contraction, her heart rate spiked and then dropped down almost to zero, slowly climbing back to a regular pulse. Regular until the next contraction, when her struggle started all over again. Every time her heart rate plunged, Ann and the nurses and the doctor on call came rushing into the room at once. Their concern was that soon, after one of these plunges, her heart wouldn't have the strength to start back up again. The doctor wanted to prep me for surgery; Ann wanted to let me labor a bit longer, in the hope that as the baby descended, she'd be released from the cord.

I slept, Dana watched the monitors, and Ann conferred with Renee. As the day wore on, it became harder and harder for the baby to recover from each contraction, and finally they decided that if her heart rate plummeted once more, she would have to be delivered by emergency C-section. But before that happened, Ann and Renee wanted to try one last thing: floating the baby. I must have awoken to this lovely phrase and not the fast-approaching likelihood of emergency surgery, because I remember coming to and feeling perfectly relaxed and rested and full of anticipation:

Yes, let's float the baby! I'd never heard of such a thing before. By injecting my womb with additional fluid, they might allow the baby to rise and free herself of the cord. It seemed like almost too simple and elegant a solution to actually work, yet it did. A tube was inserted, fluids pumped in, and, following the next contraction, her heartbeat slowed slightly but did not disappear.

Untangled and afloat, the baby descended quickly, and only minutes after removing the tube, Ann was telling me that it was time to push. As the nurse counted aloud for me, I tried to do the rhythmic breathing I'd been taught, but I kept messing it up and apologizing, promising to get it right on the next round. The nurse laughed and asked me if I had gone to Catholic school. Catholic school? I had no idea what she was talking about. I'd been raised a Unitarian. Maybe what she mistook for school-bred obedience was just my ingrained East Coast formality, my involuntary desire to do things correctly and according to directions. How strange that I was giving birth to a child who wouldn't be saddled with those mores. Who'd think of last names and closed-toe shoes as strictly optional. Who'd grow up on skateboards and surfboards and never catch fireflies or rake leaves or wake up in the morning to find snow outside her bedroom window. A child who would gaze at the alien landscape of Southern California and recognize it as her native habitat.

Which was fitting, because my baby, with her enormous head and her skinny body, with her huge, heavy-lidded eyes spaced so far apart that they almost resembled a giraffe's, did look at first like an alien to me. I remember holding her, still slick, and feeling at once startled and moved by her strangeness, and resolving to love her fiercely in spite of her extraterrestrial appearance. Dana, a good mimic, has developed a bit in which he acts out his own version of our daughter's arrival: emerging soundlessly, narrow and compressed, each scrawny limb slowly and stickily unfolding as the mouth stretches open to let out a long, rasping, hair-raising screech. It's exactly the same sound, the same insect-like unfurling, as that of the creature in Ridley Scott's *Alien*.

Willa finds this impression endlessly entertaining, even though at eight she's still too young to have seen the movie. She's turned out completely human after all, and her large, dark, wide-set eyes are very beautiful. "Do it again!" she demands, tugging on Dana and laughing. It delights her to imagine the unimaginable, to picture herself as weird and frail and unearthly, to think of herself as anything other than exactly what she is in this moment: a thriving, dog-loving, beach-going, bike-riding, kale-eating, horchata-drinking, shorts and Uggs–wearing California kid.

The Lavender Room

CHERYL STRAYED

Margaritas

In a little red cottage on a pond in the Berkshire Mountains of western Massachusetts one Saturday morning in August, I woke alone in my bed and felt a queasy swoop of something flitter through my gut. I'm pregnant! I thought, sitting up with a start. *PREGNANTPREGNANTPREGNANT!* A joyous, silent shout repeated in my head.

As I walked into the bathroom and ripped open a pregnancy test—I kept a stash of them on hand during that time—another, more reasonable voice said, No, no, NO. Don't get your hopes up. That queasy feeling is just the two margaritas you drank last night with Donna!

For once in my life that other, more reasonable voice was wrong.

Baggage Claim

My husband was out of town, but he'd be home that evening. I'd be picking him up at the Albany airport, but I wouldn't tell him about being pregnant there. I also wouldn't tell him on the drive home. The news was too momentous, too beautiful to be delivered in an airport or an automobile. I would lead him into our little red cottage on the pond where I'd open a bottle of nonalcoholic sparkling something and say the words I'd been wanting to say to him for a year.

That day, as I readied for his arrival, I bought fantastic things at the farmer's market. I wandered the stalls with the word *pregnant, pregnant, pregnant* chirping like a secret bird only I could hear. At home, I set out the organic cheeses and ridiculously expensive handmade crackers and dark chocolates I'd purchased that day, arranging them artfully on a platter. I drove to Albany while playing out the evening in my mind. How I would ask my husband all about his trip to distract him from inquiring about me. How once we got home I would finally say, "Guess what?"

When I got to the airport he was there already, his flight having arrived early. I came upon him as he was yanking his suitcase from the rotating belt in the baggage claim area.

"I'm PREGNANT!" I shrieked crazily the minute his eyes met mine. People turned and looked at us in alarm.

I've always been terrible at keeping secrets.

The One-Eyed French Guy

Ten days after I told my husband that I was pregnant in the baggage claim of the Albany airport, I returned to that same airport and flew to Brazil. I'd been awarded a residency at an arts foundation on an island near Salvador de Bahia called Itaparica. I was going there for a six-week stay so I could once and for all finish writing my first novel.

"I'll be fine! Women are pregnant all over the world!" I exclaimed to my husband whenever I worried about going to Brazil while being pregnant. It's true. They are. But as soon as I arrived,

I got the feeling I was in the very next moment going to vomit all over everyone—a feeling that didn't leave me for the entire six weeks I was in Brazil, though I never once actually vomited. I only felt like I would.

For six weeks straight.

The nausea was so bad it woke me in the night. It seemed to be a beast that lived inside me and wanted to claw its way out. I lived for weeks on nothing but bananas and grapes and fantasies about the foods I wanted but could not have because I was on an island off the coast of Brazil—pretzels and olives and pickles and bread. The primary food option on the island was fish with their heads and tails still intact that were fried in *dendê* oil—an acquired taste in even the best of circumstances.

When I wasn't writing or fantasizing about eating a pretzel, I took long walks to distract myself from my nausea, though venturing out only made me more nauseated. In the afternoons, the entire island burned their garbage in their yards. Mysterious puddles of brown liquid ran down the dirt roads. Mangy dogs snapped at me as I passed. Once, I came within a hair of stepping on a dead rat.

But one day I walked to the end of the road and smelled something delicious. I followed the scent to a house that had its door propped open. I called out an uncertain greeting and was quickly welcomed inside by a man who wore a black patch over the place where he used to have an eye. He was a French expat who'd lived on the island for years, he explained. He'd sailed here from France and never gone home. His hobby was making incredibly good pizza in his wood-fired oven. One was ready to eat that very moment. It was slathered in mozzarella and olives and cured meat. I almost fainted at the sight of it. If he'd asked me to screw him in exchange for it, I'd have instantly ripped off my pants.

"Mademoiselle," he said, holding it out to me. "Would you like a slice?"

Carver

Being pregnant meant making a lot of decisions. My husband and I decided I'd see a midwife, not a doctor. We decided I'd have a drug-free, low-tech, not-in-the-hospital-unless-it-was-actually-medically-necessary birth. We decided I'd have an ultrasound but not an amniocentesis. We decided we'd take a labor and birth class together but under no circumstances would I refer to my husband as my "coach," no matter what the official class literature instructed us to do. We decided we didn't want to know the gender of the baby, but we found out by accident anyway: a boy.

In a bar called Limey's, we decided his name would be Carver.

Big Baby

The thing I couldn't picture all through my pregnancy was his face. I tried to but I could never land on anything. It seemed like the greatest mystery I'd ever encountered, one that grew as he did inside me. He kicked and squirmed. He got the hiccups and I felt them at the top of my crotch (at which point I learned for the first time ever that my crotch had a top). I was viscerally connected to this being inside me and yet when I tried to picture him I could not.

He's going to be a big baby! people said jovially to me when they saw my enormous belly, and that's all I could imagine. Not my son's face. Just the face of a big anonymous baby that happened to belong to me.

The Burning Question

His anonymity compounded my fear that I wouldn't love him. I worried about the fact that I didn't burst into tears when we'd had the ultrasound and I'd first seen the image of him on the screen, or when I heard his heartbeat at my meetings with the midwife. I felt awfully fond of him. I did everything for him. I protected his well-being at every turn. But there was still a distance between us. I didn't know him. All through my pregnancy my burning question was this: How could I love someone I didn't know?

The Last Picture Show

His birth began on a Tuesday morning. We were living in Portland, Oregon, by then, having moved there when I was five months pregnant. I called my husband and immediately got into the shower, and by the time I got out he was there with bags of groceries that I'd instructed him to buy—snacks for labor and ingredients for baking. All through my pregnancy I'd read tales of people baking things in the early stages of labor while also watching videos. They made blueberry muffins while watching *Sleepless in Seattle*. They made a carrot cake while watching *The Last Picture Show*. So I had the same cozy idea about my own early stages of labor. That I would do what I called *putzing around*.

It didn't go like that. It went like someone was operating a jackhammer in the lower half of my body every five minutes for hours on end. I had to wander the house and lean on things and process the pain with moans and ghastly facial expressions. In between two of these contractions, my husband implored me to eat a bowl of chocolate pudding. I ate it, grateful for the small, temporary pleasure it afforded me.

Then I had a contraction and puked it all up.

What Not to Believe

1. Don't believe labor doesn't hurt more than anything you've ever felt.

2. Don't believe you might have an orgasm while pushing a head out of your hoo-ha.
3. Don't believe you can't withstand enormous amounts of pain.
4. Don't believe suffering is abnormal or permanent.
5. Don't believe your body should cooperate with some plan that a medical association made because it protects them from lawsuits and makes it easier for them to run the show— the show being your body.
6. Don't believe you shouldn't educate yourself beyond what whomever you've hired to help you with your birth tells you.
7. Don't believe a pregnant woman is psychologically fragile and should be protected from the realities of labor and birth.
8. Don't believe you can't do this. It's a rough business, but you can.

Andaluz

The thing I feared most was the drive to the birth center, a place called Andaluz, which was thirty minutes from our house. As we drove, I breathed in and I breathed out while listening to a Krishna Das CD. I chanted "Om Namah Shivaya" along with him, not knowing what it meant, only knowing it helped me. It was Tuesday around dinnertime. I'd been in labor seven hours by then. The pain had become so spectacular I figured it had to be time to go to the birth center. I looked at my husband and said excitedly, "Our baby's going to be born tonight!"

Andaluz was on the second floor of a brick building of the sort that is always described as *nondescript*. It housed dental offices and insurance firms and mortgage brokerages and psychotherapy practices. Out of respect for the regular, non-laboring, non-chocolate-pudding-puking people, I tried not to bellow and howl and moan like a madwoman as I passed by the doors of these businesses. I tried to walk upright across the vast gray carpet and to refrain from murmuring *fuckfuckfuck* while gripping the banister of the stairs as another contraction came on.

I did not succeed.

Mammals

There were three birth rooms in Andaluz, each with a peaceful-sounding name, a name that suggested that things like massage or Reiki might be going on inside. I chose the one called Lavender. There was a queen-size bed covered in a pretty quilt and throw pillows in pastel colors, and a door that opened up into a bath-room with a birthing tub at its center. I insisted on getting into the tub immediately, though the warm water only fleetingly blunted my pain. Every time I had a contraction I thought, You have got to be fucking kidding me! It seemed preposterous that this was the way birth got done. I felt solidly and profoundly connected to all the female mammals of the world. Not just the women who'd birthed, but the cats and the bears and the lemurs, too.

I howled and moaned and mooed like a cow as I contracted every two/three/four/five minutes. I walked up and down the car-peted stairs of the now-empty nondescript office building that housed the birth center. I did squats and lunges and sat on an in-flated ball and languished in the tub and vomited every time I took so much as a sip of water. I laughed with my husband and tried to concentrate on the candles he lit for me and I stared at the framed photograph of my dead mother that he propped next to them, try-ing to channel her to make me strong.

When I had a contraction my entire body would be instantly flooded with sweat, the heat unbearable. Then, as soon as the con-traction ended, I'd be freezing cold, shivering violently until the next round began. My husband and two women friends who'd joined us a few hours after we'd arrived at the birth center were what I came to think of as my contraction pit crew. They were the ones who pulled my robe off and put it back on according to my body temperature. They tried to convince me to sip the water I'd later retch up. Every fifteen minutes a midwife or one of her apprentices would crouch down and listen to the baby's heartbeat through a stethoscope and assure me that everything was okay, but otherwise the four of us were left alone, doing our circuit of stairs, ball, robe, no robe, bathtub, lunge, howl.

The Crow

By morning I was standing near a window in the Lavender Room watching the sun rise and feeling like a survivor, if only of the night. My pit crew was asleep on the bed behind me—they'd taken to dozing off in the brief minutes between my contractions—and so it seemed, in this moment, I was alone. As I gazed out the window, I prayed to be out of this misery, to muster up the courage to do whatever I had to do, for the baby to be born soon. I felt entirely at the mercy of the birth, as if I'd lost any sense of who I was outside of this. As if there was no me outside of this.

As I had these thoughts, a crow flew up and perched on the narrow brick ledge outside the window. He was only a few inches away from me. Startled, we looked at each other. After a few moments, he tapped his beak several times against the glass as if trying to tell me something—*tap tap tap*. And then he turned and flew away.

I took it as a good omen. My son would be born today.

4:07 a.m.

It went on. And on and on and on. All through the day and deep into the night. I laughed. I cried. I despaired. I pondered the possibility of going to a hospital and getting a C-section or at least an epidural. I resolved to stick it out so long as my baby was okay. I remembered to feel grateful. I told dirty jokes. I swore. I surrendered. I begged the spirit of my mother to come to me and help and she did. I refused to do another lunge or to get into the tub. I was ravaged and exhausted. I was blown away and forever altered. Aware of physical capacities and spiritual realms I hadn't known existed before. I went to the deepest place within me and found there was a place deeper still. I drifted off to sleep on the bed in the Lavender Room, and woke every few minutes with a roar. I pushed so long and hard I didn't know what I was pushing any-more—my baby's body or mine. We merged most profoundly in the panting moment that he ripped my flesh open as I forced him into the world.

At 4:07 in the dark of morning, forty-three hours after my first contraction, my son was born. He was dark and gigantic. Just shy of eleven pounds. His eyes were ancient, going to me and to his father and then back again. He looked at me like he knew everything already. Like he loved me from the start.

Neighbor

NUAR ALSADIR

thought of my unborn child as a New York neighbor—someone who, despite my awareness of her rhythms and movements, was essentially anonymous to me. Knowledge of this neighbor's name and sex may have organized my fantasies about her, but pregnancy placed me in odd relation to this being, in that she existed to the same degree in fantasy as in the real.

In an attempt to make that fantasy more real, I consulted a pregnancy book that included sketches of what a fetus looks like week by week. Around eight weeks, it has webbed fingers and toes. On the ultrasound, my fetus appeared otherworldly, an alien creature suspended in a hammock of light. It was far more pleasing, I discovered, to turn to images in my head than to envision through the diagrams what was happening inside me. For about a month, I woke every night at 1:00 a.m. with excruciating abdominal cramps. My organs were moving around, I learned, to make room for the machinery. My body, too, began to seem alien. We are, of course, always alien to ourselves (Freud would point, here, to the unconscious), but we don't often feel concretely the strange stirrings within.

The first time I experienced my fetus kick was at eighteen weeks on an airplane on my way to visit my parents. Each movement felt like a bubble popping beneath the surface of my skin. The wall separating me from the neighbor within also separated my interior from the external world, and it seemed as though I could only access the interior space through an unrecognizable variant of Morse code.

My fetus may have seemed distant to me, but already she was communicating loudly to my parents. "Look what your mother did for you!" my father said gleefully after the drive from the airport, putting my luggage down and leading me into the kitchen of my childhood home. All of my favorite foods were laid out on the counter.

"It's not for her," my mother interjected. "She's just the messenger."

Little by little, my baby made herself known. In fact, my being seemed subsumed by the goals of nourishing and knowing her. Every time I got into bed, despite all of the heavy theory I would read during the day in working on my dissertation, I had only one thought: "Soft sheets, fluffy pillow!" Within minutes of being supine, I would begin to feel the fetus kick and roll, imagine her dancing to some internal music, and revel in the ruckus.

I lived for years next door to a man I never encountered. I knew when he couldn't sleep, when agitation prompted him to pace the floor at 3:00 a.m., even when he was upset. One night, he banged on my door with a hammer during a party—the friend who opened it described him looming above her like a serial killer from a horror movie, hammer cocked, ready to hit. Days later, the neighbor slipped a note under my door. He wasn't crazy, he wrote. The music was too loud. No one could hear his knocking. I empathized. When he was sick, I'd hear his cough through the wall, and I'd hear it as I ascended the stairs. It hurt my entire body. Did I love my neighbor as myself? Is that even generous, if one is self-critical? Perhaps you should love yourself as you love your neighbor—or, preferably, as you love your unborn child. "Higher than the love for thy neighbor," Nietzsche wrote, "is the love for the man who is distant and has still to come."

The morning before my due date, I woke to use the bathroom at dawn. It was only then that I grasped what was meant by a "mucus plug." Understanding often occurs retroactively. Even in writing this piece, I feel myself far from understanding—I don't know what idea it will deliver or what meaning may be unplugged, but I'm afraid I am turning around too soon and there will be a cost.

In a recent dream, I get into my car and start driving. After a few feet, I realize someone has altered my rearview and side mirrors. Unable to see anything behind or to the sides of me, only what is directly before my eyes, I fear I will crash. The Aymara of South America conceive of the future as behind us (we cannot see it) and the past before us (what is visible, already seen). I was able, in my dream, to see the past, which was ahead of me, but the present and the future had been tampered with, adjusted to someone else's desire or need. Perhaps we are always rearranging around Nietzsche's man still to come—whether a stranger, an unborn baby, or some future self, waiting to be born.

The contractions began early on a sunny July morning, shortly after the discovery of the mucus plug. My husband and I walked across the Brooklyn Bridge, stopping when I had a contraction so he could time it—he has a knack for systems analysis, which he applied fully to this phase of my pregnancy. For much of the day, the contractions were twelve minutes apart, so I could enjoy the anticipation of finally meeting my baby without feeling overwhelmed by pain.

In the afternoon, we went swimming at our gym—the weightlessness was a relief—and it was only when I showered afterward in the cramped stall that the contractions began to speed up and feel more intense. I leaned my hands against the shower wall, hot water pouring onto my back, as I waited for each contraction to pass. My husband stood anxiously outside of the women's locker room, at one point asking a stranger to check on me. I was still able to regain composure between contractions, walk out of the locker room and into the bright afternoon. But once we were home, the contractions came at a relentless pace. I called my mother, who is an obstetrician, to ask when I should go to the hospital. "When you feel you can't take it another second," she told me. The pain was unlike anything I'd experienced, but I didn't want to go to the hospital too early and lose the parking spot outside our building I had worked so hard to obtain. Each Wednesday afternoon, I would wait in the sweltering car for more than an hour for the spot to become legal. I called it the "just-in-case space" and had begun the ritual of securing it around my thirty-fifth week.

There's a saying: People change when the pain of staying the same is greater than the pain of making the change. Well, eventually, when the pain of the contractions became greater than the pain of losing the just-in-case space, we grabbed my long-packed bag and headed to the car. I had never felt as excited as I did arriving at the hospital, even as pregnant woman after pregnant woman who had entered the ward after me was ushered past the small plastic chair in the hallway next to the reception desk where I'd been commanded to sit and wait. When my name was finally called and I was sent into the exam room, the resident was shocked to discover I was dilated four centimeters. "You look too happy to be in labor," she told me. "That's why we took everyone else ahead of you." I explained that after twelve years of ballet, I'd learned how to tolerate and mask pain. Also, the fact that I would finally meet my baby, hold her in my arms—catch a glimpse in the rearview mirror—made me able to withstand it.

No one could reach my OB. Her line was busy, I was told, and each page seemed to get lost in the ether. As soon as I got to the delivery room, I felt desperate to go to the bathroom, as though I had food poisoning. I remember being doubled over on the toilet, immobilized by pain, mentally pressing the emergency call button I could hardly turn my head to see. When I finally managed to reach out for help, the nurse assisted me out of the bathroom and onto the delivery table, where the active labor continued. I had decided ahead of time that I wanted an epidural, but the line for an anesthesiologist was so long (those women admitted before me!) that I went through much of the dilation process without drugs. After I got the epidural and was examined, the doctor told me I was dilated nine centimeters. Although it may not seem, in retrospect, as though it made sense to have had an epidural at that point, it allowed me to be present for what was about to happen. I asked my husband to play the labor mix he'd made for me, requested an elastic to tie back my sweaty hair, sucked on a sour apple Jolly Rancher. The thrill of anticipation had returned.

The same resident who had examined me earlier walked into the delivery room, looked at me as I sat up in bed, refreshed, singing along to the music, and said disdainfully, "If you don't get this baby out soon, you're going to have to have a C-section." Not a helpful thing to say. She was like an enraged driver honking for me to move, driving up to my window to shake her hands and intimidate me, even as we both knew my being stopped was out of my control. Often an epidural slows the labor down, but I was fully enjoying the reprieve. Perhaps something about my calm irritated her—or maybe it was the fact that I'd strayed from the script of a screaming, writhing woman in labor and she didn't know what to do with me.

It was then, thankfully, that my OB entered and assured me everything was okay, I wasn't going to have a C-section. Her husband and son were out of town, she explained. She had been home alone having a good long chat with an old friend from college, oblivious to the fact that her beeper's battery had died. Comforted by the image of her as a close friend, I relaxed again and began the pushing process. Something on the baby's monitor alarmed my doctor and she put an oxygen mask over my mouth and nose. I didn't understand what was happening, but there wasn't time to worry, because the baby arrived soon after. They cut the cord and rushed her, wailing, to a little incubator in the corner of the room to examine her. She was healthy!

Within minutes, someone handed her to me and my first words upon seeing the strange-looking creature that looked like she'd stepped out of a *Saturday Night Live* Coneheads sketch, was, "What's up with her head?" Then, catching myself and realizing those were not the first words I would have chosen to utter to my newborn child, I added, "Hi, sweetie. I'm your mother." Her name had already been chosen, but immediately after her birth, seeing her in the flesh, there seemed to be a disconnect. When you name what you do not know, you are naming your fantasy of what that unknown will become.

Sometimes the world has a tendency, as Stephen Dedalus had it in *A Portrait of the Artist as a Young Man*, to "give the lie rudely to [one's] phantasy." Two years later, I gave birth to another daughter, though that time I chose to be induced. I was worried about what would happen to my toddler if I suddenly had to rush to the hospital in labor. It was infinitely easier, the second time around, to envision my baby, to know what to expect. Immediately after she was born, I breast-fed her while the umbilical cord was still intact. I asked my husband to run out and buy a large Coke on ice, as I used to have in my teens after a long Saturday at the ballet studio, but the hospital where I gave birth only had Pepsi. He left the hospital and rushed to the nearest deli that sold Coke. When he returned, we were told there were no hospital rooms available, but we could stay in the delivery room with the baby and order food.

Holding my newborn baby in one hand, I ate a grilled cheese sandwich with the other. I knew exactly what to do, what was needed, but sometimes following a script can muffle the signals emitted from within. I hadn't anticipated the effect it would have on my daughter not to have been able to decide when she was ready to enter the world. To this day, seven years later, she is averse to change, has trouble transitioning from one activity to another, needs me to sing the same song to her every night at bedtime. If I nudge, she holds fast, says, "It's because you didn't let me choose my birthday." Whenever I think of an induced birth, the phrase "rude awakening" comes to mind.

But all changes aren't so sudden. The man I lived with, loved, for more than a decade, the father of my children, gradually became a neighbor to me. I explained our divorce to our daughters this way: We were two overlapping circles. The overlapping space was where we connected, but as we came to know ourselves better and pursued what was important to us—things we believed in, felt passionately about—each of us gravitated toward opposite ends of our circles. The overlapping space was diminished and we were faced with a dilemma: Would we continue toward the parts of ourselves that felt authentic, even if it meant no longer hearing the other's knocking?

My daughters play cards on the bed next to mine as I write this. It is night, and we are staying in a cabin outside the campus of the overnight camp my elder daughter, now nine, will begin attending in the morning. At one point, she reprimands her younger sister, "You're bleeding! You're bleeding!" This phrase, I recently learned, means you are holding your hand such that your cards show. Earlier, at dinner, while a conversation about the infinite excitements surrounding camp burned and spat like a sparkler, my elder daughter pulled me aside, where nobody could hear, and asked, "What if I miss you too much?"

Maybe we are all afraid of bleeding. I picture the pages of this essay streaked with red, and cringe; the image seems indulgent. I am self-conscious about turning the stories of my daughters' births into stories about myself, but also about overlaying the past with my present. We were, when my daughters were born, a happy family on clean pages—years passed before we strayed from the family script, heeded the internal hammering. Nietzsche's love for the distant one who has still to come—once, each unborn child inside me—is also potentially self-love, for a future self or a figure fashioned in the imagination. Though I am uncertain what distant figure yet knocks to be born, I know I am not this story's protagonist.

These stories belong to my daughters, as they are now and still to come. I can see the past before me, but the narrative is now in the side and rearview mirrors. At one point, I may have believed myself to be the driver of the narrative, but the threads, unraveled, have been set loose. I was, and continue to be, the messenger.

Weight

MARY BETH KEANE

My husband and I will both swear that we conceived our first child on the very same day we decided it might be time to have a baby. Aside from intense nausea until week sixteen or so, my first pregnancy was a breeze. I was living in Philadelphia at the time, and walked just about everywhere I needed to go. I did prenatal Pilates. I read a stack of books about labor. I was carrying entirely in my belly, and people in my neighborhood stopped me on the street to inform me I would be having a boy. My due date was July 20, and that summer in Philadelphia was brutally hot. I got out for a quick walk in the early mornings, and during the heat of the day I worked on edits—my first novel was scheduled for the following spring and I wanted to finish before the baby arrived. In the evenings, when my husband, Marty, was home from work, we'd make our way over to Walnut Street for a longer walk, passing along the way a baby store that had nursery furniture in the window. In my thirty-ninth week, I mailed my manuscript to my publisher, assembled my son's stroller, and put up the huge tree of life decal on the wall of what would be his bedroom. I scrubbed our bathroom. I sat on my giant exercise ball, rolled my hips, and, thinking I knew exactly what was to come, waited.

July 20 came and went. My doctor measured my belly and estimated the baby was about seven pounds and in good position. I
was dilated three centimeters, but I learned that was not uncom-
mon. She told me to go home, have a glass of wine, and relax, so
I did. As my friends were drawing up their birth plans and fine-
tuning their attitudes toward cosleeping, I listened to my own
mother, who told me to wait, meet the baby, let him teach
me. "Will you get an epidural?" a friend asked. I told her I wasn't
sure. I knew because of all the books I'd read that there were many
different types of labor, and I believed, once I was in the thick of
it, that I could categorize mine and make a decision based on how
my body felt and all the information I'd spent so many months
gathering. I believed, in other words, that I'd understand what
was happening as it was happening.

Once I was officially overdue, my doctor wanted me to check
in at the practice every day. Their offices were on Washington
Square in Center City, just over two miles round-trip from my
apartment in Old City, and I'd always walked it easily. When I
was four days past my due date, I walked to their offices as usual,
and after examining me, the doctor I saw that day told me he was
going to strip the membrane of my cervix, and that doing so might
trigger labor. He warned me that it would hurt, and it did, but
it took only a few seconds, and so I was skeptical that such a small
thing would set such a big event in motion. He measured my belly
and, like my usual doctor, estimated the baby to be around seven
pounds. I was dilated four centimeters and he assured me that
when labor started, it would be fast. Less than an hour later, after
stopping to listen to a pair of banjo players in Washington Square,
I started for home and realized I didn't feel quite as energetic as I
had that morning. I hailed a cab. I wasn't having contractions, but
I felt heavy and slow. I thought I might vomit.

I made it home and tried to find a comfortable position on the
couch, and then in our bed. I took a shower. The dull ache across
my belly and lower back was getting more pronounced. I got down

on my hands and knees, rocked gently forward and back, and finally felt some relief. I called one of my sisters: "Remember that photo of Britney Spears? Nine months pregnant and on all fours?"

"Bearskin rug?" my sister asked.

"Picture that. Minus the rug. That's me."

We laughed, and I felt a tight clench across my belly. I waited for it to happen a few more times; then I called Marty and, just like they do in the movies, told him it was time. When he walked in an hour later, I told him that I was trying to time the contractions but couldn't tell when one ended and another started. None of the books I'd read had said anything about that.

"Let's just go," he said. The hospital was just a few minutes from our apartment, but I could barely walk, so he helped me to our car. Our street was cobblestoned, and I felt every bump as a stab in my belly. Marty didn't know whether to hit the gas and fly across to the paved road or go as slowly and gently as possible. "Gun it," I said, and tried to focus on breathing.

At four o'clock, roughly six hours after the doctor had stripped my membrane, we got to the hospital. I was dilated six centimeters. A nurse put a belt on me to monitor the contractions, and I then discovered why I couldn't time them: They were riding each other. The picture on the screen looked like a series of mountain peaks, with few valleys in between. My doctor was not on call, but a midwife from my practice checked on me. I sent Marty to the car for the exercise ball I imagined I would labor on. By the time he returned with the deflated ball and the pump, it seemed like hours had passed. The contractions had gotten stronger and I was being moved to a delivery room. A nurse asked me if I wanted an epidural, and after asking for a moment to think about it, I said I did. My husband held up the sad-looking exercise ball with a question on his face. "Leave it," I said.

I got the epidural about an hour after I arrived at the hospital, and it was everything it promised to be—at first. I could still feel the pressure of contractions, but I could speak and breathe. My sisters and parents had sped from New York in record time, and each came in to see me, wish me luck, assure me they'd be waiting for the good news. I wasn't afraid. I was sure what was coming would be difficult, but I told myself I was strong. Women had been delivering babies since the beginning of time, and I would be no different (except for the epidural, of course). Around ten o'clock, twelve hours after the doctor stripped my membrane and warned me that labor would probably be fast once it started, the nurse came in and said I was at ten centimeters but that the baby had to descend a little farther. "Call for someone if you feel the urge to push." Ten or fifteen minutes later, I felt intense pressure on my pelvic floor and told my husband to get someone. Every part of my body wanted to push, but the midwife warned me not to, not yet, as the baby had to descend. I held on for a little while longer, and around ten thirty, when I said I could not hold myself back any longer, she checked the baby's position and gave me the green light.

Almost four years later, it's still difficult to wade through the blur of what came next. I think of myself folding baby clothes in those final days of my pregnancy, arranging diapers and creams, examining my belly for stretch marks, and how clueless I was, how unafraid. In those last days before labor, I was thinking more about navigating our new stroller through city streets than I was about getting the baby into the world in the first place. Delivery was not the blank that raising a baby was because I believed I'd prepared myself so well. Birth was something to be gotten through, but it didn't concern me as much as the baby himself, what he'd be like, what kind of mother I'd be to him.

Seven hours after I was admitted to the hospital, I was pushing with everything I had, but the baby was descending very slowly. The doctor's earlier prediction of a fast labor was discarded. I remember the nurses and midwife talking about me, saying to Marty that my coping strategy was to get quiet, focused, internal. I listened to all of this as if from another room, but even from that faraway place I'd sent myself in order to push as hard as I could, after a while I could sense panic creeping in, looks exchanged, small signals and nods that were not intended for me. I pushed for two hours. Three hours. At some point—I don't remember when—they turned off my epidural, explaining that it would help me feel the start and finish of each contraction better, and erected a bar over my bed so I could crouch, let gravity help me. Still, the baby stayed put. I didn't know why what I was experiencing matched up with so little of what I'd read. I asked if they were sure the baby was okay, and was told that his heartbeat was strong, they were keeping track. For the first time in my pregnancy, someone—one of the nurses—raised the possibility that the baby might be bigger than my doctor had estimated. My last ultrasound had been at twenty weeks, and since everything in my pregnancy had progressed normally, my doctor had seen no reason to order another closer to my due date. My legs were weak from the fading epidural, but I held on to that bar and pushed. The baby was finally getting closer, and when I felt his head with my fingertips, I got a second, third, fourth wind. There he was, so close, but he didn't seem to want to come any farther, and I knew without having to be told that I'd been pushing for far too long. The midwife used the phone in the room to page a doctor. After a minute, when no doctor arrived, she went out, I assume, to track one down. A nurse got out the forceps and there was a discussion about the vacuum. "Where is the damn doctor?" someone said, and like that, I was yanked from my tranquil place and pulled into the heart of the worry that was throbbing in that room. It was nearly five o'clock in the morning, and I'd been pushing for more than seven hours. My mother, who was crouched in the corner with her rosary, was reciting the same prayer over and over.

As the nurses got the forceps ready, and I tried to understand what was happening, a doctor I'd never seen before came in, looked at me, and said, "She needs an episiotomy. Now!" Who gave me the episiotomy? The doctor? The midwife? I have no idea. Not once in the many hours since I'd started pushing had anyone mentioned an episiotomy, yet the doctor who ordered it now said it in a tone that implied I'd been refusing one for hours. I'd been bracing for an emergency C-section, and so I welcomed this alternative that I'd read about as a simple procedure. The pain of the episiotomy was different from the pain of labor—sharp and focused. I remember Marty telling me in a shaky voice to push just a few more times, and then relief, a sudden emptiness, a pause, and then a cry. Someone placed my son on my chest, the cord still attached.

"Is he all right?" I asked. To me, he looked swollen, traumatized, utterly lost.

"He's perfect," the midwife said, and looked at the clock. "Enormous, but fine. Ten minutes past five."

Relieved, I began to cry, and felt something warm spread across my chest and belly. It felt good, like stepping into a bath after a long day. "Your son just peed on you," a nurse said. We laughed, and I began to shiver. A nurse took my son to be weighed and a moment later said, "Oh my God!" as the scale jumped to ten and a half pounds. I barely processed this, because a moment later I began to quake. My arms and legs vibrated in such a melodramatic fashion that I wanted to crack a joke, but I couldn't. I was very, very cold, and I realized the sound of water I was hearing was not water, but my blood, spilling to the floor as if from a faucet that had been cranked open. I saw my husband's face go white as he took a step away. Whatever panic had been in the room when my son was stalled was matched by fresh panic now. Someone reached inside me and helped draw out the placenta. Someone pressed my belly with both hands and massaged while someone else pressed from within. Another doctor arrived. I got an injection of something in my thigh, and an IV of Pitocin to contract my uterus faster.

The bleeding eventually subsided, and the doctor who'd ordered the episiotomy placed a stool between my knees and told me that I needed stitches. "It's a third-degree laceration," she said after a brief inspection, as if I had any idea what that meant. After injecting a local anesthetic, she stitched for about an hour, during which time I tried to wrap my head around the fact that my projected seven-pound baby turned out to be 50 percent larger. Was that not something my obstetrician should have noticed? Why hadn't I gotten a late ultrasound? Why hadn't I demanded it? Why hadn't I gotten an episiotomy several hours earlier? At some point during all of this, my husband and son had disappeared, as had everyone else who'd been in the room. I was alone with this stranger while my son, *my son*, was somewhere in the building. Instead of voicing any of these questions—and more questions that were lurking but unformulated until sleep and sustenance gave me the energy to think—I lifted my head as a nurse passed by and asked if anyone could bring me something to eat.

Of all the books I read to prepare for Owen's birth, none focused on those weeks after a difficult delivery, when a woman's body feels totally unfamiliar and hormones are wild. Unlike being pregnant, when my body had changed so gradually that it never felt unfamiliar, being suddenly unpregnant felt uncomfortable and far too abrupt. I was hollow, and always gasping for breath. My stitches made it so I could not sit in a hard chair for almost a month. One friend told me she was up and around her neighborhood two days after delivering her daughter, who was also a large baby, pushing the stroller to a local coffee shop and returning library books. Another friend sent a picture of herself sitting cross-legged on her hospital bed, wearing her own pajamas, nursing her son, her family looking on, just hours after delivering him. It's hard not to make comparisons, and I felt these stories as a judgment about my choices, my capabilities. I'd read about the possibility that an epidural could

slow labor, and yet I'd opted for one. I knew that although episiotomies are no longer routine, they are still necessary in certain
cases, and yet it had never crossed my mind to ask for one. During
labor, the time in which I'd expected to coolly evaluate how my
labor fit in with what was normal, my mind was almost a complete
blank. I didn't talk. I didn't cry out like the birthing-class instructor said most women do. I crouched, I breathed, I pushed, and
everything else fell away. Where giving birth had made so many
of my friends feel fierce, stronger than ever, it had left me feeling
like a complete weakling, the class dunce. Three full days after
delivering Owen, I still needed two nurses to hold me by the elbows when I peed. They handed him to me when it was time to
breast-feed, and put him in his bassinet for me when it was time
to sleep. Since I'd labored overnight and had given birth in the
early morning, I hadn't slept for a long time, and that first night in
the hospital, when Owen was about seventeen hours old, my
mother suggested I send him to the nursery for a few hours. They
could give him two ounces of formula—she insisted it would not
ruin him for breast-feeding (she was right)—and I'd get a solid
block of four or five hours of sleep. I did it, but woke in a panic
around three in the morning, needing to be with him. Against
doctor's orders, I sat up very gingerly in my hospital bed, then
stood. Keeping my hand on the wall, I walked to the door of my
room and into the hall. After a few steps, I couldn't seem to catch
my breath, and I began to sink. I knelt. I tried crawling. "What
are you doing?" a nurse said when she saw me. "I need help," I told
her, and was quickly carried back to bed.

Was my labor harder than that of other women? I doubt it. But
it was hard for me. The fear that many women have before labor
hit me full force afterward—only in retrospect did I understand
how many things could have gone wrong. I was like a dead fish for
weeks after, and though I tried to sound buoyant and sure of myself when friends and family called with their congratulations, I
cried every day. I ate as much as I could, hoping it would bring

back my strength. The iron supplements I had to take to make up for blood loss were wreaking havoc on my stomach, and with all those stitches, I was terrified of going to the bathroom. I had terrible nightmares about the forceps and vacuum—the baby getting injured, my body tearing as far up as my throat. After a few weeks, I noticed Owen's head was always tilted, and he only ever turned his neck in one direction. When I mentioned it to his pediatrician, she sent me to a specialist, who determined he had torticollis—"twisted neck"—likely as a result of delivery. I had more nightmares.

Even now, four years later, when I exchange birth stories with other women, someone often says, "But you had an epidural," and I see that person dismiss my story entirely. Or they say, "But you didn't have a transfusion. You couldn't have lost that much blood." Or they counter my story with a story about someone who had an emergency hysterectomy. Or worse. Sometimes I see in other women an impatience with my story of a difficult birth, and they go in the opposite direction and describe how easy it was for them. "Meditation," one woman advised me. "Try it your second time around." Several women I know opted for home births, and one suggested that if I'd been home, in my own bed, without the intrusion and intervention of doctors and drugs, my son would have slid out exactly as hoped. That may be true. Maybe if I'd birthed at home, I would have had fewer complications. But what if I'd had exactly the same complications? What then? My parents were both born at home, as were most of my aunts and uncles. My mother, who was the seventh of ten children, lost a baby sister when my grandmother delivered her with the cord wrapped around her throat and no one could revive her. I suppose I'd always thought of home birth as part of the Old World, the Europe my parents left behind for the bright progress of America. Whatever the reason, I never considered it. I don't know why some women can read *The*

New York Times while delivering their babies with an epidural, and why I felt like I'd been roasted alive.

When I became pregnant with my second son, all the uncertainty and confusion surrounding Owen's birth came to the surface again. No one could tell me for certain why Owen had gotten stuck in the birth canal. It wasn't necessarily his size—it could have been the width of his shoulders or the angle of my pelvis. I suggested that the epidural had slowed labor too much and caused the distress later on, but that theory was dismissed. One doctor suggested that the epidural had given me much-needed rest and that without it I might have ended up with an emergency C-section. Why an emergency C-section would have been worse than what did happen, I have no idea.

No matter what the reason, no doctor at my practice would agree to a vaginal delivery after a third-degree laceration. They explained that another episiotomy would almost certainly mean another large tear. My husband got a new job, and we ended up moving to New York when I was several months along. My chart was sent to the new practice, and the doctors there also advocated for a C-section. When I didn't acquiesce as quickly as they wanted me to, I could sense them categorizing me as a natural-birth militant, which I'm not. I wholeheartedly believe there are women whose babies must be delivered by C-section—for the safety of the child and the mother—but I was not sure I was one of those women. When I was thirty-eight weeks along and had once again left an appointment without scheduling my C-section, my new doctor called me at home to say that if I insisted on being "reckless," I'd have to find another practice. She knew, as I did, that no practice would take on a woman who was already at term. I would have had to wait for labor to start, and then go to a local ER. I am generally thick-skinned, but that sent me spinning. Reckless? I remembered Owen's delivery, the panic in that room, the dark looks exchanged between the nurses. "Fine," I said, and grudgingly agreed to a C-section.

Emmett was born at 38.5 weeks—nine and a half pounds. And at the exact moment they held him up—shocked at having been pulled from his warm nest—I felt both overwhelming guilt and absolute certainty that I could have delivered him. The number of things to feel guilty about as a parent is endless, so as my wise friend once advised, "Don't go borrowing trouble." And I won't. Emmett got here safely—happy, it seemed, from the first second. Also: hungry, curious, loud. His big brother loved him and shared his mommy with inspiring courage. The recovery period after a C-section—one of the reasons I wanted to avoid one—was not nearly as bad as my recovery after delivering Owen. I healed, and had fewer nightmares postpartum.

Neither of my children got here the way I'd dreamed, but they got here, ten fingers, ten toes, healthy, strong, big boys, and now, at nearly four years old and eighteen months, respectively, they chuff their trains, beg Daddy to throw them in the air, spray Mommy with the hose, and beg for Popsicles at breakfast. Thankfully, the sharp edges of their births have begun to fade. As they do, I find myself returned to that place of anticipated joy I lived in before Owen was born, before I knew the risks, the stakes, of getting these boys into the world. The body's ability to forget is its best talent.

"Don't forget too much," my husband warns. "Remember! Or else you'll want to do this again!"

More

AMY HERZOG

was proud of my easy pregnancy. Most days, I went to a yoga class or walked four miles around Brooklyn's Prospect Park. I gained the right amount of weight; I had no back pain; I didn't mind standing on the subway when no one gave up a seat. I would need to be strong for the natural delivery I planned in a birth center. My husband, Sam, and I read Ina May Gaskin's books aloud to each other and squealed with delight at the earnest, dated prose. Hundreds of women had their babies on Ina May's farm, not a syringe or a lab coat in sight, and these babies were just fine, their mothers elated, possessed of power and grace they hadn't known was theirs. And I had a head start. I had gotten fillings without Novocain; I had competed in a triathlon and biked over the Continental Divide. In my personal pregnancy mythology, an epidural would be a disgrace, a C-section a tragedy of Greek proportions. For some reason, every catastrophe I envisioned was labor-related. Whether out of fear or just innocence, I never imagined there would be a problem with the baby herself.

In the eighth month of my pregnancy, my belly didn't grow for two weeks in a row, and I noticed the baby was kicking less than all the websites cheerfully advertised as normal. A sonogram was reassuring, as were my midwives: "You have a peanut in there!

Easier to get out!" But the morning my water broke, I could hardly feel the baby move at all. I drank juice and ginger ale and ate pineapple and jogged around the block, trying to jolt her into action. I lay down and held the sides of my belly, hoping my hands would pick up movements that my uterus missed. I went into the hospital for another sonogram and was told, again, that everything was fine, that I should go home and wait for labor to begin.

That labor did not begin by that evening—that, twelve hours after my water broke, by hospital policy I had to be induced, forgoing the natural, birth center delivery I had envisioned—was the first disappointment in what would feel like an endless tumble over the ensuing months. I was angry; if I were on Ina May's farm, I pouted to myself, I would be allowed to wait. On my way back to the hospital, I Googled "Pitocin no epidural" and was encouraged to learn that at least a few tough women made it through induced labor without numbing their lower halves. I resolved to be one of them. I could salvage at least that piece of my birth vision.

Once I was admitted, the midwife on duty, Amanda, examined me and deemed my cervix completely closed. She inserted into my vagina something that looked like a cheap shoelace, which she called a "cervical ripener." "You don't want to start Pitocin on a closed cervix," she explained, making a tight fist with her hand. Over the next hour, I tried to picture my cervix ripening like a mango in July, but my trance was interrupted by a nurse bursting into the room. "Has it been doing that for a while?" she asked, looking unhappily at the blinking monitor. Sam and I acknowledged that it had—we didn't know what the beeping meant. The nurse left and returned moments later with our bleary-eyed midwife. "We have to take it out," she said. "The baby doesn't like it." The shoelace came out, the baby's heart rate came down, and they began IV Pitocin, despite my cervix resembling, presumably, a green mango or clenched fist.

Eleven hours of contractions later, I was dilated to about one centimeter (out of ten). I was in no state to make any calculations, but I knew at that rate I was days away from relief. I was nauseous, salivating copiously, and spitting into a cup my doula held out for me. I tried to rest between the contractions, as the experts urged, but my contractions had been less than three minutes apart since they began and were only getting closer together. I shamefacedly asked Beth, the midwife now on duty, about an epidural. I had been connected to five monitors and an IV for all that time; I reasoned it was perverse to deny myself the one hookup that would bring some relief. I slumped forward as the doctor threaded the needle into my spine. "A playwright, huh? Anything on Broadway?" Everyone waited while I withstood another grinding contraction. "No," I finally managed to say. "But I have a show at Lincoln Center." Did I just brag? I wondered, amazed and slightly disgusted. Maybe I thought that even the anesthesiologist was judging me for my failure of will, so I had to compensate. "Lincoln Center, huh?" he said, feigning interest, but in fact focused on my spinal column, which was a good thing. Minutes later, my nausea and pain were completely gone and I was dilated to three centimeters. An hour later, five centimeters. An epidural, I grudgingly acknowledged, is a fucking miracle.

But the baby felt differently. She didn't "like" the epidural any more than the ripener. So many opinions, at her tender age! The shoelace had made her heart rate race, but now her pulse rate was dipping dangerously every few hours, prompting Beth to call for a doctor and the doctor to shout commands at me. I shook and my jaw clattered as I turned to one side, then to the other, then dragged myself onto hands and numb knees. Once, Beth stabbed my thigh with a syringe of terbutaline, halting contractions altogether, and the baby's heart rate finally came back up. In addition to the monitors on my belly, Beth reached far up into my vagina and added one to the baby's head. By this time I was wearing an oxygen mask, too, which I was certain was overkill, but when I hazarded taking it off for a few minutes, the baby's heart rate slowed and the monitor beeped angrily. I put it back on, accepting the fully medicalized birth I had passionately spurned.

We had a few drama-free hours. My mom came to the room to visit, fluttery and expectant. Around 7:30 p.m., I noticed Beth's eyes glide to the monitor and rest there. "What?" I asked. She shook her head, willing the numbers to change. "We have to get this baby out," she said as she jogged into the hall. A doctor rushed in to examine me and I was vaguely aware of her decision that I would push instead of having a C-section. At last, something went right. The bottom of my bed came off, eight people gathered around it, and three minutes of shouting later, with the assistance of a vacuum device, Frances was born.

Because of her in utero distress, Franny was handed right to a pediatric resident, who examined her while the doctor stitched me up. "She's pinking up," one of the midwives declared as I craned to see my daughter. I was given Franny to hold. She was undeniably scrawny at five pounds, fourteen ounces and she made funny breathing noises, which earned her the early nickname "Gremlin," but no one seemed concerned about these adorable idiosyncrasies. I put her to my breast and she nuzzled it, with no intention of eating. "I know," I cooed, "Mama's nipples aren't very long." This apology was greeted with general hilarity. "Don't worry!" Beth assured me. "She'll draw 'em out!" Franny had improbably large lips and beautifully spaced eyes and these tiny feet—okay, so that's why rational people get that way over baby feet—and we breathed. Finally free from all the machines, I was surprised to discover I had already stopped feeling dejected about my birth experience. I was ready to fall asleep for the first time with my baby.

It wasn't until about two hours later that we began to become aware, in increments, that something was terribly wrong. We weren't particularly paying attention to the nurse doing a routine exam of the baby, when we heard her announce, "I'm calling the doctor." She seemed inconvenienced; maybe she was due for a break? She disappeared. Sam and I looked at each other, calmly surprised. We hadn't slept in almost forty hours. The scene was unhurried, unfocused, vague. The nurse returned with a young woman—presumably a resident—who examined our daughter again. She lifted both Franny's arms in a gesture that made me think of religious supplication and then abruptly let them go. Franny caught her right arm before it dropped completely, but her left arm smacked the bassinet like an overcooked noodle. The resident repeated this test a few times with increasing interest as Franny whimpered.

"Okay!" she said enthusiastically. "I'm gonna move her to the NICU for some tests."

We asked what was wrong and she rattled off a list of problems—stridor, asymmetric cry, low muscle tone. Franny was limp and weak, especially in her left arm and the left side of her face.

"She didn't grow in utero for the last month," I offered. "Maybe she's just tired and hungry."

"Maybe," the resident replied with the patient smile medical professionals reserve for laypeople's idiotic theories. "But we still need to check her out."

Someone must have set me up in my new room near the NICU, though I don't remember that at all. My next memory is of being in the NICU, holding Franny, who now had electronic leads stuck to her tiny chest and abdomen and a glowing red sensor wrapped around one of her exquisite little feet. She was crying hoarsely and the monitor at her bedside was blinking and shrilling. Sam was standing above us with his hand on my shoulder and I was telling him to go home and sleep. There was only one narrow cot for me in the room down the hall—no accommodations for NICU dads. "I'm okay, I'm okay, go," I repeated, sobbing wretchedly. Sam was tormented but exhausted. Finally, he kissed both of us and left. A nurse showed me how to put the now-sleeping baby, sensors and wires and all, back in her Isolette—the temperature-controlled glass house that was now her home. "Come at three for the next feeding," the nurse said as I hobbled toward my room.

Shortly before three, my phone alarm rang and I woke up drenched in sweat. My body was a riot of pain. I sat up, considering the possibility that my tailbone had actually been shattered. I went to the bathroom, pulled down my disposable mesh underpants, and saw that the two maxipads I'd lined up adjacent to each other were both soaked with fresh blood. I peed for what seemed like an impossibly long time. I filled my plastic squeeze bottle with warm water and aimed the spigot between my legs, watching as more blood ran into the toilet. I touched a cool witch hazel pad to the raw, swollen area, which I was glad I could not see. I lined up two more pads, flushed, and, in sweaty slippers, padded back down the hall to the NICU.

Franny was expertly swaddled in a hospital blanket and asleep. A nurse came over and showed me how to change her diaper without opening the Isolette; there were two hatches in the side, one for each hand. "I can't just open the top?" I asked as I watched her gracefully manage the blankets and wires and diapers and wipes faster than I could visually track them—I thought she would make an excellent pickpocket. "We do it this way and we expect you to, too, Mommy," she said. Then she opened the Isolette after all that trouble to keep it closed and handed me the baby.

I couldn't rouse Franny to eat. Her eyes fluttered and she opened her mouth a little wider to accommodate my breast, but she seemed content just to rest there. A different nurse, who boasted of training as a lactation consultant, happened upon us and coached me. "You really have to squeeze that whole nipple in there, like a sandwich!" she said, pleased with her simile. Then she palmed the back of Franny's skull and maneuvered the greater part of my breast into Franny's mouth. Franny snored. The nurse smiled at me as if she had seen this a million times. "She'll get it; nursing is actually easier than bottle-feeding for babies." She was the first but would not be the last lactation consultant to confuse her enthusiasm for her profession with my baby's ability to breast-feed. In that moment, it was extremely reassuring.

Back to my room, two and a half hours of fevered sleep, my bathroom ritual, then back to the NICU at 6:00 a.m. for another "feeding." The irony of this word began to seem unkind. Again, Franny couldn't get anything from my breast, and it was now approaching twelve hours since her birth, with no nutrition or hydration. I padded back to my room, where a nurse had brought a pump and showed me how to use it. I watched my nipples distend rhythmically into the plastic cones. I knew there was a joke to be made about Madonna, but I couldn't quite find it. Tiny beads of yellow colostrum appeared on my areola, but nothing collected in the enormous bottles they provided. Were there women in the world who could fill those bottles? I slept again.

When I woke up, Sam was back. In our bed without me, the empty cosleeper at his side, he had slept less than I had. We hurried to the NICU and I lifted Franny and put her in her dad's arms. "Hi, honey," he said in a voice approaching falsetto, using a pet name for the first time since I'd met him. After I tried and failed, again, to nurse Franny, the day nurse, a warm Texan named Michelle, explained that she wanted to give the baby some formula. The doctors had ordered an MRI, she said, and it would be best for Franny to have a full belly to help her sleep through it. I barely registered the part about the MRI; I was stunned to hear the word *formula*. I had been inundated with breast-feeding propaganda since long before I was pregnant. I knew breast-fed babies had fewer allergies, sounder digestive tracts, higher IQs. In my childbirth class, I learned that I would have to be vigilant in the hospital after birth, because some new moms turned their backs for a minute, only to catch the nurses in the act of feeding their babies formula. Was Michelle one of these evil nurses, intent upon disrupting my bond with my baby? I wept. I paged my midwives.

The time for the MRI was approaching and I relented, feeling obscurely like a traitor to my child. Michelle prepared the bottle and I held Franny close and nudged the nipple between her gums. That's when we learned that Franny couldn't bottle-feed, either. She spluttered. She gasped. She cried. After an agonizingly long time, I held up the bottle and saw she hadn't made a dent. I had neither the wherewithal nor the desire to protest what happened next. Michelle threaded an angel hair–size tube into Franny's tiny nostril, down her throat and into her stomach as Franny gagged weakly. She connected a syringe to the tube and poured an ounce and a half of formula into it. Gravity drew it down. Franny slept and was, once again, taken away from us.

It would be hours before the results of the MRI would come back, and Sam had to leave for work. My mother arrived to take his place, and she sat nearby in my room as I bent over with my palms on my bed, hysterical for a few minutes. "You must be so disappointed," she said, and I cried harder, making strange choking noises. Was I allowed to be disappointed in my newborn baby?

Back in the NICU, Mom made a show of her delight in her granddaughter that was too transparent to be comforting. One of the midwives came by to find out why I'd paged. I confessed that I'd given Franny formula, expecting to be chastised. But she unhesitatingly assured me I'd done the right thing, which was more unsettling—it confirmed my suspicion that I was entering into a shadowy subculture of motherhood, where different rules applied. Seeing my dismay, she helped me collect tiny drops of my colostrum. I squeezed my nipple until one appeared, and she drew it up in a small syringe. "Great," she kept saying as she flicked the upside-down syringe, trying to make the air bubbles rise through the viscous liquid into the tip. "This is so great." After about fifteen minutes, we had something short of one milliliter, which went into Franny's next tube feeding.

I pumped and slept and sweated and peed and bled. Sam came

back and my mother left. When we arrived at Franny's Isolette for the 6:00 p.m. feeding, Michelle leaned in conspiratorially. "I think the doctor has a little bit of good news for you guys."

We rushed into the hall and found the attending, a dry, mild woman in her fifties. "Yes, we received the results of the MRI," she said, and paused for effect. "Frances did not have a stroke."

I am a basically bright person who knows what an MRI is, but it had never occurred to me that Franny might have had a stroke. My grandmother had died of a stroke. I was there when she slumped forward at the dinner table a few weeks before her seventy-eighth birthday. The word *stroke* evoked her creased, baggy face, her mouth open so wide, it seemed her jaw had unhinged itself. My day-old baby—a stroke? What had I thought they were testing Franny for? I had no idea. The doctor was saying, ". . . no brain bleed, no major brain abnormalities . . ." She was smiling, pleased to be the lucky one to tell us. Between waves of vertigo, I was thinking, roughly, This is my new life . . . and in this life, this is what I can expect from "good news."

A year later, those few bewildering days seem utterly surreal. I feel deeply estranged from the woman so intent on natural birth, the woman with an almost superstitious belief in breast-feeding. Partly, I am envious of her: her blithe assurance, her optimism, her illusion of control. Isn't that why the natural-birth movement has taken hold, at least in certain subsets of the population? Pregnancy is such a vulnerable and mysterious state that it's comforting to focus on what you can achieve instead of what you can't know. Easier to blame any potential disasters on a medical establishment you can sidestep instead of on fate, which is beyond your sway.

It would be nineteen days before we were allowed to take Franny home, and almost three months until we received the diagnosis of a severe congenital muscle disease we have since learned to live with. I say learned to live with, rather than accepted, because I am still often overtaken by rage, despair, a yawning sense of injustice, and guilt for being a new mother in the throes of these feelings (a wicked distant relative to the blissed-out mamas on Ina May's farm). If I believed in a guiding intelligence in the universe, I might think my birth gone awry was a crash course in letting go: a skill I would need desperately in the ensuing months and probably for the rest of my life. But progress on the personal-evolution front is slow; I continue to find each piece of difficult news, each setback, as heartbreaking as the last. Although I now feel some peace with the knowledge that Franny can't eat by mouth and may never walk, when I imagine that she may need breathing support some day—a likelihood with her diagnosis—terror and frenzied determination grip me.

In the early months, as Sam I and began to understand the extent to which our lives would be organized around our daughter's care, we grieved for the "normal" parenthood we were missing out on while learning how to parent the child we have. Gradually, our anguish has ebbed and we focus on what she needs more than on how we feel. Franny herself is our greatest guide in this regard. At thirteen months, she can't say any words, due to weak facial muscles, but she is ravenously learning to sign. "Yes," she signs, "all done," "milk," "music," her wonder and curiosity giving us strength and something akin to joy. Her favorite and most used sign, by far, is "more."

One Year, Two Births

AMY BRILL

Here is what I remember about the moment I gave birth: the Brooklyn predawn light flooding through the car windows; the flash of stoplights as my husband blew by them, one after the other; his voice as he said, "Hold on, you two, hold on!" But I could not, because I was holding on to our baby, who had just been born. In the car.

"We are fine," I said. It was true. The newborn lay on my chest. Its nose was clear, its infant cry a strong and steady bleat, our blood still spinning through the cord that bound us.

From the initial twinges, seven hours earlier, to the final, wrenching contraction, I'd been singularly focused on one goal: avoiding a repeat of my first labor. That experience, three years before, which resulted in the birth of my daughter, had been a grueling forty-hour marathon that began at home and ended in the hospital with an IV, an epidural, and a hefty dose of Pitocin to force my cervix into compliance.

The worst part of it, though, had not been the pain itself, but my lack of control over it. Before I went into labor, I'd thought of myself as a strong person, but as pain vanquished reason and everything else, hour after hour, I reconsidered. Dehydrated, exhausted, and terrified, I'd retreated into a miserable and primal state, thrashing and shrieking like a bat in a net.

This time around, as we sped into the parking lot of our local ER, I was serene, and it wasn't because of the rush of oxytocin that occurs after childbirth, or because I'm naturally calm. It was a moment that had been in the making for fifteen years.

In 1996, I was not a mother. Nor was I married. I wasn't much of a fiction writer, either. I aspired to all of these states, though, and between fact-checking and short freelance writing assignments, I traveled, hoping that inspiration and/or love would strike on foreign shores. I strapped on a backpack year after year, exploring outback mining towns in Australia and tiny Thai islands, Greek towns where my grandfather may have been born, and the interior waterways of the Yucatán Peninsula. I found neither love nor my voice in any of these places.

Then I took a summer job at a bookstore owned by one of my college professors. It was on Cape Cod, near the beach, and it felt like a very writerly thing to do. One sunny day, I took the ferry to Nantucket and, wanting to avoid the entwined couples gazing over the rails, I ducked into the cabin and leafed through a tourist flyer. "Come and see the home of the famous girl astronomer from Nantucket," the squib implored. Girl astronomer? I thought. I pictured a teenaged girl in a gray dress, alone on her roof, searching the skies, night after night, in every kind of weather, for something new to appear, something different, something that would change her life.

When we docked, I made my way past the posh boutiques selling Nantucket Reds to the side street where Maria Mitchell's shingled gray house and small brick observatory stood. The air was salty, the dirt sandy, but a garden of wildflowers bloomed at her front door. Who had lived here? What had driven her gaze toward the stars? I felt compelled to answer these questions, not least because I, too, at age twenty-five, was desperately in search of something that would change *my* life.

For the next ten years, I wrote meandering, mediocre poems; I spent months on end learning about Maria's life, reading her journals, and immersing myself in period research. I visited many libraries; I wrote hundreds of pages of prose in what I imagined her voice to be. I learned more about nineteenth-century astronomy, whaling, and Quakers than anyone else I knew or was likely to meet at, say, a Lower East Side party at the turn of the millennium.

But I was no closer to realizing any of my major ambitions. I cycled through a difficult relationship. I published a short story and a few essays, but my "novel" languished. By 2005, I knew what was on my character's desk and what the air smelled like from her roof and even what the constellations above her on a June night at 10:00 p.m. would look like. But I could not get a handle on her heart.

In July of that year, after another breakup, I did what I always did: I packed a bag. This time I wasn't going far, just upstate to a summer house. Fourth of July weekend. Music, friends, tents.

And there he was. The love of my life. Within a week, we were an item, by Labor Day I'd met his family, and by the time the leaves fell we were on vacation in Barcelona.

Two years fluttered past. I had a full-time job. My love and I were getting married. Friends tactfully stopped asking about my novel. Four months after the wedding, we were pregnant. Reality blinked at me. A child. A *family*. I wrote furiously, gunning for the finish line. A few days before my daughter was born, I finished my first draft.

Then, for almost a year, I stopped writing. I breast-fed and made my own organic baby food, monitored tummy time and nap time, and kept on freelancing. I did the laundry. I loved my baby so much, I cried with joy when I embraced her. But I felt like I was drowning.

Desperate for a way out of my funk, I read my book. It was not great. It was more than six hundred pages long, stuffed with characters and subplots. But it had a beginning, a middle, and an end. And I could see a glimmer of who my character might be, as if she was emerging from a fog.

I began again. Three mornings a week, I rose at six and stumbled to my corner Connecticut Muffin in the dark. On weekends, I worked half a day on the book and spent the rest divvying up household tasks, as if the continued orbit of our planet depended upon the laundry being dry by lunchtime. I listened for the inner voice of my character, but she was still elusive. I sent my readers another draft. What was my character thinking? they asked. What was she feeling?

On a leather couch in a therapist's office at 7:00 a.m. once a week, I began asking similar questions of myself. Why, for example, was I so entrenched in my own views about parenting? Why did I cling rigidly to the highest standards in that and every other part of my life, from creative output to professional success to personal relationships? Why was I so critical of my writing, of myself, and of others? Why, for God's sake, couldn't I take it easy once in a while and do what I felt like doing instead of what I thought I was duty-bound to accomplish?

Each week, I chipped away at my fears and defenses, the matrix of perfectionism and criticism, defensiveness and decisiveness that had ruled my life for as long as I can remember.

At the same time, page by page, over the course of a year, I rewrote my book. As I did so, my character, Hannah, discovered that her own passions and perspectives, ambitions and beliefs—and those of others—were neither absolute nor subject purely to her will. Life was not black or white, true or false.

As Hannah allowed herself to be shaped not only by intellectual rigor and strident, unbending beliefs but also by the twin engines of what was in her heart and what was in her head—love and discipline—I did the same. I still took the most loving care of my daughter that I was able. But I reserved my discipline for where it was really needed: my book. I began leaving the dishes in the sink and ignoring the laundry pile once in a while. I ordered pizzas. I stopped feeling like I *had* to vacuum. I did not have to vacuum. I had to play with my daughter, and get my book written. With these changes, life got a little easier. So did writing.

On February 13, 2011, I finished my book. And I got pregnant that very day.

Nine months later, I stood in the dark of my bedroom, swaying as contractions racked my body. This time, though, I was armed with new power. I had already done what at one time seemed impossible: found love, created life, and—maybe most important at that moment—written (and sold!) the story I'd dreamed of for most of my adult life. I had learned that I had control over not only what I did or didn't do but over what I believed, especially about myself. My daughter was sleeping just a few yards away. In case she woke up, I had to harness the focus and direction I'd acquired while writing my book, and lose the fear and doubt. *Love and discipline.* I could help the baby come the way I wanted it to, which was, in short, *quickly.*

With every contraction, I pictured waves breaking, lilies blooming, psychedelic acid-trip swirls expanding into ever-widening spirals. I didn't focus on the pain, but what I needed it to do: open the door, release the life waiting there. I experienced each contraction as it happened, going toward the experience instead of pushing away from it.

"I don't know how people do this," I muttered to my husband in the throes of a particularly brutal contraction. "I think I'm going to need an epidural when we get to the hospital."

"Whatever you need," he reassured me, solid as a brick. "Any way you want to do this is okay."

By 5:00 a.m., I was sure it was time to go. We lumbered into the light of the living room. But in the few breathless minutes between the first phone call to our babysitter and putting on my second sock, my contractions sped up significantly. They rolled in one after the other, like weather systems colliding. And at the end of each came a deep muscle spasm, like a sudden, insistent drumbeat from inside my womb.

Our sitter wasn't there; our daughter slept on. In a panic, I dialed my upstairs neighbor, who appeared in our doorway seconds later in her pajamas. I crawled outside. My husband pulled the car up and I hurled myself into the back, between the car seats, a space the size of a Frisbee.

Ten or fifteen contraction-free seconds unfurled. Like true New Yorkers, we talked traffic. We were in Brooklyn; our OB was at New York University Hospital, fifteen or twenty minutes away, on the other side of the East River, in Manhattan. But my water hadn't broken. I figured I was in the final stage of labor—which I hadn't experienced the first time around, thanks to the epidural at hour thirty-five. I was excited, even proud, that I'd gotten myself this far. But I was ready to see my doctor—as soon as possible.

"What are you thinking?" I panted, my heart racing. "Battery Tunnel and up the West Side?"

"I was thinking Flatbush Avenue to the Brooklyn Bridge," he said. "It's five thirty in the morning. There won't be any traffic."

"Okay, just go, go," I said, my next contraction looming. He peeled out and turned the corner.

By the time he'd gone around the block, the contraction was rolling through me. But at the end, as it crested, I felt something different: an immense rush of warm pressure, accompanied by an unmistakable sensation. There was no bearing down, no pushing, but I knew what was about to happen. There was no time to be afraid. I put my hands down just in time to feel the head of my baby pop out like a cork.

"The head is out," I cried, stunned but steady. "Go to Methodist!"

Our local hospital was only ten blocks away. As my husband sped through the half-lit streets, there came a final spasm, and then, like a fish, the body of our baby slipped into my waiting hands. I leaned back and pulled the child to my breast, skin to skin, grateful for the mewling cries that proclaimed *Alive, alive, alive.*

From the front seat, my husband asked all the right questions: "Is the nose clear? Is the baby breathing? Are you okay?"

I felt no pain, no fear, no trauma, only the intoxicating rush of adoration that bound us as surely as the cord that still connected us.

"We're fine, we're fine," I crooned over and over. And we were. It was a very short trip—maybe a minute and a half—but time seemed to still even as the car rocketed on through the stoplights and the dawn. My husband pulled up and ran into the hospital, then out again.

The ER staff rolled out with a gurney and a warm blanket. I stepped out of the car, holding the most precious cargo I will ever transport in my arms. Many minutes passed before I finally lifted the sheets that covered us to discover, to my surprise, that I had another baby girl.

We

DANZY SENNA

My boy believes in magic. Not the fun magic of card tricks and rabbits popping out of top hats. He believes in a darker kind of magic—as in, if we don't abide by his rules, something bad might happen.

Lately, his rules are many.

He insists on finishing his sentences with these five words: *for real and not pretend*. If I interrupt him before these last words are out, he has to say it all over again until we get it right.

When he goes to the bathroom, he has to strip naked, including his socks, even when we are in a grimy public restroom at the back of a restaurant, even when we are in a hurry. He cannot be wearing any clothes when he uses a toilet.

When he flushes the toilet, I have to push the handle down with him. My hand has to touch the handle at the same time as his so that we press down on it together, both watching the water swirl around the white bowl.

When we open the door to the apartment building, we have to push the door at the very same moment and close it at the same moment, a synchronized dance, so it is as if there are no longer two of us, but one entity, a two-headed creature moving through the world.

His babysitter laughs. "It's extreme coupling," she says. "I feel like a third wheel when I'm around you two."

We are living in Paris and she's French and doesn't seem to see danger in his rituals. They started only recently, so she says it's a phase. She has a sense of poetry, a sense of humor, about children. His father says that he's testing me—and that if I ignore him, it will pass. But being an American mother, I live in a state of anxiety about my children. I search for a deeper meaning in his rituals.

According to my child himself, the problem stems from a mistake I made when I named him at birth. He says that he already had a name before he was born, so he doesn't need the name I gave him. The name he wants to go by—the name he has given himself, and claims to have already had when we first met—is Oui. It sounds just like the French word for yes, and that's how he spells it when he signs his paintings—but I wonder if he also means We, because there is only a we when we are together—no distinction between our bodies, our movements. There is no him and there is no me. There is only We.

He tells me bedtime stories about Oui in the dark, lying in his bed. He tells me he used to be a baby named Oui. That was the name he had before he was born. "I was Oui, and then I fell asleep and when I woke up I was inside of your tummy."

He says it's okay that I made a mistake. It's okay that I started out calling him the wrong name, but now that I know, please just call him Oui. He won't answer to anything else.

Oui, as it were, was born early—not premature, but pushed out of me a full two weeks before his due date. My doctor, witty, fun, left-wing, the favorite ob-gyn of Los Angeles's hipster elite, encouraged me to induce delivery early. He helped me pick the date. His reasons seemed sound at the time: My body had been damaged from the traumatic delivery of my older son, which had been, the doctor told me, smiling airily, "one of the most brutal natural births" he'd ever witnessed. I could see his point. The baby got stuck inside me. Nobody tells you about these things in the baby books, how violent—how like science fiction—it can really be. The baby got stuck and nobody could get him out. There was talk at one point of pushing the baby back up inside me so they could do a kind of retroactive C-section. Finally, there was a lot of tearing, there was hemorrhaging, and there was me—this part I don't remember—jumping off the table once the baby was finally out and screaming at them all to just let me die now. There was a shot of Demerol and then blackness, then waking eight hours later to unutterable pain. There were months of discomfort that followed, longer than my friends who had C-sections experienced. If that was nature, I never wanted to experience anything natural again.

And there were other factors to consider, small medical details to do with size and position and my own health that the doctor told me to think about. He assured me the boy was full-term, ready to come out. We booked an appointment for a Monday.

A few days before the birth, I had my toenails polished. I had my legs waxed. There is a picture of me in front of the hospital, about to go inside, looking very relaxed, laughing, with my small suitcase. Inside, they hooked me up to the Pitocin and I spent most of the four-hour labor reading trashy magazines and chatting to my husband. When it came time to push, I'd already had the epidural. I didn't feel a thing.

The doctor and I were determined to make it the opposite of the first birth, which had been a bloody, drug-free mess. We succeeded. It was about as painless and sterile a birth experience as I could have imagined.

But the moment that second baby slid out of me, I was filled with regret. I feared he wasn't ready. His cry sliced through me. When they placed him on top of me, his body felt so hot, almost scalding. I brought him to my breast and felt a moment of panic as I gazed wildly around the bright, cold room. *Put him back in. Listen to that cry. He's not ready.* But it was too late.

If the birth was easy, everything in his first months of life was difficult. As a baby, he was allergic to everything. The air, the sheets, the soap—everything left him red and splotchy. He seemed to be allergic to my breast milk itself. At ten months, he tested officially allergic to about ten common foods, including eggs, nuts, soy, and wheat.

He cried a lot the first six months. Eczema covered him from head to toe. He scratched himself bloody. The allergies left him weary, listless. We struggled through it. I took him to acupuncturists, homeopaths, osteopaths, witch doctors and regular doctors. I lived in a state of panic those first two years. But as my hair fell out in handfuls, he slowly grew stronger. His allergies became fewer and less acute. His skin healed. He woke up from his daze of discomfort and looked around, alert. I felt as if we were meeting for the first time.

Today, at four, he is honey-colored, with wild brown curls that pop out of his head like a hundred question marks. He is beautiful, loquacious, outgoing, the kid who charms strangers with his crooked smile and hilarious one-liners on the city bus.

But with me, and only me, lately, he insists on both of us living by his rules and rituals. They are rituals that force us to slow down, rituals that make us late.

And in my mother mind, it is as if he is reenacting that day, that medicalized, drugged-up, too-soon birth, trying to make me repeat and repeat the rituals, to get it right this time, trying to turn us into one person, not two, to return to the state we were in before we were so rudely interrupted. It's as if he's telling me, "You rushed me once, but you won't rush me again."

If you believe in the law of cause and effect, you will believe that the story of your birth holds within it the story of the life that follows. You will believe that the day you were born—how you were born, under what circumstances—echoes throughout your entire life.

But there is so much that remains a mystery about that day, for all of us. You can't remember your own birthday, so the facts you glean about it are always and already a myth, constructed by your parents or those who were there, clouded even for them by time and distance and subjectivity.

The newborn you once were becomes, retrospectively, a site of projection upon which the parents lay their own fears and fantasies, their guilt and their desires.

There are five details I know about my own birth:

There was a thunderstorm in Boston that night. My mother was at a party when the labor began, drinking something called Champale. I was born at the stroke of midnight. I had a mop of straight black hair on my head and dark downy fur on my body. My father says when he saw me, I looked like a monkey, not a baby.

I read into these five details truths about the people and relationships that will follow. My mother appears in this scene as she will always be in my mind: the life of the party, festive, tipsy, surrounded by poets and artists, undeterred from living by the fact of her female body. The storm outside that night reverberates into my future: To this day, bad weather—the sound of rain beating against my window—soothes my nerves. My father's comment that I looked like a monkey hints at his ironic distance, the crux of our relationship ever since. The claim that I was born at "the stroke of midnight" suggests a border time, the moment when one day ends and the next day begins, suggesting the person I will become—my own eternal betweenness—my lifelong state of ambivalence.

There are surely half-truths in this narrative, exaggerations and glaring omissions. But I am aware only of these five facts, and so they are the ones I attach meaning to, the ones I read into for the source of my present identity.

I will always feel remorse for having pushed my second out of me early—for inducing labor before my body clock was ready. Over the years, I have harbored resentment toward that funny, hip doctor who encouraged me to do it, who told me it would be fine, that the baby was ready. But the truth is, it was my decision, too. I didn't want to have another trauma like the first. I wanted the second one to be light and easy. I didn't want to feel too much.

The moment he left me, I felt it was too soon. That's the piece of the story I tend to remember. I leave out the other pieces of the story: the fact that he was already eight pounds; the fact that I nursed him immediately and easily; the fact that I adored him immediately and easily; the fact that his father and I hovered over him and doted on him from that moment forth.

And this, too: the fact that both boys—the first one, whose birth felt all too natural, and the second one, whose birth felt not natural enough—came into me with so much about them that was already distinct. In utero, my second thrashed about less violently, seemed quieter and more mysterious. In utero, they were already who they planned to be.

And so maybe the full answer lies not in medicine, either. Maybe my second child is trying to tell me something when he insists he was alive before he was born, when he insists he has memories of a past life, of being a baby called Oui. Maybe he's onto something when he says I made a mistake by giving him a name at birth, because he already had one. Could he be telling me, in his own peculiar, four-year-old, wise-child way, that when it comes to him, I don't have all the power, nor do I bear all the responsibility? I like to think I was the first person to leave my mark on him. But maybe there are other factors, more mysterious factors, call them DNA or karma, that are playing out in his psyche. Perhaps there are mysteries about his soul—about all of our souls—that cannot be explained by a mother's guilt or science or religion or birth narratives, and so we have to just accept them.

All I can try to affect is the aftermath—the place where we begin today. For too long, I have been indulging his rituals, entering into his magical thinking, because it is mine, too. What I sense is his grief is actually my own. Perhaps I am the one who was not ready to give birth on that day. Perhaps I am the one who felt prematurely separated. I keep trying to get it right, to make up for the moment that has long since passed, when *we* split violently into two—a him and a me—two entities. But I know I must stop.

He is already stopping. The same way that his skin healed and his body adjusted to the environment around him when he was a baby, his insistence on the rituals is fading, too, as children's mercurial habits tend to do. I can see that soon this phase will end. But for now, at six in the morning, in as calm and loving a voice as I can muster at that hour, when he's insisting I've made an error—flushed the toilet all wrong, or placed his cereal down in the wrong spot, or interrupted him before he could finish his sentence with those five magic words, *for real and not pretend*—in that moment of our mutual terror, it is up to me to pull him close and tell him what I know I'm also telling myself. "No repetitions, baby boy. We already did that. We can't go back and do it all over again. Let's try something else now. Let's do something fun. Shall we?"

The Tigers in the Room

ARIELLE GREENBERG

During my first pregnancy, my husband and I took a Birthing from Within class with a teacher who was still in training. One exercise she gave us was called "The Tiger in the Room": Think of your worst fear about childbirth, the mental tiger in your birthing room, and paint a picture of it as a way of facing it head-on.

The fear that sprang to mind instantly for me was one I'd been obsessing about during my last trimester. It is, possibly, the greatest fear of all: a dead baby. I had no reason to think I was going to have a stillborn baby—my pregnancy had been totally normal and healthy and smooth, and I was largely confident about the whole process—but it's where I put all my free-floating, first-time-mom anxiety. "Our baby could die for no reason," I'd tell my husband urgently at night as we lay in bed, about to fall asleep. "It happens. It could just die."

So when we went around the room of the Birthing from Within class declaring our tigers, I voiced this fear out loud to the group. "Stillbirth," I said . . . and was met with shocked silence. When she regained her voice, the teacher told me I *couldn't* name stillbirth as my tiger, maybe because she didn't know how to deal with it, hadn't been trained in how to talk about death as part of a childbirth class. Sure, it was an exercise about fear, but she didn't want to go *there*, not with a roomful of pregnant women and their partners.

"Okay, fine," I said, feeling put in my place, "I'll pick my second-biggest fear: a long labor." A *three-day* labor, I announced. *That's* scary. How could I *possibly* handle a labor *that* long? During the visual art part of the exercise, I painted my idea of that unimaginable challenge with watercolors—a shimmering blue arc representing an impossibly long stretch of time that would take everything I had.

If you are someone who, like me, occasionally and grudgingly believes in woo-woo stuff, then maybe you will agree that there is something about a pregnant woman's ability to tap into her psychic nature. What I painted and what I spoke turned out to be uncannily accurate clues toward my first two birth stories.

I love and take pride in my first two birth stories, each in their own way. Neither was what you might call an ideal or smooth birth. They are not particularly encouraging or inspiring stories, but they are stories of endurance, of exorcising fears: first a difficult birth, then a tragic birth. They were dramatic, powerful: Both, in fact, involve felonies.

But each, of course, resulted in a child I hold dear, and was life-changing for me.

Here's the gist of my first birth, with its satisfying kind of shock value: You know that nightmare of a three-day labor I painted? Well, I had a *five-day* labor. Yup, a five-day labor. My water broke on a Friday evening, and the baby came on Wednesday morning. At home, no drugs, no medical intervention, just me and my fantastic reservoir of stamina and endurance. Motivated by an excellent support team, fear of the hospital, and sheer determination, I kicked ass at labor, as one of my midwife's apprentices later told me. I feel like I could write a boastful hip-hop song about my first labor, if I wrote hip-hop songs.

In many ways, my first birth also fits the bill for the kind of hippie-dippy, gauzy experience one often imagines when one hears the words *home birth*. There were glowing candles. There was hushed, reverential darkness. There was Reiki and massage and essential oils and someone running around opening all the drawers in the house to "cleanse the space." There was take-out Thai food and tribal dancing. There was a house full of beautiful, wise midwives and doulas with nose rings and tattoos. There was a birthing tub and a sunrise.

But my first birth story also includes its share of difficulty: For starters, there were those five grueling days of not knowing what was going on, of labor failing to build into any kind of regular pattern or rhythm. There was the fact that the baby's position made it so that I couldn't pee, and since I was being constantly hydrated to keep my strength up, I had to be catheterized five times, each more excruciating than the pain of labor itself. There were the moments when I felt all my resources and energy leave my body, when I wept with frustration and fatigue. There was the "directed pushing" I did at the end: hours of work trying to force the baby out through sheer will and physicality, even though I wasn't feeling the urge to push and my contractions were still, after five days, not strong or close enough together to bring the baby out on their own.

And, oh, yes—that felony. Did I mention that our beloved and highly skilled midwife, emcee for the whole wild event, was illegally practicing, due to punishing laws against direct-entry midwives in the state of Illinois? So besides the endurance and weeping and beauty, my first birth is also the story of criminal activity. But the baby born of all that—my oldest, my daughter—came into the world a stunningly beautiful, serene, alert, healthy baby girl.

But maybe you can also guess what I'm about to tell you about my second birth. Because it turns out I was unerringly on target with my tigers.

My second baby died in utero at thirty-one weeks.

If you are like most people, the first question you have is, Why? And the answer is, I don't know. No one knows. As I'd told my husband while lying in bed those nights late in my first pregnancy, sometimes it just happens. Babies die at all stages of pregnancy and birth.

As with my first, my second pregnancy had been normal. This time, we'd even had an ultrasound at twenty-two weeks, which showed a robust baby boy kicking away in the womb. He was a strong kicker, an early kicker . . . and then he stopped kicking. I didn't even notice it right away—there was no event, no trauma, no sudden shriek in my throat or stab in my heart. I just sort of noticed that I wasn't feeling movement, and then I realized that I wasn't feeling *any* movement, and then I didn't really feel pregnant anymore at all—my gait felt lightened; my hunger subsided—and I knew my baby boy was dead.

To avoid another felony by being attended by a midwife who was illegal in our state, and because all the midwives we liked had left the state to avoid persecution by then anyway, we'd already made a plan to travel to Maine to have this baby there, attended by midwives we'd interviewed while on our summer vacation. We had a cute little rental house by the harbor, and plans to hunker down for the winter and wait for our baby to come, so we could wrap him in blankets and cuddle him night and day. We had just started to pack for the trip when the baby died.

We could have stayed in Illinois. I could have done what the vast majority of people do when they find out their baby will be stillborn: I could have checked into a hospital, been induced, and had our baby as quickly as possible.

But I didn't want to do that. I wanted a home birth again. After my first birth, which would have surely ended in an unnecessary cesarean had we been in the hospital (hospital policies usually don't allow a mother to labor for days on end after her water breaks), I was a card-carrying home birther. And I knew that at the end of this birth, I was not going to have a baby to cuddle and nurse and tuck into bed next to me. I was going to have a funeral home, and a burial. The only potentially *good* part of this birth—the only part that felt like it could be possibly beautiful to me—was the birth itself. To face the grief, I wanted a birth that felt sane, and intimate, and loving, and private. I wanted another home birth.

So we finished the packing job we'd started with a very different kind of trip in mind. We took a last-minute cross-country flight between two snowstorms, thereby commiting another felony: I found out later that by making this trip, I'd inadvertently done something illegal by transporting a dead body across state lines without a permit.

But we made it to Maine, to the little house by the harbor. We settled in with our two-year-old daughter to wait for our baby to be born. And waited. And waited.

It took two and a half weeks from the time we found out our son had died until the day he was born. Eighteen of the hardest, most profound, most incredible days I have ever spent. Eighteen days that ended with a smooth, quick labor marked by deep, deep mourning and also incandescent love and support from everyone around me, fearless and generous midwives and doulas and my loving husband. Eighteen days after which our sweet and brilliant daughter, two and a half, got to hold and coo at her brother after he was born as if he were the live sibling she'd hoped for, and then told her own version of the story to anyone who would listen: "My baby died. He stopped swimming. We are sad. But we'll have another one."

She was right. A year later, much to my own surprise, I was back in Maine again, entering my third trimester for the third time around. It was another healthy pregnancy, but this time, I felt haunted. Had I gotten all that hard stuff "out of the way"? My two ferocious tigers had been faced, wrestled; I'd encountered and made peace with my very worst birth fears. Would I have a clear path toward a third birth, one that could be *easy*? What I wanted most was a birth that was downright boring: uneventful, straightforward labor with a plain old healthy baby at the end.

Thank the universe, I got it.

I was thirty-seven and a half weeks pregnant. My husband, mother-in-law, now four-year-old daughter, and I went out for a delicious dinner at a restaurant in the small downtown a few blocks from where we were renting a home. It was a beautiful April night, and we started our leisurely walk home, the sun setting on the ocean just blocks away. As we passed the public library, I felt something sudden and wet between my legs. "Oh," I said, surprised, delighted. "I think my water broke." We walked the rest of the way home, my water breaking in little gushes.

We called the midwives. They were out eating fish fry. "We'll go home and go to bed," they said. We put our daughter to sleep and sent my mother-in-law back to her hotel. We ordered an infant car seat online (we weren't expecting the baby for two more weeks, and we hadn't gotten around to that yet). We went to bed. My husband fell asleep and I lay awake, waiting to feel labor kick in. I felt utterly, utterly calm and utterly, utterly thrilled all at once.

(Is there anything as delicious as spending those first hours in early labor, knowing a baby and a beautiful birth is on its way but not knowing a thing about it all yet? I wish I could feel that exact brand of anticipation every year.)

By midnight, I started having contractions. Easy contractions. I lay in bed and sort of half-noticed them, trying to figure out whether it was worth waking my husband. After a half hour or so, when it was clear that the contractions were regular and definite, I woke him, and we sat up in bed reading magazines in the dim light. Every so often I'd say calmly, "Here's another contraction," and stare placidly into space while the contraction happened, and my husband would write the time down in the margin of the article he was reading. "Okay, it's over now," I'd say, and we'd both go back to reading.

Eventually, we called the midwives. Eventually, they came. (By now it was about 3:30 a.m.) My husband was having trouble getting the birth tub set up, so one of the midwives helped him while another boiled water. When the contractions came, stronger now, I picked a midwife, doula, or husband to lean on, and made the deep moaning sounds now familiar to me from my previous two births. Then the contraction would subside and we'd all go back to chatting about the weather or someone we all knew in common. I remember one of the midwives telling a story about how she pissed off a client by clipping her nails during a labor.

We kept joking around, quietly. The baby kept kicking. The contractions kept coming. At about 5:00 a.m., the tub was finally ready and full and warm, and I got in and relaxed into the water. My whole body eased and then geared up again for harder work: the contractions coming closer together and becoming more and more difficult. *Gosh*, I remember thinking, *these are hard. I don't know if I can do this for two or three more days like I did with the first.*

But there was no need for that. One of the midwives was already getting the little newborn warming cap ready. Rosy daylight was coming in across the harbor through the windows by my birthing tub when, with one or two high-pitched screams and calls of "*I love you*," I pushed my son into the world. He came in with the dawn. He needed a little suctioning and a back rub to get him going—a couple weeks early, he was purple-tinged and slow to breathe at first—but he was also sturdy and a good size for a thirty-seven-and-a-half-week baby, almost seven pounds, and he seemed fully of this world. He met his sister, who woke up just in time to welcome him and cut his cord.

Spring birds chirped outside. My baby was alive and well. Our whole family cuddled in bed and I took pictures of our daughter with her new brother. The midwives cleaned everything up and went home. I got up and made pancakes for my family.

That's the story. It has no tigers.

Writing this now, on my third child's second birthday, I want to weep with gratitude for the plainness, the simplicity of it.

My first two birth stories *made* me. They are the experiences that have most deeply shaped every choice I've made, every path I've taken since. My third birth story is the least complicated, the least interesting, and the least told.

Last month, I gave an interview to Nora, a woman who is doing an oral history project of birth narratives. "Which birth story do you want?" I asked. "I have two exciting stories and one boring one."

"I want them all," she said.

So I told them all. I told the politically intriguing, complicated details of our underground, epic first birth, and Nora was on the edge of her seat. The telling took about two hours. I told the sorrowful story of our stillbirth, and Nora and I both wept. This story took two more hours to tell. And then I told the quick, painless story of our third baby's birth. It didn't take very long at all.

A day or two later, I got an e-mail from Nora. "My digital recorder conked out during the last twenty minutes of our interview," she apologized. "I lost the story of your last son's birth. We should get together and redo it." But it hasn't happened.

Part of me really wants to make sure this story, the story of my precious son, my third baby, is recorded, in all its boring glory. Part of me thinks that perhaps, because it's the simplest story, the least dramatic story, the story with no surprises and no tragedies and no felonies and no tigers, it's also a story I don't *need* to tell. And the not needing fills its own kind of need.

The Second Time Around

should have known better than to make any plans. Five years
before, when, after much tragedy and turmoil, I gave birth to
my first child, I had embraced the uncertainties. In the wake of
prolonged sadness and anxiety, sudden joy begets humility, wonder, and a giddy surrender to everything from the fury of a record-
breakingly blizzardous winter to the rabbit-hole vagaries of modern
medical bureaucracy.

I gave birth to my first child, Alec, precisely eight weeks before
I turned forty (no party, no sleep, and not much champagne—but
hands down the best birthday of my life). In the four years preced-
ing, I had endured a divorce, treatment for a nasty form of breast
cancer, the suicide of my only sibling, and (on the worst birthday
of my life) a miscarriage. There are no nouns or modifiers adequate
to the task of expressing the elation I felt when that baby was placed
in my arms; maybe *glory* comes close. Let the future throw at me
whatever it would: I had beaten back the dark. I knew—boy did I
ever—about the hazards of making long-term plans.

Considering my age, Alec was likely to be my only child; that
was fine. But by the time he was two, my good health holding steady, my work as a writer blossoming, I found myself missing
Carolyn more than ever—not just as my charming, risk-taking,

world-traveling sister but as the colorful aunt she would have been. And I longed for Alec to have a sibling. It was obvious even to me that I suffered from a case of covert magical thinking: that turning my son into a brother might restore to me vicarious sibling-ship. But now that I'd become a citizen of my neighborhood playground, I was also surrounded by pregnancies, nursing infants, and, among the forty-somethings, feverish talk of bucking fertility rates. New Yorkers, especially the mothers among them, don't take no for an answer. (Nor did it help that Alec's father, Dennis, had *five* siblings.)

Two years and three miscarriages later, I found myself halfway through a normal, if sternly monitored, pregnancy. As one of my too many doctors put it when he gave me the amnio results, the plane was off the ground. My cancer was seven years in the past, I had an agent eager to sell my first novel, Alec was thriving in pre-school, Y2K had just launched without global catastrophe, and it was—auspiciously, if you give credence to such things—the year of the dragon. (*The New York Times* ran an article that year about how the sudden spike in pregnancies among Chinese Americans, coupled with an apparent rise in fertility due to the widespread desire for "millennium babies," threatened to overwhelm local maternity wards.)

This time, I'm afraid I was a lot less humble about my good fortune. As December 20, my due date, approached, I started making plans.

Perhaps the only uncertainty I did not challenge was the baby's gender: Boy or girl, I would be happy. I had no hunches, and the classic superstitions had been debunked my first time around. Only if Alec had expressed a preference would I have asked to know, but he professed equal excitement at the prospect of a brother or a sister. "I wish we could be twins!" he would exclaim, pressing himself against my widening torso. (And "Will the baby shoot out like a rocket?" To which I'd laugh, quietly wishing, From your lips to God's ears.) Each time my doctor saw me, he would glance at my chart and ask if I was really sure I wanted him to withhold that information. Yes, I insisted. I honestly didn't want to know.

But here's what I blithely believed I already *did* know:

1. Second babies come earlier, right? So I could reasonably expect my water to break (as dramatically as it had the first time) about a week before Christmas. The worst of the household disruption would be over by the holiday itself, which would be, for Alec's sake, everything an almost-five-year-old could want. Tree decorating, caroling, cookie baking, new toys, and the ultimate gift: a sibling. I would be up and about, tired and tender but fully mobile. (By the time Alec was about a week old, I had learned to work at my keyboard, single-handed, while nursing him in my lap.)

2. I would have not only a millennial Dragon baby but a Sagittarius. I regard astrology as destiny the way some people regard baptism as passport: Empirically, it's nonsense, but who really knows? All things being equal, Sagittarius is a much more compatible sign with mine than Capricorn. My Sagittarius friends were intrepid, bighearted, and made me laugh.

3. There would be timely help. I'd ask my parents to come down from Massachusetts around mid-December. Alec's preschool Christmas party was to be held on the morning of Friday, December 22. His school was only a block from our apartment; maybe I could even make an appearance in the classroom, leaving the baby at home for half an hour.

4. This time, I would have no epidural—not that I'd had one for long the first time. Due to an error by an inattentive resident, I labored for several hours under the mistaken notion that my cervix wasn't up to speed. It turned out that I was close to fully dilated by the time they hooked me up. Looking back, I was certain I could have done it without drugs after all.

5. Boy or girl, this baby would be entirely different from Alec. I couldn't wait for the surprise of a child with a brand-new face, a wholly unexpected reconfiguration of genes.
6. I'd have no trouble nursing the baby. After all, I had quickly become a pro the first time around.

That December, I was busy and mobile: I worked on a magazine article about newborn babies' brains; I undertook a project to reorganize the library of Alec's preschool; I dressed up (as best I could) to meet with an editor who might—and eventually did—buy my novel; I painted a new bookcase, went to holiday parties, walked miles on impending-baby errands. Dennis and I bought a Christmas tree at a farmers' market and, together, lugged it several blocks back to our small apartment.

One day, Christmas a scant week away, I took the subway downtown to hear a lunchtime concert of the *Messiah*. Anytime, I silently encouraged this child as it reveled in the choral drama. Anytime you're ready, so am I.

Meanwhile, my parents arrived. They sublet an apartment near ours. At the checkup three days before my due date, Dr. A performed an ultrasound. He told me that I wasn't dilating much and that I was low on fluid.

Was I at the auto mechanic or the obstetrician?

"Low?" I said. "How?"

Apparently, I had what the auto mechanic might have termed a slow leak. "Maybe you've been too busy to notice," suggested Dr. A.

"But that means the baby's about to be born. Yes?"

"Doesn't look like it," he said. "We may want to induce."

"Induce?" He might as well have said, "We may want to elope." Not that I hadn't heard stories from friends who'd gone that route. I prevaricated. "The baby is going to arrive when it wants to. Isn't that best?"

Not if I continued to lose fluid, said Dr. A. And also—he

looked at his calendar—not if it chose to arrive on Christmas Day. Personally, he didn't care; he was Jewish. But he happened to know that nurses who worked on Christmas—and he said this with a hint of glee—tended toward grumpy.

And just as *The New York Times* had promised, there was quite a bottleneck of births as the coveted birth year circled the drain. My hospital's maternity ward was operating at full capacity and beyond.

"If we induce you," said Dr. A, "look at it this way. You'll have a reservation."

"What, like it's a hotel? Like otherwise I'd have this baby in the hall?"

"It's happened." His smile doubled as a grimace. "Let's see what's up in a couple of days," said Dr. A. In other words, we'd see what was *down*—like the baby's head. "I recommend walking."

He set a deadline, reserving me a birth room for December 21. He would come on duty the following day at noon, so—since I'd only just met his new partner, Dr. B—he strategized a schedule of induction (was I joining the marines?) so that he would almost certainly deliver the baby, sometime late on the afternoon of December 22.

I hoped this strategy would be pointless. I'd heard about Pitocin, and I didn't want it.

"What you don't want," said Dr. A, "is for the baby to dry out."

Gravity was my new best friend. I walked and walked and walked some more. The weather was rainy and raw, the city sidewalks gridlocked with shoppers. Like a squirrel storing nuts, Dennis worked frantically at his freelance jobs; my parents lurked around our apartment, reading, tapping their toes, offering to help. But I was prepared. I was too prepared. I *wanted* to shop, cook, do laundry; tasks kept me vertical and moving.

My due date came and went. The afternoon of the twenty-first, I was a perambulating fiend. I mapped a human crossword puzzle along the streets of our neighborhood, the West Village, and finally, when the sun went down, when my extremities went numb, took refuge in the vast, overheated Strand Bookstore. Systematically, I cruised every aisle. Never mind that the place was crammed with shoppers who, by now, were fierce as Navy SEALs. I had, unlike my normal self, done all my Christmas shopping weeks before. But I shopped anyway. I bought booklets of themed wrapping paper: Japanese kimonos, William Morris textiles, American quilts, Walt Disney movies. I was losing my mind.

Dennis, my parents, and I had dinner that evening at an Italian restaurant. I was tempted to eat standing. Or jumping up and down. But still no signs of labor.

Defeated, I checked in to the hospital at 11:00 p.m., as scheduled, and was escorted to my room, where I changed into the universally unflattering, unwarm, ungainly hospital frock. "Now get some sleep," the nurse said, tucking me in. "Someone will be back to get you started around six."

Could they turn off the lights? How about the intercom (which hovered ominously near the head of my bed)?

"Oh, no," said the nurse. "Those things are centrally controlled."

I looked around at the mauve wallpaper, the window with its glittering vista of Central Park at midnight. I closed my eyes. Never mind that I'm not terribly good at getting to sleep in the best of circumstances; my mental accelerator tends to get stuck at the end of the day. Ten minutes later, the intercom crackled to life with a dual sound track: against a background of moaning, the crisply enunciated order "Anesthesiologist to birth room five. Anesthesiologist to birth room five." Followed by abrupt silence.

Fifteen minutes later, ditto. Like a chorus punctuating some avant-garde performance piece, variations on a theme, these gunbursts of aural distress jarred me increasingly awake, until I gave up and looked for the book I'd packed.

Who had I been kidding? Read? *Read?* I went to the window and searched in vain for signs of dawn.

A new nurse came in at six. "Awake? You're awake?" she scolded. "You were supposed to sleep!"

How could I, with a constant broadcast of my near and none-too-comfortable future?

She examined me. Baby not budging. "Okay," she announced. "Here we go." She flicked at the veins in the back of my hand. Drug one would prime me for the Pitocin. "This'll take a few hours." She looked at me sternly. "Rest."

Alone again, some crafty chemical seeping through my veins, I noticed that it had begun to snow. It was still sunny, but snowing. The view from my birth room was about as deluxe as any view you could get in the best Manhattan hotel.

Almost simultaneously, Dr. B, my friend Laura, and my designated maternity nurse—I'll call her Vera—arrived. (Dennis was with Alec at his school Christmas party and would arrive for the main event.) Dr. B, a large taciturn fellow, gazed out the window and declared, "God, I hate snow."

"You hate snow?" I said, unbelieving.

"Shoveling. It means shoveling. I hate shoveling." When he wasn't looking, Laura and I exchanged smirks. I was glad this curmudgeon wouldn't be the one to deliver this child.

Dr. B examined me (still no action) and left. Vera, a warm, chatty woman, took out her tools—pressure cuff, thermometer, oximeter—and did her busywork. She made maternity small talk. She told us that she came from Trinidad and had several grown children, grandchildren galore; she knew all about babies! This was only my second?

"Second and last. I'm forty-four."

"Oh heavens! You're a youngster by our standards here. You're good for at least one more, maybe twins!" She perused the folder Dr. B had left.

"And by the way," I said, "I don't want to know the gender. I want it to be a surprise."

She nodded and gave me a curious smile. "I don't need your chart to tell me that. I always know. I knew when I came in the room."

"No epidural this time, either."

"Well, honey, stay open-minded on that, will you?"

At about ten, Vera reentered the room with an aura of purpose. "Let's get this party started, shall we?" It was time for cocktails: mine Pitocin, rumored to be the Long Island iced tea of childbirth.

Within an hour, I knew the rumors were true. I remembered the contractions from baby one, and these contractions were not the same. Not one bit. They came on like jackhammers. I was a construction site.

Was I open-minded? I sure was. Did this make me a wimp? Who cared?

"Yes?" said Vera.

"Yes," I gasped.

She leaned toward the intercom. "Anesthesiologist to birth room twelve."

Almost instantly, an anesthesiologist showed up with his paraphernalia. I sat on the edge of the bed, preparing for the oddly intimate embrace with a stranger that getting an epidural entails. That's when I mentioned the pressure. The actually rather intense pressure. Intensely, urgently *extreme* pressure.

"Where?" asked the anesthesiologist.

Under less strenuous circumstances, I might have said, "In my left elbow, knucklehead." I whispered, "Where the baby is planning to come out. I hope."

Vera shouldered the doctor aside and asked me to lie down. The shock on her face, framed by my tented legs, was almost funny.

"Good grief!" she exclaimed. "Here she comes! She's coming *now*!"

I suppose it's absurd to let on how distressed I was by that "she," even in the midst of the hubbub that followed: Dr. B summoned loudly via intercom, excess furniture shoved aside, shiny utensils assembled, my friend Laura summarily ordered to stand back.

"Call Dennis," I told her.

It was shortly after 11:00 a.m. Dennis would still be at Alec's party, one hundred city blocks south of me and our soon-to-be daughter. At lunchtime on the last shopping weekday before Christmas, in Manhattan, in the falling snow. Later, I would hear about his comic attempt to get a cabdriver to "step on it" as they sat in stalled traffic on Fourteenth Street (a mere ninety-eight blocks to go). "Your wife's having a baby? I recommend the subway," the driver told him—whereupon Dennis sprinted to the nearest express stop.

Dr. B came into the room, looking startled. He, too, had a look at the view between my legs. He, too, said something along the lines of "Good grief!"

"You're going to start pushing," he said, "now." He pulled up his mask.

"She's in a hurry, this baby!" said Vera, grinning broadly. "This is a baby on a mission!"

A daughter, I thought, an arrow passing through the pain. Wow, I'm having a *daughter*. Had I known it all along? I pictured, briefly, a little girl. We walked down an imaginary street, holding hands.

I will always remember the long, hard push toward having my son Alec. We had flirted with the notion of a C-section, though Dr. A had been patient (which was why I wanted him with me again). But the second time around? What I remember is the burlesque rush of it all. Hardly had Dr. B pulled on his mask than he was ushering my second child into the snowy luminescence of that room overlooking the park.

One last time, Vera exulted, "Here she is!" And out she slid.

"It's a boy," said Dr. B. "You have another son. Congratulations."

Vera smiled, unruffled. Dr. B made no comment on the alarming contradiction. Together, they performed the duet of the Apgar, the rituals of cleaning up. Vera hustled her tools together, wished me luck, and left to find her next patient. I never saw her again.

The baby I held in my arms was, as it turned out, virtually the same weight as his brother at birth. He looked a bit like a lobster—his skin red and dessicated, thanks to my "slow leak"—but he was all there (and yes—I had to triple-check—he was a he). But aside from that, unless my memory was deceiving me, he looked exactly like his older brother as a newborn. *Exactly.*

I kept this observation to myself but verified it in baby photos once I got home. (Not only had Alec been prescient about this birth as—once it finally happened—a Canaveral-style launch but his repeated wish that he and this baby be twins seemed to be coming true, as well.)

A few minutes later, Dr. A showed up, still in his coat. "Wow, that was fast," he said. "You didn't need me after all, did you?" At almost the same time, in barged Dennis, dripping with sweat, erupting in tears.

Dennis would tell me later how he burst from the hospital elevator and said to the nurse at the reception desk, "I'm having a baby!" only to have her check the board, turn back to him quite slowly, and pause before announcing, "Mister, you *had* a baby." Her expression, according to Dennis, was pure accusation. What kind of modern dad shows up *after* the birth?

Oliver—a name arrived at more swiftly than his older brother's—was perfectly healthy, and we returned home together on the evening of Saturday, December 23. Was it easy to nurse him? Decidedly not. Was I up and about, supermom on skates? Hardly. Was Alec thrilled at his "ultimate Christmas gift"? For about three hours. His first glimpse of Oliver's umbilical knot so disturbed him that he backed away, declaring conclusively, "Ick."

All too soon, my parents left. Winter grew colder; more snow arrived. Our small apartment seemed to grow even smaller. Oliver learned to nurse without biting me. The year came to an end.

In January, Alec turned five. He came to realize that a baby in the family gave him cachet, at least with his female classmates. Grudgingly, he could be coaxed to pose for photos with the tiny monster; if I tickled him, he had no choice but to smile. Having just learned to read aloud, Alec looked for every opportunity to show off his talent. One day, he discovered that, in his little brother, he had a captive audience. A truce was achieved. As the Dragon gave way to the Snake, the four of us found a new rhythm.

That was twelve and a half years ago. We've moved to another state; we live in a house. My boys have grown—continue to grow— into very distinctive people. But if I look back at pictures taken within a few months of their respective births, I can tell them apart only by context. And every year when Oliver's birthday arrives, he loves to tell the story of his birth. He recounts how the cabdriver and the woman at the maternity desk made his father feel completely foolish; how he "shot out like a rocket!"; how he looked like a lobster; how he was the best Christmas gift ever. ("Right, Alec?" he'll rib his brother. Alec rolls his eyes.) But the best part, his favorite, is how he was almost a girl. He puts on a pompous falsetto and says, "Here she comes . . . Here she comes . . . HERE . . . SHE . . . COMES . . . It's a boy!" He cracks up.

"Are you sure you're not a girl?" I tease him, the Capricorn son with whom I am utterly simpatico (and who happens to be, all stars aside, intrepid, bighearted, and funny).

I love that story, too, because it reminds me of everything I wish I could control in my life—and can't stop trying to control. It reminds me that experts aren't always right, that it's not a tragedy when fathers miss the big moment, that sometimes plans gone awry lead to better memories.

"Just be in the *I don't know*," a friend of mine used to scold me. I've never been good at that kind of calm, and parenthood makes it infinitely harder. But I've come to regard the story of Oliver's birth as a treasured fable, one that we dust off yearly, right alongside "The Night Before Christmas"—one that gives us delicious pause about the never-ending surprises, the good ones, in store for all of us.

The Waiting Room

JENNIFER GILMORE

While Kevin watched *World Wide Wrestling*, Mary Jane waited for the inducing meds to work. She asked him to change the channel, but he ignored her.

She had called us that morning, and my spouse and I, our packed suitcase ready, made the drive to Pennsylvania from New York City to pick her up at the trailer she shared with Kevin and her brother and sister-in-law and their children and several dogs they kept chained to three-legged couches. We were frantic to make it there in time, to be there for the birth. This, we were told, was one of the wonders of open adoption. In an open adoption, the baby will often be the adoptive parents' child from birth. We could even be in the delivery room, a moment that we had thought would be lost to us. And that day, we were told we'd be able to stay in the hospital if there was a room. On the highway, I imagined the three of us, me in a hospital bed, propped up by pillows, this swaddled baby boy in my arms, my husband leaning over us, stroking the baby's head: our family. Mary Jane, the twenty-year-old birth mother, who had already placed one child up for adoption when she was sixteen, and her abusive boyfriend, Kevin, were not included in the image at all.

Nothing about this path to parenthood was what we expected: first the inability to get pregnant, then the pregnancy, the miscarriage, the financially and physically punishing rounds of IVF, the long, labyrinthine road of domestic adoption.

Domestic adoption is open in roughly 55 percent of cases. Open means the perspective adoptive parents have a relationship to some degree with the birth mother and often the birth father, so the child can know them as she grows. In theory, this eliminates the fantasy so many children of closed adoptions have: Their birth parents can be anyone, and some adoptees spend their lives imagining their alternative lives. With open adoption, there is transparency. The child's background can be celebrated and she will not have to make the life-changing decision to search out, or not search out, her biological parents.

In the delivery room, I watched men hold other men over their heads, throwing them into the ropes. It was Sunday night. *Mad Men* was also on, if we were going to watch television, but I didn't say this. I told the nurse that my husband—outside in the waiting room—and I were the adoptive parents. When Mary Jane was in the bathroom and Kevin, well aware that he might not be the father of this child, had to go to the vending machines in the lobby, I told the nurse it could be one father or another, that we didn't know. Mary Jane had told me it could be Kevin's or it could be Hector's, a man she had loved when Kevin had gone to jail for domestic violence; the police record of him punching her in the face before the cops came was the only item that came up when I Googled Mary Jane. Hector, though, had left the country for Mexico and would not be allowed in again. Because she said Hector had no interest in her or the baby, and because Kevin would perhaps want to keep his own child, we hoped Hector was the birth father.

The nurse nodded. I'm glad you told me, she said. Hispanic

children, they often look light. African American newborns, too. They take a while to darken up. What gives it away are the balls.

The balls? I admit it was not what I expected her to say.

Yes, it's foolproof. The balls tell you the race before anything else.

As the drugs took effect, Mary Jane began to moan, and I went to hold her hand. Without turning off the television, Kevin held her other hand, and the nurse said, "This is going to be quick." She called the doctor from the intercom by the door.

I don't remember the doctor. But the nurse guided me by the elbow and had me sit by her. Look, she said. A head was emerging, splitting Mary Jane in two. And suddenly—this is how I remember it, as sudden and surprising as a mugging, a summer downpour—the baby slipped out, grayish blue, slick as a seal, his scalp ringed by a crown of dark brown hair. The sound of men screaming and grunting played loudly from the television.

Quick! The nurse rushed me over. Take a picture! Quick, she said, her hands wrapped in see-through blue gloves, bringing me closer. A video! She grabbed my phone. Cut the umbilical cord!

It was all so fast. I had not been prepared. I had no idea what my role here was. I looked up at Mary Jane, whose head was lolling from one side to the other and took what—scissors?—the nurse handed me. I snipped then. That was all. The smallest cut and I severed the boy from his mother. Another nurse picked him up and slathered his eyes with bacterial ointment and took him, screaming, wriggling, to be weighed. I went over to the baby and watched him come to life, color emerging like a photograph in a dark room.

And then I went to Mary Jane, who was sitting upright, leaning into Kevin, who had stopped his active television watching to place his arm around her.

I love you, I told her. And I really meant it.

The nurse who had delivered the baby whispered in my ear. He's white, she said.

A lump rose in my throat. I looked over at Mary Jane, who stared at the infant on the scale, a nurse measuring his head and length, Kevin's smooth tattooed head rising behind her. He's Hector's, Mary Jane said. Look at the nose. The gums. He's Hector's. Slowly, Kevin turned his attention back to the television. Look at his eyes, his mouth, too. It's Hector's. Mary Jane began to weep.

It's Hector's, I thought, and now my heart sang in my chest, because everything would go as planned.

The nurse turned to me. She's right, she said. The balls are definitely of color. I spoke too soon.

I smiled at her.

I ran out to tell my husband. He's here! I said. And he's Mexican! Look! I showed him the short video of the baby slipping out from Mary Jane's body and then my own hands reaching to cut him from her. My husband hugged me and we both went into the delivery room to hug Mary Jane. Then he trundled off with Kevin to get Mary Jane the dinner she'd been talking about since the labor began: something from McDonald's called a McGangBang, a combination of two cheeseburgers and a spicy chicken sandwich smooshed together.

When they were gone, the nurse took my hand. That boy is so damn lucky, she said.

Lucky. The first time we met Mary Jane, we drove to her trailer with a soft stuffed animal for her child—the one she'd had with Kevin—and a bottle of gardenia-scented lotion.

Is this it? I said as we pulled into the trailer park.

This is it, my husband said.

It was a clear day, one of those brisk, bright days that can come only in early March. The sky was robin's egg blue. The windows of the trailer were boarded up, but for an open one, where a Mexican blanket hung crookedly. Disintegrating Sheetrock was propped against the decomposing side of the trailer, and when we walked to the door, we stepped along rotting wood placed over holes in the stairs. I struggle now with the details: smoke in thick, striated layers; children—three, at varying ages of toddlerhood—crawling along a floor laid down with that same rotting wood; ashtrays spilled over; a hole in the wall, the mark of a punch; two whining pit bulls straining against chains attached to two couches that faced each other. There was a smell—stale smoke, body odor, feces, wet dog, rotten wood—I will never shake.

We took Mary Jane and her daughter to lunch in the town. The town was blighted. Buildings were boarded up, telephone poles were strung with low-slung cables, and all the traffic lights were broken. Mary Jane was smart and funny and filled with regret that she had made bad decisions in life. She tended so sweetly to her daughter—and it was clear to us that placing her child with us was an act of big love. Here was where she confessed that the child might be her boyfriend's or it could be another boy she'd loved when her boyfriend was in prison. Perhaps she still loved him.

We will save this baby! we thought. And also? We will save Mary Jane. We will help her get her GED. We will help her daughter get to preschool. The baby would be lucky. The baby, my husband and I told each other, would never set foot in that wretched trailer.

She also told us that day that she wanted me to be in the delivery room. To give you the chance to be there at the moment he arrives, she said, and I was so touched and so grateful. And then we went to the mall to buy a case of diapers and wipes and teething gel for her daughter. Do you want the organic ones? I asked, and my husband hit me on the arm.

It had been a long road. We'd been scammed by birth mothers. We'd had to switch agencies. We had been paying and paying. But now, finally, a baby would be ours. We would be parents. We would tell our son all about his mother, who had placed him with us out of love and was now making a whole new start in life. This is your birth mother, we imagined saying every year when we came back to visit her. The three of us. A family. This was my thinking as I marched into that delivery room.

Mary Jane and Kevin stayed next door in the hospital and she came in often to hold the baby, at length, which upset me. She had every right to do this—she was dealing with her own grief—but I was scared. Every time she entered the room, my throat closed. She took pictures with her flip phone and texted them to her mother.

We need to get out of here, I told my husband.

The lawyer came to sign the papers and we took pictures with Mary Jane and then we put the boy—our about-to-be-son—in a car seat and buckled him in. Kevin sat up front with my husband, Mary Jane and I flanking the car seat, so we could drop them off at home.

When we pulled up in front, Mary Jane said, Can we just bring him in so everyone can say goodbye?

Oh God, I thought, the baby is going into the trailer.

Of *course*, my husband and I said at exactly the same time.

We carried him inside in his car seat. That smell. I can't forget it. Mary Jane unbuckled him and passed him to her brother, her sister-in-law, to a nephew who had shown up to say goodbye. The trailer was packed with relatives. Everyone was crying. I thought I would throw up.

And then it was over and we headed to this peaceful farmhouse we were renting near Philadelphia to wait out the time it took to get the paperwork filed that would legally allow us to leave the state with the baby.

It was the setting for a fairy tale. The owners of the farm made cheese from the milk of the goats who wandered freely on the property, along with the chickens. Each day, fresh eggs and a round of

soft cheese wrapped in wax paper were placed in a basket covered in a folded blue cloth and left outside the front door. Sheets
swayed on a line. Crocuses were breaking through the earth. It
was spring.

We thought that was our birth story, but that was not our birth
story. Because Hector, the birth father, had not been deported. He
was not in Mexico. He was in the next town. He had been supporting Mary Jane through her entire pregnancy; we had been cast
to keep the child safe so she could escape Kevin, who had threatened to kill her Mexican child. She was keeping her child with us
so she could make her way back to the man she loved. She had
placed a child for adoption before; she knew that she had thirty
days to change her mind.

Mary Jane did not need our help getting a GED or with anything else, for that matter, but she needed us to think she did. I
Google her now and see that she and Hector have had another
child a year to the day after they had the child we had thought was
ours.

Will he ever know about this couple who took care of him,
who loved him, who fed him at night, who lay down next to him
on the softest blue blankets, who strapped him to our chests and
walked with him along the creek during the first two weeks of his
life? This is what my husband asked me. We were in the car; I was
in the back with the baby, and we were driving him to a family
who would take care of him until the birth parents came for him. I
was weeping. Will he know that we named him and that we loved
him? he asked. I cannot write this part of the story now without
weeping.

I didn't know then what I know now, which is that our birth
story would take place nine months later, in a different state, with

a different birth mother and birth father. From the waiting room, we could look out and see the Rockies, jagged and topped with snow, and before them the foothills, brown and rising against the mountains.

In the rental car on the way to the hospital—his early birth as sudden as a summer downpour—my husband and I didn't speak. And then we sat in the sparkling waiting area, far from the delivery room. I can't go in there, I said. I didn't even wonder if the birth mother would want me there with her. No, my husband agreed. We're staying here. Let's just see what happens.

Hours passed. My husband took the birth father back and forth to his house for a change of clothes. I went out and brought him chicken sandwiches, potato chips, an iced tea. And then, finally, a nurse came out into the lobby, which was as clean and pure as Mary Jane's town was ruined. He's here, the nurse told us.

My husband and I stood.

He's here, she said again, but we couldn't move.

This is the story of how our son slipped into the world, a moment we didn't see. But that moment is not the only story of his arrival.

In the waiting room, my husband and I stood there, nodding. Then we stepped forward.

Still, he is here.

After Everything

CRISTINA HENRÍQUEZ

This is not a story about infertility. It's not a story about three miscarriages, four rounds of failed fertility intervention, and countless injections; about blood tests, surgeries, and outpatient procedures; about endless, infuriating phone calls with insurance personnel; about repeatedly journeying up the mountain of hope, only to tumble again down the face of disappointment. This is a story about what happened after all of that. This is the happy ending.

The first thing I remember, at six in the morning, is a small gush between my legs. I thought I had peed myself. I thought perhaps I hadn't done as many Kegel exercises as I was supposed to have done. I was four days overdue with my second child, so of course I should have known better.

I rolled myself out of the nest of pillows that I constructed every night to help support my belly, my back, the space between my knees, and walked to the bathroom. When I came back out, I announced to my husband, Ryan, "I think something might be happening."

An hour later, when I hadn't yet had a contraction, I decided that maybe nothing was happening after all. I convinced Ryan to go to work, promising to call him if there was any news. I made breakfast for my five-year-old, checked my e-mail, then sat down to eat a bagel. When I stood up again, there was another gush. I called my doctor's office.

"Do you think my water broke?" I asked the nurse who answered the phone.

"Is it watery?" the nurse said.

"Yes."

She told me to head to the hospital.

"But I'm not having contractions," I said.

"Go to the hospital," she repeated.

I called Ryan, who had just gotten to the office, and told him to turn around. I called my in-laws and asked them to come over to watch my daughter, who kept rubbing my belly and saying things like, "Come on, baby. Time to come out now." She, like Ryan and me, had been waiting for so long. Then I threw a few extra things—slippers that I wouldn't end up wearing, granola bars that I wouldn't end up eating—into the suitcase and waited again for contractions to begin. Without contractions, it didn't seem real, and I wanted so badly for it finally to be real.

By the time Ryan and I made it to the hospital, I was still periodically leaking but feeling no pain. The two of us walked up to the labor and delivery unit together, leaving the suitcase in the trunk of the car just in case it was a false alarm. I remember Ryan said to me, "Maybe this will be the first labor in the history of childbirth without contractions," and the two of us laughed, as if such a thing were possible.

In labor and delivery, a nurse named Patty led us to a room with a bed and told me to undress from the waist down so she could check the fluid. She swiped some of it onto a strip of paper, which promptly turned bright purple.

"It's amniotic fluid," she reported. "Let's get you checked in."

"I'm staying?" I asked in disbelief.

"You're staying," she said. "You're having this baby today."

I got dressed in a pilled cotton gown, pulled on the giant disposable mesh underwear that Patty affectionately referred to as "our Victoria's Secret best," and then Ryan and I followed her down the hall to a birthing room.

"What's your birth plan?" Patty asked as I was taking off my shoes.

The room was large and bright, equipped with a beautiful Kohler tub for anyone who wanted a water birth. It was spacious enough to walk laps in for anyone who wanted to go natural. I was neither of those people.

"Epidural," I said.

Patty nodded and I squirmed up onto the hospital bed, feeling giddy and, for the moment, pain-free. Patty Velcroed a fetal monitor around my belly. Because my water had already broken and she wanted to get things moving (so did I), she hooked me up to an IV, which started pumping Pitocin into my system. My husband dragged a chair to the bedside. He took out a newspaper and handed me my Kindle. The fetal monitor beeped happily beside us. We sat and read and waited for whatever would happen next.

About half an hour later, I had my first contraction. After a few more, I turned off my Kindle and rolled onto my side to breathe. When the contractions got stronger, I started moaning because I'd heard that something about the physiology of moaning helped a person's body stay relaxed.

An OB resident—a ruddy-faced young woman in blue scrubs—came to check me. Four centimeters, she said, and then she sat at the foot of the bed and tried to engage me in conversation while I grunted and willed myself to relax. The conversation went something like this:

Resident: "Have you thought about names?"

Me, with my eyes closed: silence.

Resident: "Names. Have you thought about names?"

Me, in between breaths: "Ben."

Resident: "We have someone on the staff named Ben. Actually Benjamin. He plays guitar, so we call him Ben Jammin'. You could call your son that. Ben Jammin'!"

Me: low moan.

Resident: "Do you know who Louis C.K. is?"

Me: low moan.

Resident: "He has this hilarious bit about naming your kids. Have you ever seen it?"

Me, gripping the side rail of the bed while telling myself not to grip the side rail of the bed because I was supposed to be staying loose and relaxed: inhale, exhale, inhale, exhale.

Resident: "Yeah, well. His show is really funny, too. Do you ever watch it?"

And on and on.

Maybe she thought she was helping, that she could distract me from the pain, but what I needed was to focus, and I was too polite, even in the throes of labor, to tell her. But while she talked, the pain got stronger, tightening its grip on me with every new contraction. Somehow in between the birth of my first child and now, I had forgotten the precise sensations of labor—I remembered the concept but not the feeling, that particular dull and wrenching pain expanding out to every part of me, the way it burrowed so relentlessly, a vise turning, squeezing, wringing me over and over, tighter and tighter—but now, as the pain rushed through me with force and purpose, it all came back to me with shocking clarity. And now, like then, all I wanted was for it to stop.

I'll be the first to admit that I hadn't done much to prepare for delivery. After a glorious epidural with my first child (months after it, I had run into the anesthesiologist in an elevator one day and told him that he'd saved my life), I knew without question that I would get one again. Besides, for the majority of my pregnancy, I had been preoccupied with *keeping* the baby, which hadn't left much time for thinking about actually *having* the baby.

About a week before my due date, though, I spotted a book at Barnes & Noble about mindful birthing. I picked it up and opened at random to a page where the author was describing a preparedness exercise that involved holding an ice cube in your bare hand for one full minute. The point was to practice steering your thoughts away from the sensations brought on by the cube— the burn of the ice against your skin, the water sliding past your wrist as the cube began to melt, anything at all—and toward the kind of focused mindfulness that would, supposedly, be key in getting through labor. Once you could successfully manage one minute with one cube, you were supposed to try one minute with two cubes, one in each hand.

On the way home from the bookstore, I mentioned the exercise to Ryan. He didn't think it would be that hard, he said. I laughed. Of course it would be hard. An ice cube! In your bare hand! For one full minute! He shook his head. Seems easy, he said. So I suggested we try it. I thought perhaps he didn't grasp the full nature of the assignment. I thought perhaps he didn't understand how long one minute could seem when he was in pain. I thought, This will teach him to appreciate what we women have to go through, even though an ice cube in the hand is nothing in comparison to a baby in the birth canal.

In the kitchen, I dispensed the ice cubes—one for Ryan and one for me. We stood across the counter from each other, ready to duel. I glanced at the clock on the microwave, waiting for high noon. When it turned from one minute to the next, I said, "Go!" and both of us picked up our cubes.

I lasted for approximately twelve seconds, which, to my credit, was nearly ten seconds longer than I'd thought I would last. I gasped and flung the ice cube into the sink, watching it career up and down the sides of the bowl like a skateboarder on a half-pipe while I alternately shook my hand and pressed it to the thigh of my pants in a desperate attempt to stop the sting of the cold. "Oh my God!" I kept saying. Across from me, Ryan stood perfectly still, the ice cube clutched in his hand, grinning. When the full minute was up, he calmly placed it on the counter. "No problem," he said.

After that, eager for some tips about how to retrain my mind (in a week), I called a friend who had used hypnobirthing to get through labor. Even though I was planning on an epidural, I would still have to contend with hours of contractions in the lead-up to it.

My friend sent me links to YouTube videos showing women using birthing balls and various massage techniques. She told me to slump into the contractions, to let them take me, rather than trying to fight them. And she had me visualize the place where I felt relaxed, which in my case was Kansas, a state I'd driven through about ten years earlier and which had achieved a sort of mythic status in my mind for its lush, open fields, absent of houses, telephone wires, and billboards, and filled instead with swaying green grass as far as the eye could see. I was supposed to imagine myself on the front porch of a farmhouse there, gazing out across the land, and when the pain (or discomfort, as she urged me to think of it) of labor intensified, I should imagine myself slowly descending the stairs that led off the porch and walking out into the field. When it got really bad, I was supposed to lie down in the grass and tune my senses to the smell of the air, the warmth of the sun on my face, the soft rush of the breeze scampering over my skin. The underlying idea behind Kansas and the ice cube was the same: If I could direct my thoughts away from the immediate sensations, I would be okay.

Well, we all know how it went with the ice cube.

It wasn't long before I started asking for the epidural. Did I ask? Does one ask? Maybe I begged. By the time the anesthesiologist arrived, I was still only at four centimeters, but I felt sure that I was going to die. "Boy," the doctor said when he checked me. "The way you sounded, I would have thought you were further along." I didn't have the strength to thank him for calling me a wimp.

Ryan left the room (spouses aren't allowed to stay during epidurals), and Patty and the anesthesiologist sat me up on the edge of the bed. I did everything I could to stay still through another contraction, to lean forward the way I was supposed to, to keep my hands where they told me, and then—sweet, sweet relief.

By the time Ryan came back into the room, my legs felt huge and rubbery, like two whales newly attached to my body, and if I wanted to move even an inch, Ryan had to slide his arms under me like a forklift and shift me. Periodically, Ryan walked down the hall to get me small plastic cups of orange Jell-O, which he held to my lips and fed me in bed. Nurses came and went. They glanced at a screen; they checked my dilation. I closed my eyes for a little while. And then, nearly twelve hours after it had all begun, it was time to push.

There were five people in the room: Ryan, nurse Patty, the OB resident, the doctor, and me. Ryan held one of my numb legs while Patty held the other, angling them back until my knees were nearly at my ears. The resident and the doctor huddled together at the end of the bed, coaching me and occasionally conferring among themselves. The doctor kept telling me to get mad. "You've got to get madder than that!" he would shout, and I would bear down and try my best to be mad, even though I was anything but. Excited, nervous, hopeful, anxious? Check. Mad? Not so much.

In between pushes, there was a lot of chitchat. About what I don't remember. But I do know that the five of us were very convivial with one another, as if we were all out on a picnic together, during which I just happened to be squeezing a human being out of my body.

I had no concept of how much time was passing. Eventually, Patty turned off the epidural drip and enough feeling returned to my legs that I could sense better when I needed to push and how hard I was doing it. At some point, the resident said she could see hair—lots of it. Patty looked and confirmed. Lots of hair! There's the head! The doctor invited Ryan to look. He appeared conflicted, as if he wasn't sure whether it would be miraculous or gross, but he sneaked a peek anyway and managed to say, "Uh-huh."

And then, fourteen hours after my water broke and three hours after I started pushing, our baby boy was born. I remember being desperate to hear him cry. I kept asking, "Is he okay? Is he okay?"

"Yes," the doctor said.

Ryan burst into tears and collapsed on a chair next to the bed, sobbing with joy. Patty put the baby directly on my chest while she checked him out and did all the postbirth things that happen in a modern hospital setting. The doctor and the resident must have been doing something, too, but I barely registered it. At that moment, all I could see was this bleary-eyed baby with a full head of hair, slippery and warm on top of me. Very gently, I put my hand on his wrinkled back. Tears ran down my face. Here he is, I thought. After nine months filled with anxious nights and careful days and a million superstitions and sonograms and kick counts and weekly nonstress tests, where I sat in a room at the doctor's office and listened to the amplified sounds of the baby rolling and hiccupping inside me, after the five years before that—the story I don't want to tell, the one that consumed me for so long and then, at the moment he arrived, instantly receded and seemed so small, like the pain itself—here he was. After everything.

Not Telling

CLAIRE DEDERER

We're sitting around the dinner table: my husband and I, our daughter, Lucy, our son, Willie, and all the grandparents. We've just finished dinner. It's a cold December night, but cozy here in our dining room, which is painted a bosky forest green. Candles are guttering; Willie, a little bored, blows gently at the flames, not quite extinguishing them. It's Lucy's fourteenth birthday. She sits curled on her dining room chair—as always, she has a foot tucked beneath her, a born cat—snug between two grandfathers. She's quiet, which is her way, but she giggles along with her grandfathers' clowning.

There's a lull in the conversation. My mom—an inveterate storyteller and also a hater of social silences—says brightly, "Remember the day Lucy was born?" She begins to launch into the story of Lucy's delivery and the rest of us, gobsmacked, gaze at her across the cluttered landscape of the postdinner table. *Really? The birth* story? Are you fucking *kidding* us? Lucy had had a rough birth; none of us felt like talking about it, including her—she'd heard the story once or twice, and that was plenty for her.

"Gigi," says Lucy, addressing my mother by her nom de grandparenting (the *G* is hard). "Stop! Stop it right now. Please." For such a soft-spoken girl, Lucy can be quite fierce. When she was in kindergarten, one of her classmates described her as a gentle cheetah, and that's about right.

I smile at my mom and shake my head. I say, "It's time for cake." I go into the kitchen and lean against the counter for just a little minute. I stick the candles into the crown of the cake, a beautiful tall yellow layer cake I made this morning. I frosted it—chocolate—with the kids after school. Over the years, I've made a seemingly endless succession of yellow cakes covered in chocolate frosting. Lucy has been here a long time. Today might be her birthday, but we're sailing ever farther away from her actual birth, which seems a distant, abandoned shore, and way less important than everything that's happened since.

I don't think about my daughter's birth story very often anymore. But at one time, it was incredibly important to me. It was the story of this new person coming into the world; it was also a story of how I myself became a new person.

When I gave birth for the first time, I wasn't a mother, even after the baby came out. I was a regular person in the process of becoming a mother. It's not as if the baby arrives and suddenly you're a mom, freshly baked with a lovely brown crust on you. You're the same person you were, but now you've got this creature utterly dependent on you. It's a lot to take in.

When it happened to me, I wasn't any too crazy about the whole setup. I mean, I liked the baby fine—all right, I *adored* the baby—but I found the transformation into mother to be quite a shock. All of a sudden, I was a slave to this creature. My slavery was intensified by the fact that my baby had almost died in birth—my need to take perfect care of her was doubled and trebled, in the manner of a deal with God. I will do anything, anything, I thought, just don't take her.

I gave my whole heart to her, but this giving was very confusing to my sense of self. I had been the whole deal, the big cheese. I had been hot shit. Now I was supposed to live my life in service to someone else.

I entered this new world of motherhood tentatively, a little fawn-like, teetering on unsure legs. I wasn't sure what to do in this new world; there were all kinds of rules that needed to be sifted and sorted. Time and sleep and what to eat—the simplest things in life—these were all suddenly up for grabs. One thing I knew for sure: I wanted to talk about the birth. I wanted to tell what had happened. I wanted this with a fervor that felt almost biological. I told it to new friends and old, told it over and over. Every conversation seemed to end up in the same place. It was a bead I worried; a catechism that upset me and consoled me all at once.

The birth story, I believe, is not so much about the baby as about the mother and her wonder and horror at the whole crazy fucking incomprehensible transformative gestalt alteration she's undergoing. The birth story is an expression of the dying throes of an egoism that is in the process of being brutally impaired. Look what I did, says the birth story. Look what I endured. Look at this adventure/trauma/love affair I just went through.

Fourteen years after Lucy's birthday I'm a mother over and over; my cells have grown and regrown into this shape. I'm like that hammer from philosophy class: First the handle breaks, so you replace the handle. Then the head breaks, so you replace the head. Is it still the same hammer? All parts of me have been remade as mother. But when I was first becoming one, I needed the birth story to remind me of what I was in the process of becoming. What am I again? Oh yeah, a mom.

Recently, a newish friend asked me about the births of my children as we bent our heads together over coffee and talked, talked, talked in that excited, new-friend way. I glossed it: two C-sections, a little scary. She, the mother of college-age kids, made a few sympathetic noises and our conversation easily slipped down another path.

It has been a long time since I've told my birth stories, or at least told them with the old zeal. In fact, I'm bored with them. I treasure memories of my children's births, but those memories are put away, like blankets in a chest.

My children's births seem the least interesting thing about them. The babies got out; they got on their way; they started to become the people they are now. These people are of infinite interest to me. I rabidly follow Lucy's eighth-grade gossip and at least try to learn to play whatever insanely complex trading-card game Willie is currently fired up over—at one point, I almost understood how Pokémon works. I'm besotted by these small people. If my new friend had been asking me about my children themselves, I could've gone on and on with a recitation of their virtues and what we in contemporary parenting call their "challenges." I could've happily bored my friend for hours.

I'm a mother, defined and penned and held by my children. I can't imagine myself minus my tribe of two and their wide blue eyes and their stubborn temperaments and their elegantly solid limbs and their love of wordplay. The birth story helped me get here, and then I didn't need it anymore.

But I'm pretending I'm not a special case, and I am. (Though, Jesus, who isn't?) Because I haven't just told my birth stories; I've also written them. And I haven't just written them; I've published them, too. My birth stories have been professionalized, commodified, sold and bought and read.

Everybody knows that when you tell a story, you kill it. You remove the actual memory and replace it with the written memory. So it is with my children's births. I say I don't want to tell their stories, but the fact is, I've told them in print. And in doing that, I've replaced them. The birth stories now live between covers.

Which is to say, my relationship to the birth stories is fatally disrupted.

When you write a memoir, a funny thing happens. People— friends and strangers alike—assume you're sorry you wrote it. They assume you regret it. As though after all those years of work, you woke up on your publication date and slapped your forehead and said, "Oh shit! Why'd I do that?" They assume your memoir ruined your relationship with your parents and that your friends who appear in your memoir's pages won't speak to you anymore.

In fact, I do not regret writing a single word of my memoir— even the parts that my parents were not, strictly speaking, in love with. Except the birth stories. They feel stolen from me. They're mere words now.

Memoir is the saddest genre. It's driven by the desire to capture what's about to be lost forever. Nabokov says it best, as is his way: "The years are passing, my dear, and presently nobody will know what you and I know." Thus, the sad impetus to memoir: Write the memory down, quickly as you can, as a hedge against oblivion. And so you follow the impulse (which seems to have the same biological urgency that telling the birth stories once did). But guess what? It gets even sadder! When you write it, you surrender the memory; it no longer quite belongs to you.

When the babies came, I told their birth stories over and over, and the telling sustained me. It helped me become a mother. When I wrote them down, something else happened. I lost the stories. But I still had the children. And maybe the stories helped someone else become a mother. Is that too much to hope for?

Now my daughter is turning fourteen. I set the candles aflame using the butane lighter, which my kids call the "lighty lighty thing." Every object I pick up is infused with the stories of their lives. I enter the dining room, where she's waiting for the cake with the same shining eyes she had when she was an infant, when she was three, when she was seven and ten. Her brother is as visibly hungry as a cartoon character, his giant eyes fixed on the cake. Isn't the shining infinitude of this moment enough? Does it need to be told as a story? The candles flicker a little as I carry the cake to the table and everyone begins to sing.

Two Lines

ELEANOR HENDERSON

My mother had been declared infertile. A blocked fallopian tube was to blame. After three years of trying to get pregnant, she and my father adopted a son; then, to her surprise, three years later, she became pregnant with another. She may have had one blocked tube, but the other seemed to function just fine. She did the math, counting the odd months when she would ovulate from the clear tube. Three more years later, while living in Greece with my father and two little boys, she got pregnant with me. She had outwitted the doctor's diagnosis. She had detected the key to her own fickle body.

When my husband, Aaron, and I had been together ten years, and we were ready to try to conceive, I felt in my bones that the odds were against us. Luck would render me infertile, if not my genes. I sat on the toilet, inspecting my underwear for signs of fertility, watching for a sign. The telltale cervical mucus of ovulation. The blood of menstruation—or could it be implantation? Inside my body was a biological process beyond my control, a system as concealed and perplexing as modern plumbing.

So when, a few months into my quest to get pregnant, I underwent an HSG—the same procedure that revealed my mother's infertility—I felt as though I were visiting a palm reader. I lay on my back while a doctor fitted me with a catheter and injected me with blue dye. On the X-ray monitor, it flushed through my uterus like a squid's ink cloud, then burst victoriously through my fallopian tubes. They were open! The plumbing was working.

Then, a couple of months later, I went to my internist with sharp abdominal cramps. All the baby-making sex we'd been having had become uncomfortable, and then painful. "Could I have endometriosis?" I asked her. I hadn't heard of the disease before, but I'd done some research online, and the symptoms rang true.

"What does it feel like?" she asked.

I couldn't say "It feels like tissue from the lining of my uterus is growing in other parts of my abdomen." I didn't know what that felt like. I said, "It feels like gas."

"Then it's probably gas," she said. Months passed, and the cramps came and went, and still I couldn't get pregnant, despite our well-timed and often excruciating efforts. My tubes were open, so what was the problem? And then there were my periods, which had become cascades of pain. For days at a time, I ached in my belly, in my back, in the backs of my knees. The blood coursing through me ached.

Then one day, paging through Toni Weschler's classic *Taking Charge of Your Fertility*, I took a break from studying the close-ups of egg-white cervical mucus between two manicured fingers and came across another, more detailed description of endometriosis. I'd dismissed the possibility of the disease, taking the doctor's word. But this time, the symptoms shouted off the page. For all my careful monitoring of my underwear, I hadn't made a connection between my abdominal cramps, my menstrual pain, and my inability to conceive.

The internist referred me to an OB, and on a morning that happened to coincide with the first hours of my period—adding injury to insult—a nurse fit a giant condom over an ultrasound wand and probed me with it, searching deep inside for ovarian cysts or some other cause of my pain, which had abruptly become intergalactic. Aaron and I had been trying, at this point, for eight months.

"No cysts," said the OB afterward.

"I think I have endometriosis," I told her.

"I think so, too," she said.

Her name was Jennifer, she was blond, and I loved her.

A few weeks later, Aaron and my mother accompanied me to the hospital, where I underwent laparoscopic surgery—the only way to diagnose and treat endometriosis. When I woke up, groggy, Jennifer handed me a photograph of my uterus, the pink tissue of my ovaries clustered with endometriosis, like ripening berries. She had made three punctures in my belly—one through my navel for the camera and two on either side for what appeared to be a pair of knitting needles, which she used to remove the endometriosis. A decade of birth control pills had suppressed it, but there it was now—not blocking my tubes, but my ovaries. The mystery hidden inside me had been revealed and remedied.

No one really knows what causes endometriosis, or how it causes infertility. But Jennifer assured me that after the procedure, our odds would be good. For months, my underwear bore the uncertain pattern of rust-colored blood, my body healing itself, I hoped. But three cycles later, I still wasn't pregnant, and already, I'd been told, the endometriosis could be returning. After we'd been trying for a year, officially hitting the infertile mark, Jennifer referred us to a reproductive specialist, who recommended Clomid and intrauterine insemination. I picked up the prescription at the pharmacy. It was too late to begin the treatment that cycle, so one more time, on month thirteen, we gave it a try the old-fashioned way. Two weeks later, I woke up drooling on my pillow. Aaron smelled like mustard. And on the stick, there were two lines.

And then, on another early morning nine and a half months later, one week after my due date, a cramp rocked me awake. It felt as though my uterus was being choked from the inside. Now *that* feels like a contraction, I thought. I sat up in bed, riveted. Had I dreamed it? One second later, my water broke. I gasped a Christmas-morning gasp.

The exciting thing about your water breaking is that you know that you're in business. I crouched on the floor next to the bed to avoid soaking the sheets further, and called Erin, my midwife, who was thirty-eight weeks pregnant herself. She told me to go to the hospital.

Later, Aaron wouldn't remember any of the car ride, though he was the one driving. He didn't remember stopping at the bank to withdraw cash for the valet, though it was his idea. There was no valet parking at the hospital, and what man with a wife in labor stops at the ATM anyway? He has this thing where he blacks out during traumatic experiences. It's his brain's way of protecting itself from what it can't process, I guess. For him, birth was a trauma.

It was a trauma for me, too, in the most exhilarating way possible. I had been that obnoxious woman who enjoys every minute of pregnancy, including the nausea, the pain through my hips that made me feel every morning as though I'd been dropped from a great height, the burning itch of a varicose vein that bulged in my left calf. (The following year, Jennifer's husband, a vascular surgeon, would remove the vein in a fierce spousal competition for the most modest scar.) I was fascinated by the science experiment that was my pregnant body.

And now I was fascinated by labor. I felt the waves of contractions come, steady, sure. They *did* hurt! No wonder even Erin, a certified midwife, had gotten an epidural during her first labor. A year before, in the very hospital room in which I was now settled, she'd screamed, "I can't get an epidural! I'm a midwife!" But she'd swallowed her pride and chosen the pain relief. I worried that I'd get to that point myself, but I wanted an unmedicated birth, badly. I wanted the full, level-ten experience. I breathed; I dilated; I moaned. It was hell. I was so into it.

Aaron, though, he was not so into it. He grows nauseous at the sight of blood. When he wakes up in the morning and is brushing his teeth and the cat takes a dump in the litter box at just the wrong time, sometimes he will throw up in the sink. In our final childbirth preparation class, another of the dads passed out during a video featuring an epidural needle. Aaron wasn't that queasy, but he was close.

Aaron and the passed-out dad were the only dads who didn't attend every class. Aaron came for the first week and the last, excusing himself for the middle four; he had a new job he couldn't miss. I missed him, but I didn't really mind. On the other nights, my mom and my friend Gina took turns standing in as my birth partner, massaging my back as I sat on a birthing ball. My mother supported me on a gym mat as I tried to practice a very unpretty sideways push in my skinny jeans and flats. ("I don't think I'll be trying *that* one!" I said.) After the class ended, Gina filled Aaron in on all he'd need to know, quizzing him on the TACO acronym he'd have to remember if my water broke, but even this was enough to gross him out. Gina was a little grossed out, too. Me? I couldn't wait to determine the Time, Amount, Color, and Odor of my amniotic fluid.

So, Aaron did not breathe with me in the delivery room or time my contractions or play me a lovingly crafted MP3 mix. He surfed the Internet on his laptop. He handed me a cup of water between contractions. He stood at my shoulder and hid behind a camera. He cheered me on, mostly from a distance of about two yards. He was terrified.

I guess I was a little disappointed that he wasn't more involved. Early in my pregnancy, when I pictured my labor, I imagined him holding back the meaty drumstick of my thigh, my mother holding back the other, just like I'd seen on all those birthing documentaries. His gloved hands would catch our baby, and my mother would capture the whole miraculous thing on-camera.

Then again, the greedy part of me, the part of me that looked forward to childbirth like an athlete looks forward to the Big Game, wanted labor all to myself. I did not need a coach! I did not need cheerleaders! I did not need fans. Stand back, people, I was going to have myself a baby. So, I was resigned to the fact that Aaron wasn't the kind of dad who instinctively grabs a thigh. Two yards away was just about perfect. And the same logic determined my decision not to have my mother in the room when I delivered. I wanted to push without distraction.

That didn't mean that I didn't want her within close range for the early stages of labor. Two hours after we'd checked into the hospital, she arrived with my sister-in-law and her newborn son, and I walked the hospital halls with them, admiring my nephew, stopping to rest and breathe when a contraction took over. I talked with them while I tried to find a comfortable spot on an inflatable birthing device shaped like a gel capsule. The baby, Erin discovered, was tilted. To encourage him or her into place—we still didn't know the sex—I needed to be upright. Then, when I grew restless, Erin drew a tubful of warm water in the bathroom—not a big, luxurious birthing tub, but a regular hotel bathtub—and I tried sitting in it for a while, wearing a brown bikini top, while my mother and sister-in-law waited with Aaron outside the door. While I bobbed in the water, Erin told me the story of how her husband, during the early part of her labor, had filled this tub and gotten into it himself, along with a bucket of Kentucky Fried Chicken and his BlackBerry. Maybe it was that image that ruined the tub for me. I'd expected to find great comfort there, but instead I felt claustrophobic, a goldfish thrashing in a glass bowl. Also, because I'd tested positive for Group B strep, I needed antibiotics, so every twenty minutes I had to be tethered to an IV pole, which the nurse rolled into the bathroom. I leaned over the edge of the tub, moaning, trying to keep the IV tube dry. The contractions were coming hard and fast now, a minute on, a minute off. On the other side of the door, my mother whispered to my sister-in-law, "I think she's having another one!" and I screamed, "I can totally hear you in here!"

Erin suggested that it might be best if they returned to the waiting room. I got out of the tub and back into bed, but I couldn't lie down. I couldn't even sit. The instant I put pressure on my tailbone, I leaped up in pain.

"Is it your back?" Erin asked me.

"It's my ass," I told her. "Is it possible to have ass labor?"

I shed my bikini top. Even clothing was distracting. Aaron paced over to the window and observed me like a spectator at one of those staged safari tours: How cool to be this close to the wildlife, but did he really want me to leap onto the roof of his car?

Suddenly I had to poop. I lumbered back into the bathroom. Sitting on the toilet was unbearable. After returning home from my laparoscopy, against doctor's orders, I'd skipped the recommended stool softeners and asked my mother to make me pasta. Sometimes doctors are right. In labor, I felt like that again: constipated from three days' worth of carbohydrates. I strained. Nothing. Instead, I stood up, waddled over to the sink, and threw up into it. Oh God! I felt awful. I fumbled for my toothbrush, ran it over my teeth. "For God's sake, don't worry about brushing your teeth!" Erin laughed.

"God, I have to poop!" I said, my mouth full of foam. If only I could poop! I would feel so much better. Then I would be able to deliver this baby.

Erin coaxed me back to the bed. I tried sitting down again. I sprang back up. I lay on my side, moaning. Then Erin raised the back of the bed to a vertical position and I turned around and knelt on the bed, leaning over the pillows. She checked me. "You don't have to poop," she said. "You have to push. You're fully dilated!"

Oh God, was I happy to hear that! It would be over! Soon, it would be over.

"Are you ready?" she asked.

"I don't know," I admitted. I'd thought I'd be able to recognize the urge to push when it came. "All I can think of is how to poop."

"Yes!" Erin said, getting into position. "Just like that."

There was no way I could lie on my back, so I continued to kneel there on the bed, naked, growling. Aaron increased the pace of his pacing. He paced closer, close enough for a brave kiss on the forehead. And then another contraction was coming and I was pushing, pushing as if taking a shit in the woods. The baby was moving down! I could feel it with each push. After a few pushes, I turned around and squatted, holding on to a bar Erin wheeled into the room. Jennifer, my beloved OB, popped her head around the curtain just as I was moaning through a contraction. Erin, new to the practice, still had to be observed during deliveries. I smiled and waved. Jennifer smiled and waved, then disappeared behind the curtain.

"I can see hair!" Erin said.

"Oh my God!" I said.

"Aaron, do you want to see?"

"No thanks," he said, his voice tiny. "I'm good."

"Eleanor, do you want to feel it?"

Of course I wanted to feel it! I wanted to feel everything. I reached my hand between my legs, and there was the warm, wet scalp, the first time I ever touched my baby.

There was the head—right there!—but I couldn't push it out. Contraction after contraction, I tried and tried. The head remained there, crowning, a little lemon wedge of scalp, for half an hour. I lay down on one side, then the other. I squatted again. I pushed and pushed. With two fingers, Erin swept the inside of my vagina, trying to open me up as though stretching open the neck of a new sweater.

"You have excellent tissue!" she told me, leaning over the bulk of her belly.

Was that a compliment? "Thanks!" I said. A contraction came— they were back-to-back now, consuming me—and I pushed.

"I don't want to have to give you an episiotomy. Not with this excellent tissue!"

I didn't think I could push any harder. But after that comment, I did. When the next contraction came, I rolled over onto my left side—just as I'd practiced with my mother in birth class—and pushed with every muscle in my body. Then I could feel my baby's head moving.

"Here comes the ring of fire!" Erin called.

To this day, I can't hear the Johnny Cash song without wincing.

And then, one more push, and there was my baby, spilling out of my body and into Erin's deft arms.

"It's a boy!"

She placed him on my chest. He cried and cried. I cried and cried. Even Aaron cried. He kissed my forehead again. Helpless with awe, he took a thousand pictures. "Oh my God, oh my God!" we said again and again. There really was a baby in there. At 5:30 in the evening, exactly twelve hours after my water had broken in bed, our beautiful mystery had been revealed to us. A boy.

After all that crowning, he had a nice, bloody cone head. He had been stuck, Erin told me, with his fist pressed to his left cheek, so that I gave birth to his head and his arm at the same time. "No wonder you had a hard time pushing him out!"

"Ah, yes," said the nurse. "We see that every once in a while. Always the boys." She imitated, her arm stretched over her head. "They're holding their hands out for the car keys already."

"Dad," Erin asked, "do you want to cut the cord?"

Aaron took a step back, as though Erin were about to stab him with the scissors. "No thanks," he said. "I'm good."

My mother, who had been listening outside the door—all my life, it seemed, she had been listening, safely, patiently, outside the door—came tumbling in. She kissed me, and Aaron, and the baby. "This is Nicolas," I told her. Had I been a boy—and my mother had been sure that I was—I would have had the same name.

Nicolas was still crying. He would cry for the next half hour. I thought it was an appropriate response to the experience of being born.

Me? I felt as though I had just run a marathon. I felt as though I could run *another* marathon. My baby's naked skin pressed to mine. The oxytocin coursed through me. "I'm so happy!" I told them. "I'm not in labor anymore!"

And Nicolas—he was pretty great, too.

The nurse bathed and swaddled him, and by the time she handed him to Aaron, he had stopped crying. Aaron looked down at him, nervous but blissful. He sighed. It was over.

"That was some primal stuff," my husband said to our son, shaking his head with pride. "Your mom just earned some serious respect."

Then Aaron's face lit up with alarm. "Something's happening!" he said, pushing the baby into my arms.

"What's happening?"

"He's, like, shaking!"

But the baby looked fine. Aaron patted down his chest. From the pocket of his flannel shirt, he withdrew his cell phone, which had been vibrating. A call from a well-wisher. He sighed again.

"It's going to be fine," I said.

Three years after Nico was born, while he napped in the backseat, I sat parked in the driveway in our air-conditioned car, breathing through the labor of our second child. This time, we knew it would be another boy. This time, labor didn't start with my water breaking, but with contractions, three days before my due date. This time, I knew just how hard natural labor would be, but I didn't look forward to it any less. A different college town, a different cheerful midwife, a different doctor who performed a different laparoscopy, a different whole year before we conceived: The differences were so negligible that the memories of my sons' births blend into one.

The real difference was that this time, Aaron was sick. Two months before, overnight, his body had broken out into painful lesions, dime-size wounds that wouldn't heal. Eventually, the diagnosis that would stick was prurigo nodularis—two words that were as useless as they were excruciating. But at that point, his doctor believed it was a staph infection and had prescribed a powerful dose of antibiotics, and Aaron had to get permission to be in the delivery room. His whole body ached. He'd lost thirty pounds. He was consumed by a cycle of insomnia and fatigue. He'd barely slept the night before, and shortly after we settled into the hospital, into the steady rhythm of contractions in a dark room, he nodded off.

Mahrie, my midwife, eyed him snoring softly in his armchair. She looked puzzled. I stifled the urge to tell her about what a good father he was to Nico. Would he love this child any less because he was unconscious for part of his birth? A stay-at-home dad, he now spends his days waging light saber battles, sanitizing sippy cups, dispensing Band-Aids, and changing diapers with an expertise that puts to shame those clueless-dad diaper commercials. He couldn't love either child any more.

Instead, I just said, "I'll wake him up for the good part."

While he slept—he in his own private pain, I in mine—I took a shower. The warm water pounding my back was so much better than the bath. Every once in a while, Mahrie came in to check on me. "I'm fine," I told her. My parents were on the way. Nico was at home with a sitter. My husband slept in the next room, and I labored there for an hour under the falling water. I stood, I squatted, I knelt. I wasn't lonely. By now, solitude was an unwritten line of my birth plan, and besides, my baby was there with me. So was my grandmother, who had birthed my mother while her husband was overseas during World War II. So was my mother, who before her C-section in Athens, wearing nothing but a shower cap, freezing on the gurney, tried to remember the Greek word for cold. They, too, were without their husbands, and yet none of us was alone. I think we'd never been less alone, in those quiet moments before we met our babies.

Henry was born just after midnight. I wouldn't see my mother until the morning. We didn't know it yet, but already cancer was growing quietly in her lungs, as she drove through the night toward me, as I swayed in the shower, as Aaron slept. Despite her fifty years of smoking, her doctor had never ordered a chest X-ray. When Henry was six months old, just after gathering with all six of her grandsons for my father's surprise eightieth birthday party (my sister-in-law was pregnant with the seventh), my mother would climb into the car for her radiation treatment and say to me and my brothers, "Goodbye. You're wonderful children." From her diagnosis to her death, three weeks passed.

(I should have asked her into the delivery room.)

Aaron woke up for the last few hours of labor, the finale of which he captured on film from the respectful site of my left elbow. A year later, his sores vanished as inexplicably as they had appeared. Who knows at any time what mysteries are inside us, what cells and spirits conspire to shut down life, or bring it forth? Sometimes modern medicine, with its X-ray vision, helps to reveal our bodies' secrets. Sometimes it reveals them too late. Sometimes it fails us. Sometimes we get lucky and we triumph over our own bodies, and what we believed them capable of.

I've never felt luckier than the hour after first giving birth, my hormones soaring, Nicolas bundled in my arms. During the depths of labor, I'd had the autonomy and privacy I'd craved, but now, there was nothing sweeter than the company of my mother and my husband, the people who—with my son—had made me a mother. There we were, huddled together, all of us dazed with happiness. I'd almost forgotten Erin, standing pregnant in the corner. In just a couple of weeks, she'd be the one with the new baby in her arms.

"Get the present," I told Aaron, and he handed our midwife— this woman who had sat at my side for hours, who had protected my space, who had been wrist-deep in my tissue, who had delivered not just a healthy baby but the day of my dreams—a gift bag of maternity lotions and soaps, a box of Mother's Milk tea.

"Thanks for bringing my child into the world," I joked. "I wish I could give you more."

Her smile was exhausted, expectant. "I'd take a labor like yours," she said.

So I closed my eyes and made a wish. I wished it on her.

Reader, I wish it on you.

Contributors

NUAR ALSADIR is the author of the poetry collection *More Shadow Than Bird* (Salt Publishing, 2012). Her poems and essays have been published in numerous periodicals, including *The Kenyon Review*, *Ploughshares*, *Slate*, *The New York Times Magazine*, and *Tin House*. She teaches writing at NYU's Tisch School of the Arts and is currently training to become a psychoanalyst.

AMY BRILL's fiction and nonfiction have appeared or are forthcoming in *One Story*, *The Common*, *Salon*, *Real Simple*, *Redbook*, *Guernica*, and other publications. A Pushcart Prize nominee, she's been awarded fiction fellowships by the Edward F. Albee Foundation, Jentel, Fundación Valparaiso, the Constance Saltonstall Foundation for the Arts, the Millay Colony for the Arts, and the American Antiquarian Society. Amy's first novel, *The Movement of Stars*, was published by Riverhead Books in 2013.

SUSAN BURTON is at work on a memoir, *The Invention of the Teenage Girl*, to be published by Random House. Her writing has appeared in publications including *The New Yorker*, *New York* magazine, and *The New York Times Book Review*. She is a former editor of *Harper's* and a former producer of *This American Life*. The feature film *Unaccompanied Minors* is based upon one of her radio essays. She lives in Brooklyn with her husband and their two sons.

SARAH SHUN-LIEN BYNUM is the author of two novels, *Ms. Hempel Chronicles*, a finalist for the 2009 PEN/Faulkner Award for Fiction, and *Madeleine*

Is Sleeping, a finalist for the 2004 National Book Award. Her short fiction has been published in *The New Yorker*, *Tin House*, *The Georgia Review*, and *The Best American Short Stories 2004* and *2009*. In 2010, she was named one of "20 Under 40" fiction writers by *The New Yorker*. She lives in Los Angeles and teaches in the Graduate Writing Program at Otis College of Art and Design.

LAN SAMANTHA CHANG is the director of the Iowa Writers' Workshop at the University of Iowa. Her fiction has appeared in *The Atlantic*, *Story*, and *The Best American Short Stories*. A 2008 Guggenheim fellow, Chang is the author of *Hunger: A Novella and Stories* and the novels *Inheritance* and *All Is Forgotten, Nothing Is Lost*. She lives in Iowa City with her husband and daughter.

PHOEBE DAMROSCH is the author of *Service Included: Four-Star Secrets of an Eavesdropping Waiter* (William Morrow), which was a 2007 *New York Times* Notable Book of the Year. She has written for *The New York Times*, *Food & Wine*, and the *New York Daily News*. A graduate of the M.F.A. program at Sarah Lawrence College, she now occupies the ground level of a house in Brooklyn with her husband, two sons, and French bulldog.

CLAIRE DEDERER is the author of the bestselling memoir *Poser: My Life in Twenty-three Yoga Poses*. Her writing has appeared in *The New York Times*, *Vogue*, *The Nation*, *Slate*, *New York* magazine, and many other publications. She lives on an island near Seattle with her family.

JENNIFER GILMORE's latest novel, *The Mothers*, was published by Scribner in 2013. She is also the author of *Golden Country*, a *New York Times* Notable Book of the Year and a finalist for the *Los Angeles Times* Art Seidenbaum Award for First Fiction and the National Jewish Book Award, and *Something Red*, a *New York Times* Notable Book. Her work has appeared in *The Atlantic*, *Bomb*, *BookForum*, *The Huffington Post*, *The Los Angeles Times*, *The New York Times*, *The New York Times Book Review*, *Salon*, *Tin House*, *Vogue*, and *The Washington Post*. She has taught writing and literature at Barnard College, Cornell University, and the New School. Currently she teaches at Princeton University.

JULIA GLASS is the author of the novels *And the Dark Sacred Night*, *The Widower's Tale*, *The Whole World Over*, and *Three Junes*, for which she won the

2002 National Book Award. *I See You Everywhere*, a collection of linked stories, won the 2009 Binghamton University John Gardner Fiction Book Award. She has also won fellowships from the National Endowment for the Arts, the New York Foundation for the Arts, and the Radcliffe Institute for Advanced Study. Her essays have been widely anthologized, most recently in *Bound to Last: 30 Writers on Their Most Cherished Book*. Glass lives with her two sons and their father in Massachusetts.

ARIELLE GREENBERG is the coauthor, with Rachel Zucker, of the nonfiction book *Home/Birth: A Poemic*, and the author of the poetry collections *My Kafka Century* and *Given* and the chapbooks *Shake Her* and *Farther Down: Songs from the Allergy Trials*. She is the coeditor of three anthologies: with Rachel Zucker, *Starting Today: 100 Poems for Obama's First 100 Days* and *Women Poets on Mentorship: Efforts and Affections*; and with Lara Glenum, *Gurlesque: the new grrly, grotesque, burlesque poetics*. Twice featured in *Best American Poetry*, she lives with her family in a small town in rural Maine.

LAUREN GROFF is the author of *Arcadia*, a *New York Times* Notable Book of the Year, bestseller, and finalist for the *Los Angeles Times* Book Prize for fiction. Her first novel, *The Monsters of Templeton*, was short-listed for the Orange Award for New Writers. She has a collection of short fiction called *Delicate Edible Birds*, and her stories have won Pushcart and O. Henry Prizes and have appeared in publications including *The New Yorker*, *The Atlantic*, *One Story*, *Tin House*, and *Ploughshares*, as well as two editions of the *Best American Short Stories* anthology. She lives in Gainesville, Florida, with her husband and two sons.

ELEANOR HENDERSON is the author of the novel *Ten Thousand Saints*, which was named one of the Top 10 Books of 2011 by *The New York Times* and a finalist for the Art Seidenbaum Award for First Fiction from the *Los Angeles Times*. Her stories and essays have appeared in *Poets & Writers*, *The Wall Street Journal*, *Virginia Quarterly Review*, *AGNI*, *Salon*, *The New York Times*, and *Best American Short Stories*. An assistant professor in the Department of Writing at Ithaca College, she lives in Ithaca, New York, with her husband and two sons.

CRISTINA HENRÍQUEZ is the author of the forthcoming novel *The Book of Unknown Americans*, as well as the novel *The World in Half* and the short story collection *Come Together, Fall Apart*, which was a *New York Times* Editors' Choice selection. Her stories have appeared in *The New Yorker*, *The Atlantic*, *The American Scholar*, *Glimmer Train*, *Ploughshares*, *TriQuarterly*, *AGNI*, and the *Virginia Quarterly Review*, where she was named one of "Fiction's New Luminaries." A graduate of the Iowa Writers' Workshop, she is also the recipient of an Alfredo Cisneros Del Moral Foundation Award. Henríquez lives outside Chicago with her husband, daughter, and son.

AMY HERZOG'S plays include *After the Revolution*, *The Great God Pan*, *Belleville*, and *4000 Miles*, a finalist for the Pulitzer Prize and winner of an Obie Award for the Best New American Play. A recipient of the Whiting Writers' Award, the Benjamin H. Danks Award from the American Academy of Arts and Letters, the Helen Merrill Playwriting Award, the Joan and Joseph F. Cullman Award for Extraordinary Creativity, and the *New York Times* Outstanding Playwright Award, Herzog has taught playwriting at Bryn Mawr and Yale.

ANN HOOD is the author of thirteen books, including the bestsellers *The Knitting Circle*, *The Red Thread*, and *Somewhere Off the Coast of Maine*; the memoir *Comfort: A Journey Through Grief*, which was selected as a *New York Times* Editors' Choice and as one of the top ten nonfiction books of 2008 by *Entertainment Weekly*; and the critically acclaimed short story collection *An Ornithologist's Guide to Life*. She has won two Pushcart Prizes, the Paul Bowles Prize for Short Fiction, and Best American Spiritual Writing, Best American Travel Writing, and Best Food Writing awards. Her new novel, *The Obituary Writer*, was an *O, The Oprah Magazine* Best New Book of April 2013 and was chosen as one of the Best Books of the Year So Far by Amazon.

SARAH JEFFERIS is the author of the poetry collection *Forgetting the Salt* (Foothills Publishing, 2008). Her poems and nonfiction have appeared in the *American Literary Review*, the *Mississippi Review*, *Icon*, *The Hollins Critic*, *The Patterson Literary Review*, *Icarus*, *The Healing Muse*, and other journals. She holds an M.A. from Hollins University, an M.F.A. from Cornell University, and a Ph.D. from SUNY Binghamton. She is working on a novel and a second book of poetry. A professor of creative writing and women's studies for thirteen years, she lives in Ithaca, New York, with her wife and their two daughters.

HEIDI JULAVITS is the author of four novels, most recently *The Vanishers*. Her fiction and nonfiction have appeared in *Harper's*, *McSweeney's*, *Elle*, and *The New York Times*, among other places. She's the recipient of a Guggenheim fellowship, a founding editor of *The Believer* magazine, and an associate professor at Columbia University. Along with Leanne Shapton and Sheila Heti, she is coeditor of *Women in Clothes: Why We Wear What We Wear* (2014).

MARY BETH KEANE graduated from Barnard College and received an M.F.A from the University of Virginia. Her debut novel, *The Walking People*, was a runner-up at the 2010 PEN/Hemingway Awards, and in 2011, Julia Glass selected her as one of the National Book Foundation's "5 under 35." Her second novel, *Fever* (Scribner), was published in the spring of 2013, with foreign editions forthcoming from Simon & Schuster U.K., Edizioni Piemme in Italy, and Presses de la Cité in France. Keane lives in Rockland County, New York, with her husband and their two sons.

MARIE MYUNG-OK LEE is an essayist and novelist. She is the author of the novel *Somebody's Daughter*, and her current novel is forthcoming in 2015 from Simon & Schuster. She has been a recipient of a Fulbright Scholarship, the Robert & Margaret MacColl Johnson and Rhode Island State Council on the Arts Fellowships, and fellowship residencies at Yaddo and MacDowell. Her work has appeared in *The Kenyon Review*, *Witness*, *Five Chapters*, *Slate*, *Salon*, *The New York Times*, and *The Nation*, and she is a regular contributor to *The Atlantic*. She teaches writing at Columbia University.

EDAN LEPUCKI is a staff writer for *The Millions* and the author of the novel *California*. Her short fiction has been published in *McSweeney's*, *Narrative* magazine, and *Meridian*, among others. A graduate of the Iowa Writers' Workshop, she is the founder of Writing Workshops Los Angeles.

HEIDI PITLOR has been the series editor of *The Best American Short Stories* since 2007. In 2015, Houghton Mifflin Harcourt will publish *100 Years of "The Best American Short Stories,"* which Heidi also edited. She is the author of the novel *The Birthdays*. Her second novel, *We All Fall Down*, is forthcoming from Algonquin in 2015. She lives outside Boston with her husband and twins.

JOANNA RAKOFF   is the author of the novel *A Fortunate Age*, which won the 2010 Goldberg Prize for Outstanding Debut Fiction, and the memoir *My Salinger Year* (Knopf, 2014). She has written for *The New York Times*, *Vogue*, *Marie Claire*, and many other publications. She lives in Cambridge with her two children.

JANE ROPER   is the author of a memoir, *Double Time: How I Survived—and Mostly Thrived—Through the First Three Years of Mothering Twins* (St. Martin's Press, 2012), and a novel, *Eden Lake* (Last Light Studio, 2011). Jane received her M.F.A. in fiction from the Iowa Writers' Workshop, and her writing has appeared in *Salon*, *Poets & Writers*, *The Rumpus*, and elsewhere. She lives in the Boston area with her husband and twin daughters.

DANZY SENNA   is the author of the national bestselling novel *Caucasia*, winner of the American Library Association's Alex Award, the novel *Symptomatic*, and the memoir *Where Did You Sleep Last Night? A Personal History*. Her latest work, a story collection titled *You Are Free*, was published by Riverhead Books in 2011. A recipient of the Whiting Writers' Award, she lives in Los Angeles with her husband, the novelist Percival Everett, and their sons.

DANI SHAPIRO   is the bestselling author of the memoirs *Devotion* and *Slow Motion*, and five novels, including *Black & White* and *Family History*. Her stories and essays have appeared in *The New Yorker*, *Granta*, *Ploughshares*, *Tin House*, *One Story*, *Elle*, *Vogue*, *The New York Times Book Review*, and many other publications. She has taught in the writing programs at Columbia University, NYU, the New School, Brooklyn College, and Wesleyan University. Her new book, *Still Writing: The Pleasures and Perils of a Creative Life*, was published in 2013. She lives with her family in Litchfield County, Connecticut.

ANNA SOLOMON   is the author of the novel *The Little Bride*, a *Boston Globe* bestseller. Her writing has appeared in *The New York Times Magazine*, *More*, *One Story*, *Ploughshares*, *The Georgia Review*, *Harvard Review*, and elsewhere. Her short stories have twice been awarded the Pushcart Prize. A graduate of the Iowa Writers' Workshop, she lives with her husband and two children in Providence, Rhode Island.

CHERYL STRAYED   is the author of the number one *New York Times* best-seller *Wild*, which was chosen for Oprah's Book Club 2.0 and has been made into a film starring Reese Witherspoon. She is also the author of the novel *Torch* and the *New York Times* bestseller *Tiny Beautiful Things*, a collection of the Dear Sugar columns she wrote for *The Rumpus*. Her writing has appeared in *The New York Times Magazine*, *The Washington Post Magazine*, *Vogue*, *Tin House*, *Creative Nonfiction*, *The Sun*, *The Best American Essays*, *Best New American Voices*, and elsewhere. She lives in Portland, Oregon, with her husband and two children.

SARAH A. STRICKLEY   is the recipient of a National Endowment for the Arts Literature Fellowship, an Ohio Arts Council grant, a Glenn Schaeffer Prize from the International Institute of Modern Letters, and other honors. Her fiction and essays have appeared in *Oxford American* magazine, *A Public Space*, *Harvard Review*, *Gulf Coast*, *The Barcelona Review*, and elsewhere. She is a graduate of the Iowa Writers' Workshop and is currently a doctoral candidate in the University of Cincinnati's Department of English and Comparative Literature. She lives in Cincinnati with her husband, the writer Ian Stansel, and their daughter.

RACHEL JAMISON WEBSTER   is the author of the poetry collection *September* (TriQuarterly Books, 2013), and has published poems and essays in many journals and anthologies, including *Poetry*, *The Paris Review*, *The Southern Review*, *The Madison Review*, and *Not a Muse*. She teaches at Northwestern University, where she is artist in residence, and edits an on-line anthology of international poetry, *UniVerse*. For several years, she worked with Chicago's first lady Maggie Daley to design and teach writing workshops for city teens. In this capacity, she edited two anthologies of writing by youth, *Alchemy* and *Paper Atrium*.

GINA ZUCKER   has published fiction and nonfiction in journals such as *Tin House*, *Salt Hill*, *Self*, *Elle*, *Glamour*, *GQ*, *Cosmopolitan*, *Rolling Stone*, and *Babble*. Her work has been anthologized several times, including in *Fantastic Women*, published by Tin House Books. She directs the Writers' Forum reading series at Pratt Institute in Brooklyn.